HOMO, MEMENTO FINIS

**Early Drama, Art, and Music
Monograph Series, 6**

HOMO, MEMENTO FINIS:

The Iconography of Just Judgment in Medieval Art and Drama

papers by
David Bevington, Huston Diehl, Richard Kenneth Emmerson,
Ronald Herzman, and Pamela Sheingorn

Early Drama, Art and Music
Monograph Series, 6

MEDIEVAL INSTITUTE PUBLICATIONS
Western Michigan University
Kalamazoo, Michigan
1985

ISBN 0-918720-60-5
ISBN 0-918720-61-3 (paperback)

CONTENTS

ILLUSTRATIONS

Frontispiece. Angel locking the door of Hell. Winchester Psalter.

Figures (following page 212)
1. Separation of the Sheep and Goats. Early Christian sarcophagus lid.
2. The Last Judgment. Tympanum, Church of St. Faith, Conques.
3. The Last Judgment. Anglo-Saxon Ivory.
4. St. Foy asks God's forgiveness. Detail from tympanum, Church of St. Faith, Conques.
5. Poacher receives reward. Detail from tympanum, Church of St. Faith, Conques.
6. The Magi. Tympanum, Church of St. Mary Magdalene, Neuilly-en-Donjon.
7. Resurrection of the Witnesses. Cloisters Apocalypse.
8. Ascension. Biblia Pauperum.
9. Pentecost. Biblia Pauperum.
10. Life of Elias. Bodleian Library MS. 270b.
11. Two Witnesses. British Library, Harley MS. 1527.
12. Destruction of Antichrist. Woodcut.
13. The Last Judgment. Bolton Hours.
14. The Last Judgment. Wall painting, St. Thomas of Canterbury Church, Salisbury.
15. Rogier van der Weyden, Last Judgment Altarpiece.
16. Hubert and/or Jan van Eyck, *The Last Judgment*. Panel painting.
17. The Last Judgment. Church of St. Peter, Wenhaston.
18. The Last Judgment. Devotional woodcut, from Syon Abbey.
19. The coming together of Peace and Righteousness. Stuttgart Psalter.
20. The Castle of Love. Peterborough Psalter.
21. Hieronymus Bosch, *Death of the Miser*. Panel painting.
22. Staging Design for Valenciennes Passion.
23. Attributed to Jan Massys, *St. Jerome in His Study*. Panel painting.
24. Hans Mielich, *Meeting of the Regensburg Town Council*.
25. Jan Dadeler (after Dirck Barendsz), *Mankind before the Last Judgment*. Engraving.
26. Jan Vermeer, *A Lady Weighing Pearls*. Painting.
27. Emblem from George Wither, *A Collection of Emblemes* (1635).

vii

PREFACE

This project began during a year-long residential seminar for college teachers, sponsored by the National Endowment for the Humanities, at the University of Chicago in 1978-79. The rapport that developed that year proved exceptional for all of us, and it has led to a number of collaborations since, most of them comparative in method and focused particularly on the relationship of drama to other literature or to art. Richard Emmerson and Ronald Herzman have published jointly an essay in *Traditio*, 36 (1980), 373-98, on "Antichrist, Simon Magus, and Dante's 'Inferno' XIX." During the seminar year, Emmerson brought to completion a study, since published under the title *Antichrist in the Middle Ages: A Study of Medieval Apocalypticism, Art, and Literature* (Seattle: Univ. of Washington Press, 1981), to which the seminar made an essential contribution. Pamela Sheingorn has contributed to the EDAM (Early Drama, Art, and Music) series at Western Michigan University a forthcoming monograph on Easter Sepulchres, while Huston Diehl has completed a project, similarly concerned with the relationship of art and drama, entitled *An Index of Icons in English Emblem Books*. Sheingorn's article on "The Moment of Resurrection in the Corpus Christi Plays," *Medievalia et Hu-*

manistica, n.s. 11 (1982), 111-29, was first presented to the seminr and profited from the insights of several participants. Diehl has also published three essays based on her seminar presentations or on related material: "The Iconography of Violence in English Renaissance Tragedy," *Renaissance Drama*, 11 (1980), 27-44; "Reduce Thy Understanding to Thine Eye: Seeing and Interpreting in *The Atheist's Tragedy*," *Studies in Philology*, 78 (1981), 47-60; and "Inversion, Parody, and Irony: The Visual Rhetoric of Renaissance English Tragedy," *Studies in English Literature 1500-1900*, 22 (1982), 197-209. The consultation among seminar members on each of these endeavors has been extensive.

These same four members of our group presented a lecture with slides on the iconography of just judgment in medieval and Renaissance art and drama at a session of the Modern Language Association in December 1979 at San Francisco. This session was sponsored by Comparative Studies in Medieval Literature, and I served as its chairman on that occasion. Our hope was to make a continuous presentation and argument, unlike many programs at learned meetings where papers, even in related fields, have no direct bearing on one another. This present book, while allowing for the various interests of five different individuals, similarly aims at something more coherent than an edited collection of essays.

This group has met repeatedly since 1979, especially at the annual International Congress on Medieval Studies at Western Michigan University in Kalamazoo, where all of us have given papers. Sheingorn and Emmerson participated in two sessions at Kalamazoo in 1981 on Resurrection Themes in Medieval Art and Literature which were based on a collaborative principle similar to that of our seminar. At these meetings we have planned the present book and rehearsed its argument. Although the chapters were assigned to individual members as indicated in the table of contents, we have reviewed and criticized one another's contributions to the point where collaboration marks every portion of the manuscript. At the same time we have also left room for the diversity that such a multiple authorship invites. Sheingorn's focus is that of an art historian, Emmerson's that of a student of apocalypticism. Diehl is concerned with post-Reformation drama in a volume whose title addresses itself to medieval art and drama, though what she has to say about Protestant transformation of images has important implications for medieval iconography as well. Herzman is primarily interested in artifacts of twelfth-century monasticism that do not directly portray the Last Judgment, and yet his method of "reading" both verbal and visual images in the context of meditative self-examination describes a relationship between audience and work of art that is central to our iconographic investigation. My own biases and limitations are, I suspect, so evident that I need not attempt to describe them.

We wish to thank the National Endowment for the Humanities for sponsoring our seminar in Chicago and the library staffs at the University of Chicago, Baruch College, Walla Walla College (especially Lee Johnston), the University of Oklahoma, and the State University College of Arts and Science, Geneseo. Most of these same institutions where we teach have given financial assistance so that this book could be regularly typeset. William Stephany, Paula Gerson, William Clark, Jonathan Glenn, and Martin Stevens have read portions of the manuscript and have given invaluable assistance. V. A. Kolve has provided us with a rigorous reading of the whole to which we have responded with some extensive rewriting. Appreciation is also expressed to the various museums and libraries and to Photo Marburg for permission to use photographs as illustrations in this book. Marlene Spletzer, former EDAM editorial assistant at the Medieval Institute, has done great service in the keyboarding of the entire manuscript. We are deeply indebted to our spouses, who have made sacrifices and have given us much warm support during our seminar year and ever since.

Finally, we thank our fellow members of the seminar, Thomas Berger, Michael Hall, Robert Knapp, Joan Marx, and John Wyatt, whose own projects took them in somewhat different directions but whose inspiration and friendship were, and continue to be, unceasing. We owe them all a great deal, and dedicate this book to them.

David Bevington

INTRODUCTION

David Bevington

Gay, gay, gay, gay,
Think on drydful domisday.
—Carol refrain[1]

How did the dramatic art of the Middle Ages depict just judgment? What were the iconographic means of attaching verbal signification to visual symbol when dealing with images of divine punishment and reward? What heritage did this iconographic tradition leave for art and drama after the Reformation? These are some of the questions we have addressed in this present study. We have chosen just judgment as our subject because it is, for the religious drama under consideration, the ultimate issue. Man is invited to ponder his ending day as the time of reckoning when all the conflicts of his uncertain life will be resolved for better or for worse. "Man, thinke on thin[e] endinge day," the Good Angel warns Mankind in *The Castle of Perseverance*, "Whanne thou schalt be closyd under clay!" (ll. 407-08).[2] Mercy similarly lectures the wavering protagonist in the play of *Mankind* to bear in mind the day of judgment:

1

But how then, when the angell of hevyn shall blow the
trumpe
Ande sey to the transgressors that wikkydly hath
wrought:
"Cum forth onto yowr juge, and yelde yowr
acownte"?

(ll. 175-77)[3]

Importantly, the audience too is forced into self-examination
by the process of judgment as it identifies with Mankind or
Mary Magdalene or those present at Christ's crucifixion.
Christ's warning in St. Matthew's Gospel, that the Son of
Man shall come in his glory to separate mankind "as the
shepherd separateth the sheep from the goats," offers a terrifying summons to all Christians to amend their lives lest
God say to them, "Depart from me, you cursed, into everlasting fire which was prepared for the devil and his angels"
(25.31-46).[4] Just judgment awaits all men, and for that reason
the dramatic images of judgment in medieval plays are always
both particular and universal, historical and timeless, personal and generic.

The scene of judgment is, for many a medieval drama,
the climactic final scene of reversal in which man's tragicomic saga is resolved in favor of mercy. In the alpha and
omega of the great civic cycles associated with Corpus Christi,
the omega is the Last Judgment, and, as V. A. Kolve and
others have shown,[5] it is anticipated at key points of the
cycle by such events as the Fall of Lucifer, Cain's Murder of
Abel, the Deluge, Abraham and Isaac, the Raising of Lazarus, the Resurrection, and the Journey to Emmaus. The
Advent episodes of the cycles are particularly insistent in
their foreshadowing of Doom: both Herod and Mak are figures of Antichrist in the Towneley cycle, and the Death of
Herod in the N-town cycle vividly anticipates the Last
Judgment.

The liturgy for Advent is heavily dependent on eschatological readings, and in medieval theology the season of
Advent is a penitential one in recognition of the necessity of
Christ's Second Coming; to prepare for his birth is also to
prepare for his return as judge.[6] Despite the fact that it leads

2

into the Christmas feast, Advent has not always been regarded as the beginning of the Church's sacred calendar; its
true liturgical significance points more to the end of that year
and indeed to the ending of all time. Beginning and end are
in immediate juxtaposition; the November lessons not only
of Advent but of late Pentecost repeatedly celebrate the coming of the kingdom of God and the necessity of our preparation for Christ's appearance. This Janus-faced character of
the late fall liturgy remains true after the Reformation as
before: it was for the Gospel lesson of the ten wise and
foolish virgins, with its warning of divine judgment, that
Bach wrote his chorale cantata "Wachet auf, ruft uns die
Stimme," bidding all people prepare for the arrival of the
bridegroom. Other appointed readings for Advent and the
weeks immediately preceding include a text from Amos, "But
judgment shall be revealed as water, and justice as a mighty
torrent" (5.24), and St. Paul's First Epistle to the Thessalonians, "For the Lord himself shall come down from heaven
with commandment, and with the voice of an archangel, and
with the trumpet of God: and the dead who are in Christ,
shall rise first. Then we who are alive, who are left, shall be
taken up together with them in the clouds to meet Christ,
into the air, and so shall we be always with the Lord"
(4.15-16).

Medieval art too illustrates the profound relevance of
the Day of Judgment to every part of the divine history of
the world, including Advent. Giotto's paintings for the Arena
Chapel in Padua bring together the Annunciation on the wall
of the triumphal arch and a fresco of the Last Judgment on
the west wall, so that "Christ's first appearance on earth is
contrasted with his return as Judge in Glory."[7] Similarly, as
Gertrud Schiller further observes, "from the mid-twelfth
century onwards for many decades the theme of the Incarnation of Christ in cathedral sculpture went hand in hand
with scenes of the Last Judgment." Iconographic tradition
in the visual arts associates the Last Judgment with the
Slaughter of the Innocents, with the Deluge, and with the
Baptism of Christ.[8] At Lincoln, in England, the twelfth-century west front of the cathedral presents a series of rec-

tangular panels high up over the doors in which selected Old Testament episodes such as the Temptation and Expulsion, Noah and the Ark, and Daniel in the lions' den on the south half are matched with scenes of the Last Judgment on the north. The juxtaposition underscores the profound relevance of the Day of Judgment.[9] The treatise *Pictor in Carmine*, written about 1200 probably by an Englishman as a means of providing appropriate typological subjects for illustrating the life of Christ, suggests a number of topics from Old and New Testaments—e.g., Christ's Crucifixion between two thieves—that parallel the image of Christ in Judgment with the elect to his right and the reprobate to his left. The Gothic period in England is no less rich in Last Judgment art made relevant to the whole of divine history, as at Broughton, Huntingdonshire, where a fifteenth-century Judgment scene over the chancel arch is visually related to scenes on the south wall of the nave depicting the Expulsion of Adam and Eve from Eden and Adam digging and Eve spinning.[10]

The centrality of judgment in medieval art and drama extends well beyond the actual depictions of Last Judgment or foreshadowings of it in the central episodes of the Corpus Christi "protocycle." In drama of the twelfth-century renaissance, the great theme of judgment is given eloquent form in a *Sponsus* liturgical play about the Wise and Foolish Virgins and in the Tegernsee *Antichrist*. The Chester cycle gives special prominence to two noncanonical pageants on the Coming of Antichrist; the images of just reward for Enoch and Elias and of punishment for Antichrist both recapitulate and foreshadow similar judgments throughout the cycle. Morality drama is, from its inception, deeply concerned with eschatological matters. *The Castle of Perseverance*, an early morality play (c. 1400-25), ends with the Father sitting on his throne, reconciling the debate of the four daughters of God by welcoming Mankind to sit on his right hand while the Bad Angel and his companions are thrust down into hell. The heritage of the climactic judgmental scene is evident in such diverse Renaissance plays as *Measure for Measure*, *The Atheist's Tragedy*, *The Devil's Law-Case*, and *The Malcontent*, where objects of the visible world are often signs of the

4

spiritual even though the two worlds are problematically related to one another.

The method of this study is iconographic and attempts to see medieval drama in the context of other medieval art forms. Svetlana and Paul Alpers have well said that "The endeavors of literary historians and art historians should no more be separated from each other than were the respective arts themselves in most periods of Western culture."[11] This observation is especially pertinent to the medieval period of whose beginnings Tertullian remarked, "There is no art which is not either the mother or a very close kinsman of another art."[12] Tertullian said this to discredit the whole enterprise of idolatrous image-making, to be sure, but his point remains valid. Medieval graphic art is often narrative in that it presents a number of scenes in a chronological sequence or simultaneously combines those scenes into one composition, and it is often verbal in that it includes text in painting or sculpture or offers itself as illustration to the manuscript of which it is frequently a part.[13] Medieval drama, conversely, is to an important degree one of the visual arts. In any era the drama is highly visual, but in the medieval religious drama we also find that the very images of stage action have conventional symbolic meanings found in religious painting and sculpture. Medieval drama and the visual arts share a common iconographic heritage, though we must also remember that they remain separate as genres and that an appreciation of the different expectations created by genre is essential to a viewer's proper response and understanding.[14] Because of this fundamental consanguinity among genres that nevertheless retain their separate identities, much can be discovered about the organization of parts in a medieval play, or the relationship of audience to performer, or the way in which an audience is invited to "read" images in the theater, by exploring similar modes of construction and image-making in other art forms. This is not to argue indebtedness, either from other arts to drama or from drama to other arts. In this study we have set aside for the most part the vexed issue of sources and influences on which much has already been said in any case.[15] We are concerned rather with habits of mind or of seeing, so that our basic resource is analogy.

We share a conviction that it was a medieval habit of mind to read visually when confronted with a text and, conversely, to read textually (in terms of narrative and moral lesson) when confronted with an image. Because both text and image thus served as media for ideas, we find it natural to examine and compare manifestations of those ideas in more than one medium. The drama is by its nature both textual and visual, or "interdisciplinary," and thereby affords an unusually rich opportunity for exploring the methodology of related disciplines in a way that will not violate the integrity of each. One medium possesses strengths which another lacks: literature can supply great detail in a continuous narrative, while visual art provides arresting static images in which a narrative can be inherent. If we can remain sufficiently mindful of the contexts of our various examples, and the integrity of each, the use of analogy should serve as a valid means of investigation.

The dangers of analogy have been explored by Jean Hagstrum in a lively book on *The Sister Arts* which, though concerned chiefly with the Restoration and eighteenth century, offers an incisive review of attitudes toward Horace's "ut pictura poesis" and Simonides' observation that painting is mute poetry and poetry a speaking picture.[16] Hagstrum is properly skeptical of attempts to analyze the *Zeitgeist* underlying all works of art in a given period. Although it is true, Hagstrum concedes, that "in all the works of a given epoch there is an *air de famille*,"[17] explanations of that familiar relationship too often lapse into the discovery of ingenious correspondences by means of what F. P. Pickering calls mediating terms.[18] The pictorial language of form, color, line, and space, and conversely the textual language of theme, argument, tone, and the like, are applied from one genre where such terminology has acquired an understood meaning to another genre where it is perhaps suggestive but is also technically imprecise. A Renaissance lyrical refrain is seen as parallel to the repetition of a Renaissance façade; a Gothic interior becomes a manifestation of the *sic et non* of

6

scholastic thought; *Hamlet* is "mannerist" while *Othello* is "baroque," and so on.[19] Hagstrum is surely right that a safer critical course is to focus on imagery, for, as Laurence Binyon says (quoted approvingly by Hagstrum), "it is on this side of imagery that poetry comes closely into relation with painting."[20] To begin, as Hagstrum does, with the visual side of poetry is especially fruitful in an analysis of medieval religious drama, since in text and stage action that drama is so avowedly visual and so close in its visual formulations to the iconography of other medieval art forms. At the same time, we must remember that drama is not simply a picture, and that literary pictorialism is generally more literary than pictorial.

Mario Praz, in his *Mnemosyne: The Parallel between Literature and the Visual Arts*, offers a potentially more hazardous method of analogizing, although not without use in specific instances, through attention to what he calls the "sameness of structure in a variety of media."[21] He shares the belief of Erwin Rosenthal, whose study of Dante and Giotto argues a synthesis in both artists of the earthly and supernatural, that similarity of form in different media arises in the medieval period not as "a consciously parallel tendency, but as a necessarily analogous way of becoming form, in a definite historical moment, of similar historical and spiritual premises."[22] Praz argues a similarity of panoramic construction in Chaucer's *Canterbury Tales* and in Brueghel's *St. John the Baptist Preaching*, though admitting they are two centuries apart, and contrasts their mode of construction with the Vitruvian emphasis on proportion and harmony in Renaissance art. He cites other instances of congruity of form arising from shared aesthetic assumptions, such as the correspondence between the hennin or pointed headdress of fifteenth-century ladies and a Gothic pinnacle, or a trunk hose and an Elizabethan table leg.[23] From the historian of Italian costume, Rosita Levi Pisetzky, Praz presents examples of "unity of taste" bringing together architecture and dress: the curve and the arch of Renaissance palace architecture find their parallel in dresses, particularly women's, "conceived so as to amplify the human figure without alter-

7

ing its proportions," as opposed to the slimness of Gothic fashions.[24] This way of analogizing is clearly capable of serious distortion if vaguely pursued, but can perhaps be applied with caution to representations in various media that share a common iconographic tradition. Dramatizations of the Last Judgment do seem to share with eschatological painting certain elements of form: symmetry, vertical arrangement, symbolic differentiation of right and left, and the like. A proper way to discipline analogies of form is to concentrate, as Hagstrum suggests, on the image.

The warnings of E. H. Gombrich concerning the "Aims and Limits of Iconology" are relevant to a study of medieval art and drama of the Last Judgment, even though Gombrich is specifically interested in the Renaissance.[25] Gombrich insists that the viewer's responsibility is to attempt to recover the artist's primary intention. Because images apparently occupy a position "somewhere between the statements of language, which are intended to convey a meaning, and the things of nature, to which we only can give a meaning" (p. 2), the viewer of a visual work of art must undertake an active role of interpretation; the artist depends more than the writer on "the beholder's share." Essential to this active pursuit of meaning is a knowledge of genre and of canonic texts, both religious and classical, on which artistic convention and generic programs are based. "It is from a knowledge of these texts and a knowledge of the picture that the iconologist proceeds to build a bridge from both sides to close the gap between the image and the subject matter" (p. 6). The theory of decorum, of what is fitting to a particular circumstance, is an important guide; so is the realization that images need not be limited to one meaning, but to an area of intersection. Taken in isolation, removed from their context, images can all too readily be misinterpreted by inflexible dictionary definition. This is equally true of symbol, for symbol "functions as a metaphor which only acquires its specific meaning in a given context" (p. 16). Symbolism tends to follow either an Aristotelian tradition aiming at what might be called a "method of visual definition" (p. 13), in which metaphor is a figure of speech to be applied as decoration or embroidery,

8

and by means of which we can study an abstract quality like solitude in terms of its associations; or a Neo-Platonic tradition in which the meaning of a sign is mysteriously hidden and accessible only to those who know how to seek for it. The latter tradition, as adapted to Christian ideas of revelation, gives rise to the notion of a "divine language of things" in God's created universe that "differs from the language of words as being both richer and more obscure" (p. 149). The symbol is thus "the imperfect reflection of the higher reality which arouses our longing for perfection" (p. 150).

A picture usually has several meanings rather than one, all of which to be properly understood must be seen in relation to the artist's dominant meaning, his principal intent. To interpret a Madonna and Child in terms of the doctrine of salvation "does not, by itself, introduce a different level of meaning" (p. 16). The interpreter must focus not on whatever in the artist's life or circumstance may have caused certain images to recur, but on the artist's purpose. Purpose points inevitably to use, and hence the interpreter must be knowledgeable about the institutions (such as the Church) that commission or otherwise encourage the artist's choice of genre. Taken as a whole, Gombrich's essay is a warning against overinterpretation, and can be applied to medieval art and drama by calling our attention to the need for close interrelation of text and picture (in this case, stage picture), for an awareness of institutional auspices and genre, and for an appreciation of context and decorum.

Other principles of investigation to which we are committed have been enunciated by Pamela Sheingorn and Clifford Davidson.[26] Literary critics and historians alike should be well versed in iconographic method, and should strive for a depth of approach whereby the whole history of a motif and its sources comes under consideration rather than an isolated example. Following the same line of reasoning, we have tried to avoid monolithic assumptions about medieval image-making, and have looked instead for the changes that were bound to occur as Romanesque style gave way to Gothic, or as Catholic drama and art yielded of force to Protestant drama and art in England. We have also tried to respect

9

regional differences. We are especially interested in what Sheingorn calls the "complex relationship between image and text" (p. 103). Medieval drama excels in its ability to bring together pictures (stage images) and words (speeches or dialogue), as Glynne Wickham, T. W. Craik, and others have shown,[27] and in this fruitful union lies a wealth of material for iconographic analysis.

The subject of judgment proved an unusually complex and difficult one for medieval artists and dramatists, as we shall see in Chapter I. The vastness of scope, the futurity of mysterious and unknown events, the visionary and metaphoric language in which those events are pictured in the Scriptures, the need for a hierarchical scheme to organize a representation of heaven and hell at the ending of the world—all these unusual demands obliged medieval artists and dramatists to seek out new forms. The difficulty manifested itself in lateness of development. Iconography of judgment emerged tentatively and sparingly at first, in metaphorical rather than direct presentation. In church drama of the tenth through twelfth centuries, similarly, eschatological drama emerged only belatedly in plays about the foolish and wise virgins or about Antichrist where the Last Judgment was approached indirectly through parable or caricature. The topic of judgment could apparently be explored and defined at first only through pictorial analogy, envisioning Christ as a shepherd parting his flock or a bridegroom awakening those waiting for his arrival. Judgment art lacked for a time a sure sense of its visual continuity and tradition.

These difficulties were nevertheless amply compensated for by the remarkable opportunities inherent in the subject of judgment, opportunities that are of particular relevance to this present study. One such opportunity was the limitless extent to which imagination could be brought to play in depicting a heretofore imperfectly realized subject. The unusual challenge met with unusual response, and late medieval arts including drama exploited their canvases or sculptural space or acting arena in rich and piquant detail. Another challenge and opportunity was that the subject required such a disciplining and ordering of its components as it grew in scope and complexity. No medieval religious subject asked more of artists in the way of structural design, hieratic subordination of parts to the whole, thematic interrelationships, balancing, antithesis, recapitulation. If medieval artists and dramatists were to reach for the inclusiveness and variety that the narrative content of their subject invited them to use, they had to devise new ways of arranging and disciplining the elements of their compositions. The result was that judgment art and drama, after a hesitant and belated start, came in time to lead the way in inclusiveness and complexity of form.

The success of a more elaborate and sophisticated design was an appropriate one because, as the artists and dramatists had come to recognize, the Last Judgment was their culminating performance, the last act of the play, the final chapter in the story of God's creation. For all its foreboding note of warning, it was a triumphal ending as well, one that fittingly employed all the artistry and design of which medieval art and drama had become capable. The Last Judgment was the final tableau, the scene on the tympanum at the west portal, the subject on the chancel wall dominating the nave; it summarized all divine history and provided a closure to it, and could not be anything less than splendid.

Faced with this unparalleled challenge and opportunity, medieval artists and dramatists inevitably thought alike about problems and devised solutions that shared certain broad assumptions even while the solutions were of necessity adapted to discrete media. Vertical movement, for example, became a dominant motif in presenting a story about the dead who rise from their graves and ascend into heaven or are thrust down into hell at the command of God who descends from heaven to earth and then reascends. Drama provided its actors the ability to move from one level to another on vertically-arranged stages, but the other visual arts were no less intent on implying vertical movement through a sequence of scenes juxtaposed simultaneously on a large canvas or stone sculpture. The hand-held attributes and other objects of iconographic tradition in visual art became stage properties in theatrical performance, able to offer

11

symbolic identification as in a painting or sculpture while also functioning as the focus of stage business. The relationship of audience to art work was temporally different in different media, although devoted generally to the same religious purpose. Painting and sculpture were constantly on display in the church as familiar objects to be venerated, explicated in sermon, or made the object of meditative reflection. Dramatic performance, even though it could be repeated periodically and was sometimes incorporated into church ritual, was by its nature an occasional event, dominating the audience's attention during performance but destined then to vanish. Such similarities and differences, in an age when the arts were unusually close to one another, help define not only their mutual interdependence but their generic separateness. For these reasons, iconographic study of medieval art and drama can be pursued not merely as a matter of sources and influences but of generic capabilities and of commonly pursued goals.

NOTES

1. *The Early English Carols*, 2nd ed., ed. Richard L. Greene (London: Oxford Univ. Press, 1977), no. 329, British Library Sloan MS. 2953, fols. 4ᵛ, 5; quoted in Morton W. Bloomfield, *The Seven Deadly Sins* (1952; rpt. East Lansing: Michigan State Univ. Press, 1967), p. 203.

2. Citation from David Bevington, ed., *Medieval Drama* (Boston: Houghton Mifflin, 1975), p. 811.

3. Ibid., p. 909.

4. Quotations in this and subsequent chapters are from the Douay-Rheims translation from the Vulgate unless otherwise noted; the final chapter, because it deals with the Reformation era, quotes from the Geneva Bible.

5. V. A. Kolve, *The Play Called Corpus Christi* (Stanford: Stanford Univ. Press, 1966), pp. 84-89; Edward Murray Clark, "Liturgical Influences in the Towneley Plays," *Orate Fratres*, 16 (1941), 69-79; Rosemary Woolf, *The English Mystery Plays* (Berkeley and Los Angeles: Univ. of California Press, 1972).

6. Thomas P. Campbell, "Eschatology and the Nativity in English Mystery Plays," *American Benedictine Review*, 27 (1976), 297-320; Pa-

trick Cowley, *Advent: Its Liturgical Significance* (London: Faith Press, 1960).

7. Gertrud Schiller, *Iconography of Christian Art*, trans. Janet Seligman (Greenwich, Conn.: New York Graphic Society, 1971-72), I, 10.

8. Ibid., I, 32; see also I, 45, figs. 99-100 (painting by Pacino di Bonaguida, c. 1320), and p. 108, fig. 280 (showing a tympanum at Neuilly-en-Donjon, where trumpet-blowing angels appear on each side of a composition devoted to the Adoration of the Magi and the Fall and Mary Magdalen; mentioned by Herzman in Chapter II, below). On p. 114 of Vol. I, Schiller notes that "The slaughtered innocents of Bethlehem were very early regarded by the churches of both east and west as the first martyrs," and hence that they were to be "redeemed in the context of the Apocalypse and the Last Judgment." On p. 129, Schiller notes the use of flood typology to link God's first great judgment, the flood, with his Last Judgment, both being associated with the water of baptism: "1 Peter 3, 18-21, finds a connexion between the Flood—Christ's descent into the realm of death—baptism and the Last Judgment."

9. Lawrence Stone, *Sculpture in Britain: The Middle Ages*, 2nd ed. Pelican History of Art, 9 (Baltimore: Penguin, 1972), p. 73, and A. M. Cook, *Lincoln Cathedral*, 4th ed., revised Peter B. G. Binnall (Holborn: Donald F. Beters, 1970), p. 18.

10. M. R. James, *"Pictor in Carmine,"* *Archaeologia*, 94 (1951), 141-66, and A. Caiger-Smith, *English Medieval Mural Paintings* (Oxford: Clarendon Press, 1963), p. 147; see also Newington, Kent, and Little Missenden, Buckinghamshire (Caiger-Smith, pp. 152, 133).

11. Svetlana and Paul Alpers, *"Ut Pictura Noesis*? Criticism in Literary Studies and Art History," *New Literary History*, 3 (1972), 442; quoted in Pamela Sheingorn, "On Using Medieval Art in the Study of Medieval Drama: An Introduction to Methodology," *Research Opportunities in Renaissance Drama*, 22 (1979), 101-09.

12. Tertullian, *De idolatria*, cap. 8; "Nulla ars non alterius artis aut mater propinqua est"; *Quinti Septimii Florentis Tertulliani quae Supersunt Omnia*, ed. Franciscus Oehler (Lipsiae: Weigel, 1853), I, 76. Cited in Jean H. Hagstrum, *The Sister Arts: The Tradition of Literary Pictorialism and English Poetry from Dryden to Gray* (Chicago: Univ. of Chicago Press, 1958), p. 37.

13. Meyer Schapiro, *Words and Pictures: On the Literal and the Symbolic in the Illustration of a Text* (The Hague, Paris: Mouton, 1973), pp. 13-14.

14. F. P. Pickering, *Literature and Art in the Middle Ages* (Coral Gables, Fla.: Univ. of Miami Press, 1970), pp. 3-15.

15. See, for example, M. D. Anderson, *Drama and Imagery in English Medieval Churches* (London: Cambridge Univ. Press, 1963); Clifford Davidson, *Drama and Art: An Introduction to the Use of Evidence from the Visual Arts for the Study of Early Drama*, Early Drama, Art, and

Music, Monograph Ser., 1 (Kalamazoo, Mich.: The Medieval Institute, 1977); and Otto Pächt, *The Rise of Pictorial Narrative in Twelfth-Century England* (Oxford: Clarendon Press, 1962).

16. Hagstrum, *The Sister Arts*, especially the Introduction, pp. xiii-xxii.

17. Ibid., p. xiv, referring to Mario Praz, "Modern Art and Literature: A Parallel," *English Miscellany*, 5 (1954), 217-45, especially p. 217.

18. Pickering, *Literature and Art in the Middle Ages*, p. 7. See also Ernest Gilman, *The Curious Perspective: Literary and Pictorial Wit in the Seventeenth Century* (New Haven: Yale Univ. Press, 1978), Introduction.

19. Hagstrum, *The Sister Arts*, p. xiv, citing Marco Mincoff, "Baroque Literature in England," *Annuaire de l'Université de Sofia*, 43 (1946-47), 27, and Wylie Sypher, *Four Stages of Renaissance Style* (Garden City, N.Y.: Doubleday, 1955), pp. 25, 45, 261, and *passim*.

20. Laurence Binyon, "English Poetry in Its Relation to Painting and the Other Arts," *Proceedings of the British Academy 1917-1918*, p. 383, cited by Hagstrum, *The Sister Arts*, p. xv.

21. Mario Praz, *Mnemosyne: The Parallel between Literature and the Visual Arts* (Princeton: Princeton Univ. Press, 1970), p. 55 (title to Chapter III).

22. Erwin Rosenthal, *Giotto in der mittelalterlichen Geistesentwicklung* (Augsburg: Dr. Benno Filser, 1924), pp. 202-06; cited by Enzo Carli, "Dante e l'arte del suo tempo," *Dante*, ed. Umberto Parricchi (Rome: De Luca, 1965), p. 164, and by Praz, *Mnemosyne*, p. 68 and note.

23. James Laver, *Style in Costume* (London: Oxford Univ. Press, 1949), cited in Praz, *Mnemosyne*, p. 29.

24. Rosita Levi Pisetzky, *Storia del costume in Italia* (Milan: Istituto editoriale italiano, 1964), III, 18.

25. E. H. Gombrich, *Symbolic Images: Studies in the Art of the Renaissance* (London and New York: Phaidon, 1972), Introduction, pp. 1-25, and *"Icones Symbolicae,"* pp. 123-91.

26. Sheingorn, "On Using Medieval Art," pp. 101-09, and Davidson, *Drama and Art, passim*.

27. Glynne Wickham, *Early English Stages 1300 to 1660* (New York: Columbia Univ. Press, 1959-81), III, 61, and T. W. Craik, *The Tudor Interlude: Stage, Costume, and Acting* (Leicester: Leicester Univ. Press, 1958), *passim*.

I

"FOR GOD IS SUCH A DOOMSMAN": ORIGINS AND DEVELOPMENT OF THE THEME OF LAST JUDGMENT

Pamela Sheingorn

An intriguing paradox characterizes the subject of the Last Judgment in the first twelve centuries of the Christian era. Despite the centrality to Christian doctrine of the Parousia, Christ's Second Coming to judge mankind and end world history, the subject does not receive direct artistic treatment in the early stages either of the pictorial arts or of drama. The pictorial arts of the early Christian period refer to the Last Judgment only through metaphor. Dramas concerned with Last Judgment do not emerge until the twelfth century, and even then they retain metaphorical rather than literal presentation. This chapter will closely examine the visual arts, both pictorial and dramaturgic, in their cultural context in order to come to an understanding of this paradox.

To undertake such an examination is to realize that the topic of the Last Judgment creates for the visual arts a series of special problems, including the sheer size and complexity of the task. No subject is larger than that of Christian eschatology, for it deals with the end of the world in terms of everything that has gone before; since Christ's judgment comes in response to man's behavior, the Last Judgment recapitulates the entire history of the created universe. Understandably, too, the topic invites obscurity of treatment. Scripture treats the coming judgment in visions (e.g., St. John's in the Apocalypse) or in the metaphors of parable and prophecy, such as those of Christ in the Gospels. None of these sources sets out an ordered series of events that translates easily into narrative or clearly describes one central image that would allow others to be grouped around it. In all, four major problems challenge those artists charged with creating images of the Last Judgment: its enormous scope defies the imagination; it is an event of future time; references to it are couched in visionary or metaphoric language; and it demands the invention of an organizational scheme to cope with its huge cast of characters and individual narrative episodes.

Yet because the Last Judgment is a subject of such central importance, Christian artists ultimately had no choice but to attempt to solve these problems. In studying their solutions we are really studying the expressions in visual language of a subject that stretches the limits of that language and ultimately, therefore, expands its range of artistic vision because of the abstract and eschatological dimensions of the subject. Christian artists had to develop both an iconography of complex symbolism to provide the elements of a suitable language[1] and the means of arranging those elements to communicate the specific content of the Last Judgment clearly, using compositional principles such as symmetry, hieratic ordering, triangular arrangement of forms, and organization in bands or registers. The methods of composition developed in the pictorial arts to give visual expression, first to metaphoric and then to direct statements of the Last Judgment, also inform the visual patterns of two early eschatological plays. By exploring the use of visual language in two media, the pictorial arts and drama, we are able to see how these two arts both resemble each other and differ in presenting a subject of central theological and psychological importance

16

through images both formally sophisticated and visually memorable.[2]

Our exploration of the paradox of the Last Judgment in the visual arts must be conducted against the background of changing attitudes toward the Last Judgment in Christian culture. We begin in the early Christian period when the approach of the Last Judgment was not a cause for serious apprehension. Although early Christians expected the imminent return of Christ, they looked to a Christ who promised to take all believers to their heavenly home rather than to eternal punishment. Later, in the medieval period, conversely, Christians were to view the Second Coming as a pattern of judgment offering a potential threat as well as a potential consolation to the individual Christian. Beginning with the sixth century, increased emphasis on the Last Judgment as deserved punishment for sin aroused both fear of and intense curiosity about eschatology, and helped to create the climate that eventually produced the first pictorial images of the Last Judgment in the ninth century and the first eschatological play, the *Sponsus*, a dramatization of the parable of the wise and foolish virgins, at the end of the eleventh. As part of the major cultural shift of the twelfth-century renaissance, fear of Doomsday provided a crucial development in the way in which the process of penance was understood. In order to intensify fear and consequently motivate penance, the Church began to place pictorial representations of the Last Judgment constantly before the eyes of Christians. The tendency to see present behavior in its relation to eternal destiny also marks on a grand scale the twelfth-century eschatological play *Ludus de Antichristo*, which employs the story of Antichrist's activity at the close of world history in order to urge the Holy Roman Emperor to take a course of action that would lead to the unfolding of that story. By the end of the twelfth century, concern about the coming Doom had become a significant factor in motivating both beliefs and actions. Each individual could have said, along with St. Anselm, "I know myself to be very wretched in the just judgment of God."[3]

17

In the early days of Christianity, followers of the new religion looked to the end of time, believing in the literal fulfillment of Christ's promise: "this generation shall not pass, till all these things be done" (Matthew 24.34). Apocalypticism promised a swift end to the evils of the Roman world; God would intervene, bringing history to a cataclysmic close and delivering Christians from persecution.[4] Christians were apprehensive of the trials that the events of the Last Days would bring; Cyprian, for example, wrote to an African congregation in the third century urging his "most beloved brothers" to overcome their fright at the "coming of threatening Antichrist" as "the sunset of the generation" approached.[5] Still, this fear was confined to the finite time before the Parousia because of the early Christian understanding of baptism. Justin Martyr wrote in the second century that "those who are prepared by the water, the faith, the wood, and who repented of their sins, they will escape the judgment of God which is to come!"[6] Jean Daniélou offers the following gloss on this passage: "Baptism, by the symbol of immersion, is, as it were, a sacramental anticipation, through imitation, of the final Judgment, which will be baptism of fire. And it is thanks to Baptism that the Christian will escape the Judgment because in that sense, he has already been judged."[7] Baptized Christians who had to endure threats of discovery and persecution were at least spared the fear of eternal damnation and could feel secure in the certainty of eternal life in paradise. Evil was largely external to the Christian community.

This view of the Last Judgment found direct expression in early Christian art. From the rich variety of Old Testament narratives available for illustration, early Christians selected for representation in the catacombs those subjects that also appeared in contemporary apocalyptic literature where, as Thomas Buser shows, they were read as " 'signs' of apocalyptic time."[8] Thus stories such as those of Noah and Jonah were interpreted as prefigurations of the period of persecution that Christians were then enduring,[9] a period that in turn signaled the imminent "coming of threatening Antichrist."

As well as illustrating the Old Testament stories seen as prefigurations of the apocalyptic age, early Christians drew on the metaphoric references to the Last Judgment in the New Testament. The words of Christ recorded in Matthew 25.1-13 and 31-46 offer two fundamentally important metaphors of separation, that of the wise from the foolish virgins and that of the sheep from the goats:

> Then shall the kingdom of heaven be like to ten virgins, who taking their lamps went out to meet the bridegroom and the bride. And five of them were foolish, and five wise. But the five foolish, having taken their lamps, did not take oil with them: But the wise took oil in their vessels with the lamps. And the bridegroom tarrying, they all slumbered and slept. And at midnight there was a cry made: Behold the bridegroom cometh, go ye forth to meet him. Then all those virgins arose and trimmed their lamps. And the foolish said to the wise: Give us of your oil, for our lamps are gone out. The wise answered, saying: Lest perhaps there be not enough for us and for you, go ye rather to them that sell, and buy for yourselves. Now whilst they went to buy, the bridegroom came: and they that were ready, went in with him to the marriage, and the door was shut. But at last came also the other virgins, saying: Lord, Lord, open to us. But he answering said: Amen I say to you, I know you not. Watch ye therefore, because you know not the day nor the hour.
>
> And when the Son of man shall come in his majesty, and all the angels with him, then shall he sit upon the seat of his majesty: And all nations shall be gathered together before him, and he shall separate them one from another, as the shepherd separateth the sheep from the goats: And he shall set the sheep on his right hand, but the goats on his left. Then shall the king say to them that shall be on his right hand: Come, ye blessed of my Father, possess you the kingdom prepared for you from the foundation of the world. For I was hungry, and you gave me to eat; I was thirsty, and you gave me to drink; I was a stranger, and you took me in: Naked, and you covered me: sick, and you visited me: I was in prison, and you came to me. Then shall the just answer him, saying: Lord, when did we see thee hungry, and fed thee; thirsty, and gave thee drink? And when did we see thee a stranger, and took thee in? or naked, and covered

thee? Or when did we see thee sick or in prison, and
came to thee? And the king answering, shall say to them:
Amen I say to you, as long as you did it to one of these
my least brethren, you did it to me.

Then he shall say to them also that shall be on his
left hand: Depart from me, you cursed, into everlasting
fire which was prepared for the devil and his angels. For
I was hungry, and you gave me not to eat: I was thirsty,
and you gave me not to drink. I was a stranger, and you
took me not in: naked, and you covered me not: sick
and in prison, and you did not visit me. Then they also
shall answer him, saying: Lord, when did we see thee
hungry, or thirsty, or a stranger, or naked, or sick, or in
prison, and did not minister to thee? Then he shall answer them, saying: Amen I say to you, as long as you
did it not to one of these least, neither did you do it to
me. And these shall go into everlasting punishment: but
the just, into life everlasting.

The second of these passages, expounding the good
deeds ascribed to the blessed that later came to be known
as the Seven Corporal Acts or Works of Mercy,[10] is central
to many works of medieval art and literature concerning the
Last Judgment. Early Christian artists, on the other hand,
passed over any direct descriptions of the Last Judgment in
favor of two metaphors which they interpreted as stressing
the separation of those who await certain salvation from
those unprepared persons who are outside the Christian
community.

A representation of the parable of the wise and foolish
virgins in the catacomb of St. Cyriaca in the fourth century[11]
shows how an early Christian artist translates narrative into
visual language. His representation reveals key characteristics of that visual language and illustrates the way early
Christians viewed the Last Judgment. The artist faces a
choice that those who illustrate narrative must always make:
whether to follow the narrative in a sequence of scenes or
to choose one scene that effectively calls to mind the entire
narrative.[12] The choice made by this artist is to collapse the
last few events of the story into one scene: the arrival of the
bridegroom, his reception of the wise virgins, the subsequent
return of the foolish virgins, and his refusal to recognize

them. Thus, in the painting, the long-awaited bridegroom stands between the wise and foolish virgins, dividing them into two distinct groups. His gesture of lifting his hand and turning toward the virgins with burning torches on his right simultaneously welcomes these wise virgins and rejects the foolish virgins to his left. This solution is satisfying in terms of content because it effectively recapitulates the narrative; it is an aesthetically pleasing and formally memorable composition because it both balances two groups about a strong, vertical center and differentiates these groups by gesture and by relying on the symbolism of left and right. By reducing this parable to one scene, the artist has brought out the symmetry implicit in the narrative that would have been submerged by a sequential presentation. The artist has accentuated that symmetry through the figure of the bridegroom, the central axis of the composition, who turns toward and therefore emphasizes the group to his right. The bridegroom's posture focuses attention on the reward of the wise virgins, who succeed to paradise, and reveals a lack of interest in the fate of the foolish virgins. The artist's interpretation of the parable coincides with the interpretation early Christian culture gave to it; its emphasis on the wise virgins reveals the confidence that early Christians felt in the face of judgment. It is that interpretation which renders this painting suitable for its location, the funerary chamber of a consecrated virgin, where it consoles those mourning for her with the message that she is among the blessed in paradise. In later periods, when Christians could be either wise or foolish and imagine themselves either on the right or the left sides at the Last Judgment, scenes of judgment no longer appear in funerary contexts.

Similar attitudes and compositional patterns inform a contemporary representation of the metaphor in verse 32 of Matthew 25, "as the shepherd separateth the sheep from the goats." Early Christian art frequently depicted Christ as a shepherd in reference to the parable of the shepherd who searches for and saves one sheep lost from his flock;[13] accordingly, it was easy to identify the shepherd with Christ in representations of the Last Judgment metaphor. The ear-

21

liest surviving example of the separation of the sheep and the goats by Christ the shepherd is carved in relief on a sarcophagus lid (fig. 1) dated about 300 A.D.[14] The shepherd, centrally seated and flanked by sheep and goats facing toward him, symbolizes Christ the judge; his gestures reveal his judgment, and placement of the sheep to his right and goats to his left indicates their eternal destinations. As in the representation of the parable of wise and foolish virgins discussed above, the decision to compose this scene with opposing groups balanced about a central figure creates a formal and explicit visual statement. Here it reflects the verbal balance of Matthew 25, where each act of mercy on the part of the saved is balanced by its omission on the part of the damned. The axis of reflection passes through the figure of Christ, whose position above those who flank him places him at the apex of a triangle; this arrangement creates a compositional pattern equal in its stability to the eternally valid doctrine that makes up the content of the work of art. The two compositional principles discussed thus far, bilateral symmetry and triangular composition, are basic to later representations of the Last Judgment. Even the reactions of the symbolic animals—the sheep with lifted heads, the recoiling goats—predict those of the ranks of the blessed and damned in later art. These factors were to remain consistent, although the bucolic flavor of this interpretation, and specifically the concept of Christ as shepherd, were soon to be displaced by the imperial imagery of Rome.

The legalization of Christianity in the Roman Empire early in the fourth century resulted in major shifts both in the attitudes of Christians toward apocalypticism and in all Christian iconography. With a Christian ruler in control of the Empire and the persecutions at an end, some Church Fathers perceived the time of Antichrist as retreating to an indefinite future. Augustine expresses this view in his discussion of the Last Judgment in *The City of God*, where he seems to be speaking of a distant event as he compiles and explicates scriptural passages referring to the Last Judgment. As Barbara Nolan notes, "Augustine removes a sense of climax from the day of the Last Judgment by making it only one of the judgments made by God from the time of Adam's eviction from paradise."[15] In the pictorial arts, other subjects that supported the development of church institution and hierarchy gained prominence, an example being that of the typological relationship between Melchisidek as a priest and Christ.

This change of Christianity's relationship to its host culture also reduced the sense of a Christian-Roman dichotomy and facilitated the amalgamation of Roman and Christian iconography. Even though the amalgamation was resisted by some apocalypticists who continued to view Rome with mistrust, the Church adopted many forms and procedures from imperial Rome, drawing parallels between the emperor and Christ as ruler of the universe. This comparison led to the depiction of Christ as a Roman emperor. In a sixth-century mosaic panel representing the separation of sheep and goats from Sant Apollinare Nuovo, Ravenna, for example, Christ wears the imperial purple with gold trim.[16] Like an emperor who never appears alone but is always accompanied by those assigned to protect him and implement his will, Christ is flanked by angels ready to carry out his commands. In terms of composition, these angelic assistants must be hieratically subordinated to Christ, thereby introducing a principle of organization that will become increasingly important as Last Judgment compositions become more complex. The placement of the angels also underscores the symbolism of left and right. On Christ's right is an angel clothed in red, the color of fire and thus (according to one ancient tradition) the color of light, identifying this being as a good angel; the blue of the angel's garb to Christ's left symbolizes air without light, or darkness, identifying a fallen angel or demon, in accordance with Paul's reference in Ephesians 2.2 to "the spirit that now worketh on the children of unbelief" as "the prince of the power of this air."

These earliest, allusive representations of the Last Judgment have little emotional content. Their timeless serenity is typical of early Christian art. As Frederick van der Meer argues, "What distinguishes Early Christian art in general from the art of later times, is that most distinctive feature of

23

the Greek spirit: the keeping of the measure of the reasonable mean, called *sophrosyne* by the ancients. Not even the friends of Plato were able to define this idea, though everyone understood what it meant, and regarded it as the crown of all virtues: the sense of measure, the feeling of what is fitting; restraint, self-control, dignity, good taste; it was all these and much more. And these qualities, moreover, are those which distinguish Early Christian art from all that comes after."[17]

On the other hand, the Christian community had begun to move away from *sophrosyne*, with a concomitant gradual rise of interest in the Last Judgment as an event of personal warning. The Christian religion, intent upon absorbing many of the Germanic tribes that had infiltrated and then invaded the Roman Empire, was itself changed in the process. One result of wholesale conversion was that evil was no longer external; it was evident in the behavior of the greatly enlarged and increasingly disparate Christian community. Recognizing the existence of sinful Christians, the Church adjusted its views on penance and provided priests with penitentials, handbooks to guide them in assigning appropriate penances. These books characterize sins as discrete debts to be paid by means of specific actions rather than as more general evidence of the nature of postlapsarian humankind; as Charles Radding observes, "the penitentials were almost invariably concerned with *satisfactio*, the actions by which reparation was offered God for the sin."[18] Caesarius of Arles, who was intimately involved in the conversion of the Franks at the beginning of the sixth century, and whose teachings continued to have a profound effect into the Carolingian period and beyond because his sermons were repeatedly used or paraphrased, also promulgated the view that discrete actions in this world determined one's fate in the next world: "do good works, for the time of judgment will come soon."[19] In nearly every one of his over two hundred surviving sermons, Caesarius introduces the Last Judgment, often as a motivating force for concrete actions in this life. Thus, in discussing the Lord's Prayer, he comments: "There our Lord will without doubt so carry out his judgment against us, that, whatever verdict we have given will be given against us, and we will be forgiven according to the same measure as we have forgiven our neighbor. For whoever has not fulfilled this, himself closes the door to divine mercy." Herbert Kolb, commenting on the attitudes expressed toward the Last Judgment in early Germanic Christianity, emphasizes that it is conceived of as a process with just preconditions and legal results.[20]

Apocalypticism, which was to reassert itself repeatedly whenever conditions could conceivably be interpreted as coinciding with those described in St. John's vision of the Apocalypse, found in the massive social and cultural disruptions of the early medieval period a further impetus toward awareness of a time of reckoning. Contemporary evil was one of the multiple signs of the Last Days that pointed to the imminence of the Last Judgment. As Richard Emmerson observes, "Eschatology remained a major preoccupation of commentaries, especially after the eighth century, when the Apocalypse became a major object of study for exegetes and of illustration for artists."[21] Commentators drew on eschatological references throughout Scripture, augmenting the Apocalypse in order to construct a detailed sequence of events that included the attack of Antichrist, the Fifteen Signs of Doomsday, and the Resurrection of the Dead.

In this climate of increased concern about the Last Judgment, artists discarded the static non-narrative metaphor of the shepherd and drew instead on the wealth of narrative detail about the Last Days now available for their use. Organizing the vast amount of material that belonged to the subject of Last Judgment required compositions much more complex than those of the separation of the sheep and the goats. The individual steps in the development of these compositions remain hidden in obscurity. Nonetheless analysis of one of the earliest examples of a Last Judgment from Western Europe will reveal both the content of the new Last Judgment and the compositional principles artists employed to arrange that content in coherent form.[22]

A scene of the Last Judgment on an Anglo-Saxon ivory (fig. 3) of about 800 A.D. speaks to the emotions of the viewer through a composition that presents the actual events of the coming Last Judgment in a narrative sequence, but retains at its center the hieratic formula of earlier metaphorical representations.[23] The inherited pattern consists of three figures in a symmetrical and triangular arrangement. No longer cloaked by the metaphor of parable, they are directly identifiable as Christ the judge and two resurrected humans, one of the elect and one of the damned. Christ is recognizable not only by means of his cruciform halo, but also by a mandorla. With its almond-shaped form, the mandorla enframes the entire body of Christ while serving as a way to represent emanating light. The image of Christ thus is derived less from imperial iconography paralleling the heavenly ruler with an earthly one than from biblical visions such as that of Ezekiel and of St. John in the Apocalypse. Such an image, called the *Maestas Domini*, always refers to Christ both as eternal ruler and as judge.[24] Scrolls that extend diagonally from each of Christ's outstretched arms toward the two naked human figures confirm the source of this grouping as Matthew 25. The scroll in Christ's right hand invites the blessed in the words of verse 34: "Come, ye blessed of my Father, possess you the kingdom prepared for you" ("*Venite benedic[ti P]atr[is] mei p[er]cipite reg[num] vo[bis]*").[25] The figure touched by this scroll reaches his hands toward Christ as if in response to its message, whereas the figure to Christ's left (the scroll is blank) looks down and away from him, recoiling as did the goats in early Christian art.

This old pattern has been imbedded in narrative content by the superimposition of its triangular form onto a series of horizontal zones or bands that can be read sequentially from top to bottom. By adding an arrangement of horizontal bands to the triangular, symmetrical pattern found in early Christian art, the artist creates a complex design giving visual expression to the narrative of the Last Judgment as compiled by contemporary commentators without discarding the imposing formality of the inherited pattern. The resulting compositional type communicates so successfully that it is to remain in use for representations of the Last Judgment from the ninth century through the end of the Middle Ages.

Beginning at the top of the ivory, the narrative of the Last Judgment opens with six trumpeting angels who may refer in abbreviated fashion to the events following the sounding of each of the six trumpets as detailed in Apocalypse 6-11. Next in succession, forming a second zone, is the resurrection of the dead, an event destined to occur after the blowing of the seventh or last trumpet: "thy wrath is come, and the time of the dead, that they should be judged, and that thou shouldest render reward to thy servants the prophets and the saints, and to them that fear thy name, little and great, and shouldest destroy them who have corrupted the earth" (Apocalypse 11.18). The claim that physical bodies of the dead would be resurrected had attracted both speculation and ridicule beginning in the early years of Christianity, so that St. Augustine, for example, felt compelled to discuss the issue at length in *The City of God*. The notoriety of this issue may explain why the designer of the ivory states the orthodox position in an unmistakable sequence of images. We see open coffins, the shrouded bodies in them not yet animate; half-length naked figures rising from their coffins whose souls, envisioned as birds, fly into their mouths; and, just above this zone, the two fully alert figures who are being judged by Christ. Dominating this band, an angel identified as the archangel Michael stands on a crescent moon in a lively twisted pose suggestive of dance. The gesture of a hand placed on the head of one of the resurrected is unusual; Michael's standard role in later examples is weigher of souls or combatant of the devil. This gesture, one capable of various interpretations in early Christian art, may here refer to the bestowal of the Holy Spirit in baptism, for angels were believed to participate in that sacrament.[26] If such an interpretation is correct, then the gesture here may allude to the belief, enunciated by Justin Martyr but already fading by the time this ivory was made, that baptized Christians will escape the Last Judgment.

In compositional terms the most important expansion of the Last Judgment pattern occurs in the lowest zone. As the final phase in the narrative of this ivory panel, this zone illustrates the results of the Last Judgment: the blessed and

27

the damned arriving at their eternal homes. Architectural structures symbolize both heaven and hell. What is striking is the way this zone picks up the symbolism of right and left. By placing paradise to Christ's right and hell to his left, the artist makes explicit what is implied in the Last Judgment above and gives it a terrifying finality. Continuation of the directional symbolism integrates this zone both into the narrative sequence of the Last Judgment and into the overall composition of the panel.

One compositional problem unsolved in this ivory is the lack of visual interest at the center of the lowest zone. The content demands eternal separation of blessed and damned so that there can be no central focus here; yet the overall symmetry of the panel demands one, and so it is weakly supplied by a decorated crescent shape. In later representations of the Last Judgment, artists handle this problem more successfully.

In the expansion of the lowest zone, the ivory speaks most pointedly to an intensified fear of the Last Judgment that was weakening inherited trust in the efficacy of baptism. Viewers are forced to contemplate the results of the Last Judgment: either they will stride confidently with the blessed toward the welcoming gesture of the angel at the entrance to paradise or they will join the damned, shivering and cowering, forced into the open mouth of a monster. This monster received its form from the Leviathan extensively described in Job 41 that commentators on the chapter saw as one of Satan's creatures. Thus it was logical to identify the spread jaws of Leviathan, capable of opening "the doors of his face" to swallow the wicked, with the gates of hell—such an identification is present in Gregory the Great's *Moralia*—and to include this monster in scenes of the Last Judgment.[27] Later drama of the Last Judgment consistently calls for a hell mouth, indicating that the identification of the entrance to hell with the mouth of a monster had become a commonplace of Christian iconography.

The early medieval period, in which as we have seen both the iconography and the composition of the Last Judgment reached a stage of high development, also saw the birth of medieval drama. That drama arose within a liturgy, moreover, that seemed to offer a rich opportunity for the expression of eschatological themes.[28] The liturgy that had been practiced in northern Europe, the Gallican rite, was not only inherently dramatic in character but reflected concern about the Last Judgment in the ceremonies through which converts prepared for baptism during Advent. Because the attitude of repentance that must precede baptism held a special relevance for the season of Advent, that penitential season was seen as preparation both for the first Advent and for the second, the return of Christ and his subsequent judgment. We find in this conjunction the earliest association in the West of the Second Coming and Last Judgment with any liturgical season. The Carolingians suppressed the Gallican rite in favor of the Roman rite, to be sure, because of their reverence for the past as embodied in Christian Rome, but in the process they retained important characteristics of the Gallican rite through which the rather austere and intellectual Roman liturgy that took its place underwent a significant change. First, the Roman rite absorbed the penitential aspect of Advent, which it had entirely lacked, even if it did so rather slowly and unevenly.[29] Also, as C. Clifford Flanigan has suggested, the need for dramatic ritual, thwarted by the suppression of the Gallican rite, found a vehicle for expression in newly emerging liturgical drama, and may even have motivated the rise of that drama.[30] Thus the new liturgy and the nascent liturgical drama would seem to have provided encouragement for the expression of Last Things.

Despite this apparent sympathy of interest, the Last Judgment did not in fact provide the theme of any early liturgical ceremonials or dramas. We are faced with a paradox similar to that we encountered before, in which the Last Judgment received no direct treatment during the initial centuries of early Christian art when the Parousia was nonetheless of such immediate concern. How are we to understand the lateness of dramatic treatment in the tenth through twelfth centuries? Perhaps if we examine the themes that were actually developed in dramatic form, we will see why the Last Judgment is not among them.

Early church dramas share a number of common characteristics, none of them suitable for the presentation of the
Last Judgment. Because early dramatic ceremonies grew
directly out of the liturgy, the occasions of dramatic presentation were closely tied to the liturgical year. Easter, the most
important event of the calendar, provided the first focus for
ceremonials and plays in the *Visitatio Sepulchri* and later the
Peregrinus. The next most important season, Christmas, gave
rise to Nativity plays featuring the shepherds, the Magi, or
both. The celebrations on saints' days, of liturgical importance in the local communities in which they were observed,
encouraged the performance of plays recounting the lives of
the saints. All of the events so dramatized, whether at Easter,
Christmas, or on saints' days, took place on earth in historical time. Those in which Christ made his appearance presented him as the incarnate Christ, not as the Christ-logos
or the second person of the Trinity. Defenders of the pictorial
arts had long argued that it was permissible to represent
Christ incarnate because God had given him human form;
artists portrayed that human flesh, not the divine being without form. Finally, the first subjects of drama featured central
characters that were among the first subjects for monumental
Christian sculpture: the Virgin and Child, the crucifix, statues of saints. In some cases these statues "played" roles in
drama, thereby avoiding the problem of impersonating central figures in the Christian myth.

During the period in which liturgical drama originated,
the subject of the Last Judgment met none of these criteria.
The liturgy presented a recurring cycle of moments of cultic
celebration in which the Christian community re-enacted and
thus experienced its central myth. The Last Judgment was
not yet a part of that pattern. Despite the increasingly penitential nature of Advent, no liturgical season concentrated
on the Last Judgment as such. Further, the nature of the
Last Judgment made it a particularly challenging subject for
drama: both in size of cast and in spatial organization the
Last Judgment demanded much more dramatic complexity
than plays such as the *Visitatio Sepulchri*. Whereas the events
in the life of Christ that received dramatic treatment had the

concrete character of the historical, the Last Judgment presented the problem of representing a visionary event yet to occur. Finally, the role of Christ in a play adapted from Matthew 25 would have to be a major speaking part, hardly able to be filled by a statue, nor do any statues of Christ with iconography appropriate for plays of the Last Judgment survive from this period. Solutions to some of the problems of making the Last Day visible in the arts were to be found in images of the Last Judgment such as the Anglo-Saxon ivory discussed above, but the subject had to impinge more directly on the daily lives and behavior of Christians before these solutions would be brought to bear either on the liturgical music-drama or on the later vernacular religious stage.

We can see evidence of this necessary impingement in the work of the Carolingian writer Rabanus Maurus, whose warnings are indebted in turn to Caesarius of Arles' emphasis on the imminence of Last Judgment. Rabanus cautions, for example, that "he who is looking out for the coming of the Judge who snatches the soul secretly should hasten to meet his coming by repenting, lest he perish impenitent."[31] No longer do we find an attitude toward Last Judgment like that of Cyprian in the third century who could prepare for the Second Coming by focusing on the glory of eternal life that would come after the suffering of the Last Days. Rabanus, writing in the ninth century, is intensely aware of man's sinful nature and of the need for the repentance that must precede Christ's arrival. Rabanus' emphasis on preparedness for the Last Judgment illustrates the context that seems at length to have generated our earliest surviving eschatological play, written at the end of the eleventh century, the *Sponsus*.[32]

The *Sponsus* thus shows at last one way in which church drama could begin to reflect the heightening of concern with the Last Judgment that had already led, in the pictorial arts, to Last Judgment compositions such as the Anglo-Saxon ivory. The play's method of presenting eschatological subject matter through metaphor adopts a strategy similar to that of early Christian eschatological art. The *Sponsus* also uses compositional principles that pictorial artists had discovered

31

to be appropriate and effective for presenting this subject matter. A closer look at this play in the light of its cultural milieu and the pictorial tradition it inherited will reveal both parallels to the pictorial arts and the uniqueness of drama as a new genre of eschatological art.

Concerned directly with preparation for the Last Judgment rather than with the reward of blessed virgins, the *Sponsus* reveals a turning away from early Christian interpretation of the parable in which the emphasis had been on the salvation of all those who were baptized. The play highlights its theme of watchfulness from the very beginning, opening with an admonition of wakeful vigilance, sung probably by a chorus: "The bridegroom is coming, who is Christ, virgins, be watchful" (*"Adest Sponsus, qui est Christus, vigilate, virgines"*). By providing a key to interpretation in the first few words, and by directly identifying the Sponsus with Christ, the play partially unveils its metaphor in order to inform the spectators that this story concerns them directly; they are the benefactors of the salvation history which the chorus goes on to narrate. The next speaker, Gabriel, reiterates the theme in Provençal: "Gaire noi dormet" ("Watchers may not slumber").

What did the metaphor of watchfulness mean to those who saw the first presentation of this play? Although anticipation of the Second Coming had always been an appropriate attitude for Christians, in early medieval times the sense of urgency increased perceptibly. St. Gregory the Great (590-604) counsels: "Therefore it ought to be the more feared as if always coming, in proportion as we are unable to foreknow when it is about to come."[33] Rabanus Maurus, writing in the ninth century, calls for unceasing vigilance: "For that very man watches well who, when he holds his body back from sleep, does not permit his heart to be made heavier in perverse desires, but holds the eyes of his mind opened to the sight of true light: he watches, who saves by working hard at what he believes; he watches by pushing away from himself the shadows of torpor and negligence."[34] In the late eleventh century, St. Anselm gives this idea still more forceful impact by presenting it in personal and emotional terms.

After passionately lamenting that he was not present during the events of Christ's life on earth, Anselm yearns unrestrainedly for the Second Coming—"I want you, I hope for you, I seek you"—and closes with an expression of the penitent attitude he seeks to maintain until that time:

> Lord, meanwhile, let my tears be my meat day and
> night,
> until they say to me: "Behold your God,"
> until I hear, "Soul, behold your bridegroom."[35]

Even though the *Sponsus* is not so emotionally charged, it reflects, through its emphasis on watchfulness, a growing sense of direct relationship between repentance and the coming Last Judgment.

Text, stage picture, and dramatic action all contribute to the effectiveness of the *Sponsus* in dramatizing its concern with watchfulness. The text seems to give the foolish virgins the central role, whereas stage picture gives emphasis to the wise virgins as well. Dramatic action maintains the balance between the two groups, carries the narrative forward, and provides a memorable ending in the deserved rewards of both wise and foolish virgins.

The heavy concentration of the text of the *Sponsus* on the foolish virgins reinforces the theme of timely repentance. They seem almost to be its protagonists, for, after the opening, the play apportions most of the dialogue to them. This dialogue consists largely of their lamenting over their situation—"too long have we slept"—and begging for relief from the wise virgins, the merchants, and the bridegroom, all of whom refuse them.

The visual composition of the play, to the extent that it draws on traditional ways of portraying eschatological subjects, operates to give the wise virgins an important place in stage picture. The opening of the play strongly suggests a processional during which the actors can take their places. Thereafter, the content of the play, in the balancing of the dramatis personae and their contrasted fates, demands a symmetrical visual composition. Thus a likely and effective

33

stage picture for the beginning of the play is one in which the central axis is an expectant void, to be filled only by the arrival of the bridegroom. The foolish virgins are to his left, near a hell mouth on the same side, while the wise virgins to the right are near a door that functions as the gate to paradise. No rubrics specify such an arrangement, but the presence of foolish and wise virgins necessarily invokes a compositional pattern that was familiar to dramatist and audience alike and was suited to any depiction of judgment.[36] The merchants' booth does not belong in the charged space of this composition and would have been outside the main playing area. The wise virgins remain in their places, keeping their vigil, while the foolish virgins futilely petition first them and then the merchants for oil. By maintaining their position stage right through much of the play, the wise virgins not only demand visual attention but proclaim their spiritual steadfastness through their physical presence. Because they are in the right place when the bridegroom arrives, activating the central axis of the visual picture, they are invited to join him in his wedding feast.

Like the metaphorical scenes of judgment in early Christian art, this play uses a small cast, a minimal set, and visual symbolism of left and right, but as a play it is also able to add dramatic action. The movement of the foolish virgins in their search for oil helps characterize them as lacking in constancy. This sequence of actions builds tension toward the climax of the bridegroom's sudden appearance and allows for the intriguing possibility of simultaneous staging. If the bridegroom receives the wise virgins while the foolish virgins process from the merchants' booth back toward their places, and if the attention of the audience is held by the lament of the foolish virgins, then the audience too will have failed, like the foolish virgins, by not "looking out for the coming of the judge who snatches the soul." In the pictorial arts this moment is portrayed with a satisfying symmetry but without the excitement of surprise inherent in drama. Drama is also able to employ mimed action to convey meaning and emotional impact. The wise virgins must be received into paradise entirely by means of gestures and movement without dialogue. Similar action visualizes the fate of the foolish virgins, underscoring the effect of Christ's refusal to receive or even recognize them. The play, in one of its very few stage directions, explicitly sends demons to carry them to hell: "Then let demons seize them, and let them be thrown into hell" ("*Modo accipiant eas Demones, et precipitentur in infernum*"). This final action has dramaturgic value as well, for it disposes of the remaining actors, the foolish virgins, clearing the playing area for the resumption of the day's liturgy.

In its use of stage action to balance dialogue and picture, this play successfully presents the alternative consequences of wise watchfulness and of foolish heedlessness. Previously, the pictorial arts tended to concentrate on the wise virgins. In the early Christian period pictorial interpretation of the parable saw it as a lesson that those who remained steadfast, like the holy virgins, would be rewarded with participation in the heavenly banquet. Even in the Carolingian period we find a wall painting or mosaic of the Last Judgment at Gorze, showing the wise virgins but apparently deliberately omitting the foolish virgins.[37] The *Sponsus* shifts this emphasis in the direction of a more even presentation, reflecting a comparable shift in the way Christians of the eleventh and twelfth centuries came to view themselves. As Philippe Ariès comments, "Gone is the old idea that all believers are saints. No one among the people of God is assured of his salvation, not even those who have preferred the solitude of the cloisters to the profane world."[38] In this context the *Sponsus* transforms the parable of the wise and foolish virgins into a liturgical drama that presents, through metaphor, two opposed models of behavior against which Christians could measure their own lives.

Such a metaphoric treatment is appropriate to eschatological drama in this eleventh-century period for a number of reasons. To begin with, the Last Judgment, with its visionary nature and its infinite dimensions, is unlike any other subject treated in liturgical drama before the twelfth century and would have been very difficult to render literally. Also the parable is more suited to liturgical occasion than is the actual Last Judgment. So long as drama maintained even a

35

loose connection with liturgy, it partook of the liturgy's function as cultic ritual. Such ritual, according to Flanigan, involves actions that stand at the center of the culture's myths and include "an act in which its celebrants seek to imitate the actions . . . in such a way that the past events which are commemorated are thought to be rendered present once again for the benefit of the cultic community."[39] The Last Judgment was not a part of the recurrent liturgical cycle made up of central events in Christian mythology and was therefore not a suitable subject for drama in such a system. The *Sponsus* is likely to have been played on feasts of holy virgins, when the passage from Matthew 25 on which it is based was usually read, and on such an occasion the play would have avoided an explicitly eschatological context. Alternatively, its performance may have come during Advent because of the growing association of this season with preparation for the Second Coming, or at Easter because of language in a Mass of the Easter Vigil that speaks of waiting "for the advent of the radiant bridegroom."[40]

The metaphor of the wise and foolish virgins speaks to the concern for timely repentance in a way that the Last Judgment did not during the early medieval period. Although it later would serve such a function, in this period the Last Judgment was seen only as the finality after which it was too late to repent. As St. Gregory the Great comments, "For now [Christ] is not seen and is near; then he will be seen and will not be near. He has not yet appeared in judgment, and if he is sought he is found. For in a wonderful way, when he will have appeared in judgment he is both able to be seen and unable to be found."[41] That is, until the Second Coming, Christ's mercy is present, but when he returns and is himself present, his mercy will be absent and those who are deserving of doom will not be spared. So long as an eschatological play remained metaphorical, it did not enact Christ's actual judgment at the end of time. Drama of the Last Judgment would become possible only after the rise of imaginative devotion that encouraged Christians to take figures such as Christ and the Virgin Mary as exemplars—in the words of Giles Constable, they are to be "personal spiritual model[s] whose least actions were to be imitated by the devout Christian"[42]—and who are to envision themselves as present at events described in Scripture such as the Last Judgment.

The rise of imaginative devotion forms one facet of the cultural shift called the "renaissance of the twelfth century," which brought about major changes in virtually every area of western culture from technology to theology. To understand the underlying causes that explain these "intimate, irreversible, and delicately interrelated changes," as Peter Brown terms them, is difficult.[43] Brown suggests that the boundary between the sacred and the profane was redrawn in this period, and he provides an extended example in the decline of trial by ordeal. These ordeals had enabled a community to submit difficult issues *ad judicium Dei* often with results sufficiently ambiguous that the actual determination was made by the community as interpreters of the evidence. Two factors are significant here: first, the whole community, rather than the clergy alone, judged the outcome of the ordeal; second, as a result of this public trial, the accused, if found innocent, could feel secure that God's judgment had been pronounced. Trials by ordeal thus, to a certain extent, obviated fear of the Last Judgment; conversely, with the decline of such trials, fear of the Last Judgment rose sharply.

Another approach to understanding the renaissance of the twelfth century is taken by Charles Radding, who proposes a shift in mentalities—"the beliefs and ways of reasoning shared by actual people living at a given time"—to explain "the sudden predominance of cognitive structures that were different from those of the early Middle Ages."[44] Drawing on the research of psychologists on stages of moral reasoning, Radding sees a shift in the twelfth century toward a higher stage of moral reasoning characterized by increased concern with interpersonal relationships and the interior aspects of human nature. This shift affected every aspect of human thought. As interpersonal relationships came to be more highly valued, people developed emotionally, seeing their responsibilities to others, as well as to themselves, more seriously. Thus, as ethics developed in the direction of considering the intention of a person in evaluating that person's actions, this development in turn changed the view of penance. Whereas previously, as shown by early medieval penitentials, penance had been understood as a transaction in which the penitent performed assigned actions, it now required an emotional state of interior contrition. Radding further observes that, correlating with a general rise in the place of the imaginative and the emotional in human nature, even the judicial system (to which analogies to the Last Judgment were often drawn) developed a new "ability to test hypotheses by consideration of imaginary situations."

All of these changes impinged on attitudes toward the Last Judgment. Part of the movement that withdrew the Church's support of trial by ordeal clarified the boundary between the sacred and the profane so as to define certain areas in which the authority of the Church was unquestioned, among them the determination of the state of the soul through confession. Clergy quickly realized that fear of the Last Judgment could motivate contrition. With intermediate trials by ordeal no longer functioning as determinants of God's will, all lay in uncertainty until the final judgment. Christians, attentive to their spiritual states, were susceptible to imaginative visions of the Last Judgment and learned to fear the punishments of hell.

The direct use of imagery of the Last Judgment to motivate repentance is clearly evident in the prayers and meditations of St. Anselm, written at the end of the eleventh century. Unlike Gregory the Great, who saw God acting to bring man to awareness of sin, Anselm assumes that it is the responsibility of the individual to initiate the process of penance, and he directs his writings to aid in that process. First, in order to stir the mind from its torpor, Anselm describes man as a foul sinner thoroughly deserving the punishment of hell. Only when filled with fear of eternal condemnation, Anselm reasons, can man be provoked to repentance. Thus Anselm's first meditation, entitled "A meditation to stir up fear," contains a highly emotional description of the Last Judgment: "Alas for me, here are sins accusing me—there is the terror of judgment. Below the horrible chaos of hell lies open—above is the wrath of the judge. Inside is the burning conscience—outside is the burning of the world. Scarcely shall the just be saved—and thus overtaken where can a sinner turn?"[45]

Such vivid imagery suggests a sculptural representation of the type that St. Hugh of Lincoln and King John contemplated while Hugh admonished the latter concerning his sins:

> Then the bishop pointed to the left hand of the Judge, where kings in their regalia were being consigned to damnation. . . . The bishop turned to his companion and said, "A man's conscience ought continually to remind him of the lamentations and interminable torments of these wretches. One should keep the thought of these eternal pains before one's mind all the time. . . . Let the memory of these pains remind you how severe will be the charge against those who are set for a short time to rule others in this world, but fail to govern themselves. In this life we still have a chance to avoid this terrible fate, and to do so we ought to dread it in our whole being. . . ." He said that images like this were very rightly placed at the entrance of churches. For thus the people going inside to pray for their needs were reminded of this greatest need of all. . . . If only [the king] could be warned in time of the wrath so soon to come! That even so late he might endeavour to escape eternal punishment, and remove himself from the left hand to the right of that Eternal Judge![46]

With such a crucial role for the process of penance, monumental representations of the Last Judgment like the one Hugh so skillfully employed became ubiquitous. Often a Last Judgment took the place of the *Maestas Domini*, an image of Christ as eternal ruler and judge, which in the Romanesque period (c. 1050-1200) had occupied a central location in the church. Inspired by Apocalypse 4.4-6 and hence called the Apocalyptic Christ, the Apocalyptic Vision, or the Second Coming, the *Maestas Domini* portrayed Christ enthroned in a mandorla, seated on a rainbow, surrounded by the four beasts of the Apocalypse (commonly interpreted as symbols of the Evangelists), and flanked by the twenty-four elders.[47] Romanesque art, with its abstract, two-dimensional style that isolated the main thread of a narrative and conveyed its spiritual content, was especially well suited to put into imagery this visionary scene, lacking reference to linear time or the solid, three-dimensional matter of earth, its landscapes, or inhabitants. The Apocalyptic Vision, frequently painted in the half-domes of apses, above and behind an altar, transformed the interior of the church into God's space, completely separate from the external world. The same subject was also carved in relief on tympana, lunette-shaped or triangular areas over the doors of churches placed so as to dominate the vision of beholders just before they entered the church.

When, under the impact of increased concern with the Last Judgment in the twelfth century, the subject of Last Judgment absorbed or displaced the Apocalyptic Vision, it did so in one of the most prominent locations of the church, its western wall. The fact that the sun setting in the West is a universal metaphor for finality and death made the choice of the western wall for imagery of the Last Judgment especially appropriate. On the façade, Last Judgments appeared in tympana; on the inside, as Otto Demus describes wall paintings of the Last Judgment, "they would normally have spread over the whole wall, a powerful reminder of the Last Things for the congregation as they left the church."[48]

Not only did representations of the Last Judgment flourish during the Romanesque period because of fear of the Last Judgment, but their content also changed in order to inspire that fear more effectively. The compositional formula first developed in the Carolingian period, one that combined a triangular arrangement with narrative bands, lies at the basis of Romanesque Last Judgments. This formula both organizes increasingly detailed components into a clearly legible whole and imparts an impressive monumentality to its subject. A detailed study of the Last Judgment on the western tympanum at Conques (fig. 2), variously dated from the beginning to the second half of the twelfth century, will reveal significant changes both in iconography and in composition when it is compared with the ivory discussed above.[49]

The overall composition of the tympanum at Conques shows increased sophistication both in its adaptation to the shape of its frame and in its strong central axis. This sculpture exploits the shape of the lunette much more effectively than is the case with the triangular composition of the ivory within its rectangular shape. The resulting congruence makes a more cohesive statement of hierarchy. Especially impressive is the development of the central axis, a weak point in the composition of the ivory. The large cross above and behind Christ significantly strengthens both the vertical axis at the center of the tympanum and the symmetry of the whole composition. The partition between the entrances to heaven and hell in the lowest register of the tympanum extends the axis visually so that it can hold in balance the strong horizontals of the narrative bands.

The narrative of the Last Judgment unfolding around the central figure of Christ in Romanesque Last Judgments such as the example at Conques seems to reveal a rhetorical strategy paralleling that exemplified by St. Anselm's prayers and meditations. It represents horrifying scenes of hell's torment in order to rouse the mind from its torpor; then it urges a course of action that, if taken, would result in the avoidance of hellfire and suggests the contrasting bliss of paradise. Finally it reminds its audience that two ways lie open and that each individual must make a personal choice.

On the lower right hand side of the tympanum, a spot likely to catch the eye of the viewer approaching the main western door of Conques, scenes of hell effectively shake the viewer out of any false complacency. The demons that are so ubiquitous in Romanesque art are often thought to be as much expressions of artistic imagination run riot as of deeply felt conviction that such creatures exist. Yet there is seriousness of intent behind their ubiquity: the intent of urging man to repentance by means of the sheer terror which these creatures inspire as they display unending inventiveness in devising tortures for condemned humanity. Romanesque artists excite the fear of punishment both by conjuring up specific tortures for particular sins and by supplying horrifying details as to the instruments and machinery of torture. At Conques, the hell that lies behind the open mouth of Leviathan seems an incarnation of that imagined by Anselm in his "Prayer to St. Stephen":

> A prison with no remedy gapes;
> in that prison lie great torments,
>
> . . .
>
> Torments without end, without interval, without respite,
> horrible tortures which never slacken,
> on which no one has pity.[50]

Anselm might almost have been describing the experience of approaching such a tympanum as he continues:

> Fear shakes the accused, his conscience confounds him,
>   thoughts beset him and he cannot flee.
>   Thus he stands,
>   with the heaviest of sentences hanging over him.[51]

Having been convinced of the need to act before it is too late, the viewer of the tympanum eagerly searching for help finds figures to Christ's right that call to mind two things each person can do on his own behalf. First, angels display scrolls on which the names of the virtues are inscribed, a variant of a theme that often appears in association with Last Judgment portals from this time onward: the pairing of personified virtues with defeated vices. As Adolf Katzenellenbogen observes, "the special function of the triumph of the virtues is now that of encouraging the faithful even before they enter the church, to emulate the virtues in view of the coming Judgment Day."[52] And while the virtues refer to efficacious actions the viewer can take, the procession below them illustrates the potency of prayer. The Virgin Mary leads this procession, followed by St. Peter, a hermit, a monk, and an emperor. Mary was first associated with the Last Judgment in the Byzantine East, specifically in the Deësis scene where she and John the Baptist stand before the enthroned Christ as intercessors for the souls of humankind.[53] Mary's presence in Western Last Judgments inspires the viewer to pray to her, in words like those of St. Anselm's "Prayer to St. Mary when the mind is anxious with fear":

> Lady, it seems to me as if I were already
> before the all-powerful justice of the stern judge
> facing the intolerable vehemence of his wrath,
> while hanging over me is the enormity of my sins,
>   and the huge torments they deserve.
>   Most gentle Lady,
> whose intercession should I implore
> when I am troubled with horror and shake with fear,
>   but hers, whose womb embraced
>   the reconciliation of the world?[54]

Similarly Anselm calls upon St. Peter, who stands behind the Virgin in the tympanum at Conques, holding the large key that is his attribute:

> To the door-keeper of the kingdom of heaven,
>   the prince of the apostles,
> I will show a faithful soul, unhappy in the kingdom of sin,
>   longing for the kingdom of heaven.[55]

Following Mary and St. Peter come additional saints to whom prayers might be offered. Representations of the Last Judgment from this time forward contain figures of saints; by so doing they provide the viewer with a course of action, a means of diminishing the paralyzing fear of hell. The inclusion of saints also contributes to the hieratic nature of the scene by adding a layer of intercessors between God and man.

The composition of the tympanum works to reinforce the impact of the content, constantly reminding the beholder that the Last Judgment to come, concentrated on the central axis of the tympanum, will result in one of two fates, eternally separated on Christ's left and right sides. The half of the middle zone to Christ's right, in which the procession led by the Virgin Mary and St. Peter appears, serves the important function of moving the eye from left to right in a steady rhythm toward Christ. The calm order of this portion of the tympanum contrasts sharply with the chaos of hell that seethes on the opposite side of Christ. The same ordered harmony reigns in paradise in the zone below the procession, again contrasted with the scene of frenzied torture symmetrically opposite. The two sides of the tympanum maintain a visual balance that is pleasing to the eye while offering antithetical content. The complex relationship between the two sides of the tympanum, both iconographic and compositional, is seen most clearly in a comparison of the figures at the center of each side of the lowest zone. Frontally seated, these two figures repeat the posture of the judging Christ (though not his gestures) and form the lower corners of a triangle which has Christ at its apex. In paradise reigns Abraham, placidly holding two blissful souls to his bosom. Abraham's presence here derives from the story in Luke 16 of a rich man (called Dives in apocryphal sources) and Lazarus, a beggar.[56] As if in mocking response to Abraham's protective gestures, Satan, seated symmetrically opposite Abraham, tramples a prostrate sinner and points to Judas, the suicide hanging next to him.[57] The eye recoils, seeking again the serenity of paradise behind its stately arcade. Neither Anselm nor Romanesque artists explore the pleasures of paradise, but the composition itself speaks clearly of its positive qualities.[58]

Because the central axis of the tympanum exerts a dominant force over the entire composition, the eye of the viewer returns to it, just as the soul returns to the contemplation of God and the need for God's mercy. The cross, through which the top of the central axis passes, is a new—and from this time forward a ubiquitous—element in Last Judgment compositions. Iconographically the cross functions as the "sign of the Son of man" that was to appear in the heavens at the time of the Last Judgment (Matthew 24.30). The presence of the cross and Christ's displaying of the wounds in his hands, both calling attention to the physical suffering Christ endured during his crucifixion, underscore his humanity. In so doing, they reflect St. Anselm's new theory of the Atonement which says that Christ, through his Incarnation and Passion, has redeemed mankind by being the perfect sacrifice, the God-man.[59] In most contexts emphasis on *Christus patiens* encourages the viewer to imagine and empathize with Christ's suffering, but in the context of the Last Judgment it states forcefully that, through his suffering, Christ earned the right to judge mankind. The angels censing Christ recall the scene of the *Maestas Domini*, further stressing Christ's authority as judge. With majestic gestures, Christ communicates his judgment in visual language. These gestures also establish vertical associations for paradise and hell and create a dynamic rather than static balance of the two sides of the tympanum.

The space on the central axis between paradise and hell, left as an unsatisfying void in the Anglo-Saxon ivory discussed above, here contains two scenes of great visual interest that amplify Christ's message of the separation of blessed and damned. These scenes also apply that message to viewers and are thus most effectively placed nearest to them. Directly below Christ, an angel holding a balance scale enacts the action known as the Psychostasis or weighing of souls. The immediate scriptural source for this image is the metaphor of Daniel 5.27, "thou art weighed in the balance, and art found wanting." The concept is still more venerable, however, for ancient Egyptians were familiar with it; there the judge supervised the weighing of a man's heart against the symbol for *ma'at* (truth, justice, righteousness, right-dealing, order).[60] Whether the Psychostasis was adopted into Christian art by Egyptian Christians or inspired directly by biblical language,[61] its inclusion in the Last Judgment greatly enhances the impact of that scene. Often, as at Conques, demons attempt to pervert Christ's justice by insinuating extra weight on their side of the scale. This is the only portion of the tympanum where the central axis does not receive visual reinforcement. Its absence effectively focuses attention on the Psychostasis, giving this scene more prominence than its size alone would suggest. In terms of content, the viewer sees the moment when eternal fate is determined, when destiny literally hangs in the balance.

At the center of the lowest zone, the central axis reasserts itself as a visible partition between the antechambers of paradise and hell. Here the artist inserts a scene of anecdotal interest, balancing the remote grandeur of Christ the judge far above. As one of the elect glances over his shoulder across what is at once a narrow partition and an immeasurable gulf, a wild-haired demon brandishing a club also looks back. Their glances lock, not only to emphasize the tension of balanced opposites on either side of the central axis, but also in tacit acknowledgment that the escape was a narrow one.

The achievement of the Romanesque in regard to the Last Judgment, as exemplified by Conques, lies in its having found ways of amplifying the content of the scene so that it can speak effectively to evoke repentance as well as ways of organizing the composition so that it not only presents that content in a coherent fashion but even enhances the total impact. The next few centuries introduce changes in style, though the basic solutions found in the Romanesque period continue to inform representations of the Last Judgment throughout the remainder of the Middle Ages.

In summary, the pattern of development of the subject of the Last Judgment in the pictorial arts begins hesitantly in the era of primitive Christianity. The earliest representations are metaphorical; compositionally they present a few figures symmetrically balanced about a central axis; a triangular arrangement of figures introduces the hieratic principle. The first direct presentations of the Last Judgment use these compositional principles and add to them horizontal bands of narrative, responding to increased curiosity about and fear of the Last Judgment in the early medieval period. Comprehensive Last Judgments become ubiquitous in the Romanesque period, reminding Christians that they are responsible for the state of their souls in the face of the Last Judgment. These works of art contain a huge number of figures, held in legible configurations by tightly organized compositions in which relative placement has symbolic value.

The development of medieval drama concerned with the Last Judgment repeats this pattern of slow, tentative problem-solving. We have already seen that in its initial stages liturgical drama, or church music-drama, does not include the subject of the Last Judgment. At the end of the eleventh century, the *Sponsus* treats an eschatological subject, the parable of the wise and foolish virgins, but declines to enact the actual Last Judgment. In choosing a metaphor rather than a literal representation of the Last Judgment itself, the *Sponsus*, like the early Christian representations of the wise and foolish virgins, demonstrates a preference for a simply presented scene made up essentially of one episode and acted out by a cast of relatively few characters. A later twelfth-century eschatological play, the *Ludus de Antichristo*, moves, like eschatology in the pictorial arts, from the metaphorical to the literal level.[62] The *Ludus de Antichristo* rehearses the events to precede the Last Judgment, stopping just short of staging the final moments of history. Its visual composition reflects that of complex Last Judgments like Conques, and its content shows the influence of the twelfth-century renaissance on eschatological thinking.

Even in the context of experiment with many new subjects that characterizes twelfth-century drama, the *Ludus de Antichristo* stands out. It is, in Karl Young's words, "the best literary product of German ecclesiastical life in the twelfth century."[63] Compiling an account closely based in Adso's *Libellus de Antichristo*, Pseudo-Methodius, the Vulgate, and the liturgy, the dramatist expresses the twelfth-century view of Antichrist, the devilish man who brings the world's rulers into submission through a skillful combination of terror, bribery, and display of miracles. Antichrist kills Enoch and Elias after they have won the Jews from him, converting them to Christianity, and, when a great noise is heard from above, he collapses as his followers flee. The play then ends quickly with the Christians joining Ecclesia, the personification of the Church, in praise of God.

In its use of certain features of liturgical drama, the *Ludus de Antichristo* is reminiscent of its eschatological predecessor, the *Sponsus*. Both display a tendency toward processional movement, especially marked in the *Ludus*. Further, both plays rely on the symbolic spatial orientation inherent in the performance of the liturgy. According to Elie Konigson, "sacred space is always oriented: the officiants and the place of the dramatized liturgy are situated and move themselves along an axis, sometimes from west to east, sometimes from east to west, sometimes, starting from these two poles, toward the center marked by the crossing of the transept or the middle of the nave."[64] Orientation "according to the axis of the world" allows a performance of the *Sponsus* to place the entrance of the bridegroom at a point on this axis as he separates wise and foolish virgins to his right and left. The *Ludus de Antichristo*, whether performed in sacred space or not, structures its action along such an axis, placing the Temple of God to the east and the seat of the emperor to the west.

In spite of these similarities, the *Ludus de Antichristo* differs fundamentally from the *Sponsus* both in its visual composition and in its content. The *Ludus* is drama on a much grander scale than the *Sponsus*. More than sixty actors, in a wide variety of colorful costumes, enact numerous episodes in a huge playing area containing *platea* and *sedes*. In purely objective terms, the *Ludus* is a much longer play, taking, in Richard Axton's estimation, well over two hours to perform.[65] Its very length gives it an identity of its own separate from the liturgy.

In its approach to its content, the *Ludus* also separates itself from the liturgy. The liturgy, like the *Sponsus*, takes no notice of secular affairs: its application is universal, general, unchanging from year to year, just as the allegory of the *Sponsus* applies to all mankind without reference to time. The *Ludus* works on two distinct levels. Many critics have seen the *Ludus* as a political play, urging Frederick Barbarossa "to realize his ambition of becoming emperor of the East and West and military defender of Christendom."[66] Certainly much in the play refers to a specific moment in history. On the other hand, as Richard Emmerson reminds us, the course of action urged on Frederick is that in which Frederick would become the Last World Emperor, an agent in the unfolding of universal eschatology. Ultimately, as Emmerson shows, "the eschatological motivations are stronger than the political,"[67] for the Last World Emperor, faithful to the Antichrist tradition, gives up his *imperium* as Frederick would scarcely have done. The stage of the play is the entire

48

world, its actors have the names of generic figures, and its action brings world history to its penultimate moment. The twelfth-century historian, Otto of Freising, who was uncle to Frederick, may have inspired the application of the universal to the particular seen in the *Ludus*, but, on a deeper level, it is a reflection of a new interest in history attributable to the twelfth-century renaissance. As Marie-Dominique Chenu observes, "Christendom became aware of its historical evolution in the twelfth century."[68]

Both in its ability to manipulate two levels of reference and in its visual composition, the *Ludus de Antichristo* is analogous to pictorial treatments of the Last Judgment such as the tympanum at Conques. The universal vision of final judgment at Conques contains figures of purely local content (see Chapter II, below). Both at Conques and in the *Ludus* these two levels fit into a highly structured visual pattern controlled by symmetry and hierarchy. Symmetry plays a key role in visual organization of both play and sculpture. The many battles in the play, which could easily cause visual confusion, sort themselves out by reference to the symmetrically arranged *sedes* of the combatants just as the many individual incidents in the tympanum can be interpreted only by reference to their placement on left or right sides. As Richard Axton observes, symmetry in the contrast between the rule of the Last World Emperor and of Antichrist gives the play its overall sense of structure.[69] Symmetry also emerges through repetition: songs are sung repeatedly, especially in the elaborate processional visits to the various kings. The acts of doing homage and swearing fealty in the play create visual images of hieratic order which are like those of the tympanum. In both tympanum and play, every episode is held in a tight visual relationship to the whole through the pervasive conflict between good and evil.

Visual picture communicates much of the play's content. Confrontations between good and evil are direct and physical. The exploits of evil lend themselves especially well to visualization, as we have already seen in the pictorial arts of the Romanesque period. As John Wright observes of the *Ludus*, "The playwright is interested only in the graphic de-

49

piction of the enormous power of evil."[70] Antichrist's false
miracles of healing and raising the dead are enacted, and his
followers acknowledge his authority by receiving an imprint
of the letter "A" on their foreheads. Standard iconography
provides visual identification of the characters. Synagogue
appears here with her blindfold as she does frequently within
Last Judgment compositions in the great sculptural programs
of the twelfth century. Misericordia and Justitia, who carry
their attributes in the *Ludus*, also play roles in the late medieval English play, *The Castle of Perseverance*, discussed
below in Chapter V. Thus, both the monumental Last Judgment compositions of the twelfth century and the *Ludus de
Antichristo* are impressive presentations of eschatological
content, similar in the spatial organization they employ to
handle visual complexity.

The underlying similarities between the pictorial arts
and the visual aspects of drama emphasized in this chapter
should not be allowed to obscure the differences between
these media. The functions of the pictorial arts are importantly different from those of early drama, to which the liturgy had made a significant contribution. In fact, these
differences of function between pictorial art and drama in
their representations of Last Judgment help explain the paradox of the contrast between doctrinal importance and late
development with which we began. The pictorial arts of the
early Christian and early medieval periods served a primarily
didactic purpose, supplying images through which Christians
read lessons essential to their understanding of their religion.
The Last Judgment was not one of those lessons so long as
Christians believed themselves free of condemnation, either
because of the efficacy of baptism or because satisfaction
for individual sins had been given. As assurance of salvation
waned, under the impact of writers like Caesarius of Arles
and St. Gregory the Great the contemplation of an image of
the Last Judgment became a way of apprehending the nature
of events to come. In the wake of the twelfth-century renaissance, Last Judgment images acquired a related function:
the need for repentance was learned through fear of judgment.

On the other hand, the liturgy and the earliest of liturgical dramas functioned in an inherently different way from that of pictorial art, seeking to make present the events being celebrated so that the congregation could re-experience them. Perhaps for this reason, the first drama with eschatological content, the *Sponsus*, did not enact a scene of the actual Last Judgment and may have been written for feast days of holy virgins rather than for an eschatological context. The *Ludus de Antichristo*, more distinct from the liturgy, turned to, but still did not complete, eschatological time, ending with the death or collapse of Antichrist. As Emmerson observes, the end of the play may have been meant to suggest that the next event would be the period, believed to be forty or forty-five days, in which those who followed Antichrist would have a chance to repent.[71] If so, then the message of the *Ludus*—that the time to repent is at hand—is the same as that of the Last Judgment in the pictorial arts. If the *Ludus* were to enact the actual Last Judgment, it would bring that time prematurely to an end.

Drama of the actual Last Judgment does not appear until the changes begun in the twelfth century have had sufficient time for their impact to be felt. When the concept of religious drama separates from that of liturgy to the point that drama is no longer restricted to the liturgy's function of re-presenting, then drama acquires a new function, imparted to the pictorial arts as well: that of providing an imaginative, emotional experience for the viewer as part of affective devotional practices. The relationship between the pictorial arts and later medieval plays that treat the subject of Last Judgment directly lies outside the scope of this chapter. Nonetheless, the increase in interest in the Last Judgment traced here created a climate receptive to plays of the Last Judgment, and the compositional principles laid out here inform the examples of the pictorial and dramatic arts discussed in the later chapters of this book.

NOTES

1. For the subject of the Last Judgment in the visual arts, see Beat Brenk, *Tradition und Neuerung in der christlichen Kunst des ersten Jahr-*

tausends: Studien zur Geschichte des Weltgerichtbildes, Wiener Byzantinische Studien, 3 (Graz, Vienna, and Cologne, 1966); Yves Christe, *La Vision de Matthieu* (Paris: Klincksieck, 1973); H. Sachs, "Jungfrauen, Kluge und Töriche," in *Lexikon der christlichen Ikonographie*, ed. Engelbert Kirschbaum (Freiburg: Herder, 1968-76), II, 458-63; W. Kemp, "Seelenreise," in *Lexikon der christlichen Ikonographie*, IV, 142-45; B. Brenk, "Weltgericht," in *Lexikon der christlichen Ikonographie*, IV, 514-23; Louis Réau, *Iconographie de l'art chrétien* (Paris: Presses Universitaires de France, 1955-59), II, Pt. 2; Louis Réau, "Eschatology: The Christian World," in *Encyclopedia of World Art*, IV, 820-27. The volume on the Last Judgment in Gertrud Schiller's *Ikonographie der christlichen Kunst*—projected to be Vol. VI—has not yet appeared.

2. Pamela Sheingorn, "The Visual Language of Drama," in *Contexts of English Medieval Drama*, ed. Marianne Briscoe and John Coldeway (Toronto: Univ. of Toronto Press, forthcoming).

3. *The Prayers and Meditations of Saint Anselm*, trans. Sister Benedicta Ward (1973; Harmondsworth: Penguin, 1979), p. 164.

4. On apocalypticism in the early Christian period, see Jaroslav Pelikan, *The Christian Tradition: A History of the Development of Doctrine*, I: *The Emergence of the Catholic Tradition (100-600)* (Chicago: Univ. of Chicago Press, 1971); William A. Beardslee, "New Testament Apocalyptic in Recent Interpretation," *Interpretation*, 25 (1971), 419-35; and for pertinent texts, Bernard McGinn, ed., *Visions of the End: Apocalyptic Traditions in the Middle Ages* (New York: Columbia Univ. Press, 1979).

5. "Scire enim debetis et pro certo credere ac tenere pressurae diem super caput esse coepisse et occasum saeculi atque antichristi tempus adpropinquasse, ut parati omnes ad proelium stemus nec quicquam nisi gloriam vitae aeternae et coronam confessionis dominicae cogitemus. Neque aliquis ex vobis, fratres dilectissimi, futurae persecutionis metu aut antichristi imminentis adventu sic terreatur ut non evangelicis exhortationibus et praeceptis ac monitis caelestibus ad omnia inveniatur armatus"; quoted in Karl Heisig, "Über den geistesgeschichtlichen Standort des Sponsus," *Romanistisches Jahrbuch*, 5 (1952), 246.

6. *Dialogue*, CXXXVIII, 2-3, quoted in Jean Daniélou, *The Bible and the Liturgy* (Notre Dame, Indiana: Univ. of Notre Dame Press, 1956), p. 78.

7. Ibid., p. 79.

8. Thomas Buser, "Early Catacomb Iconography and Apocalypticism," *Studies in Iconography*, 6 (1980), 13.

9. The New Testament itself had linked these stories to the apocalyptic. For Noah see Matthew 24.37, "And as in the days of Noe, so shall also the coming of the Son of man be." For Jonah, Luke 11.30, "For as Jonas was a sign to the Ninivites; so shall the Son of man also be to this generation."

10. Six charitable acts are actually listed; a seventh, the burial of

the dead, was added later. This enabled the Seven Acts of Mercy to be contrasted with the Seven Deadly Sins.

11. Josef Wilpert, *Die Malereien des Katakomben Roms* (Freiburg im Breisgau: Herder, 1903), I, 428-29; II, 241.

12. For a penetrating study of the relationship between text and illustration, see Kurt Weitzmann, *Illustrations in Roll and Codex: A Study in the Origin and Method of Text Illustration* (1947; rpt. Princeton: Princeton Univ. Press, 1970).

13. "In the Gospels of Luke (15:3-7) and John (10:1-16), Christ is characterized as the shepherd who protects and loves his flock and who will bring the soul of man to salvation as a shepherd retrieves lost sheep. The model for this Christ derives from a classical bucolic ram-bearing shepherd, which personified philanthropy and when used in funerary monuments implied the promise of salvation"—Margaret E. Frazer, "Iconic Representations," in *The Age of Spirituality: Late Antique and Early Christian Art, Third to Seventh Century*, ed. Kurt Weitzmann (New York: Metropolitan Museum of Art, 1979), p. 558.

14. For further discussion of this object, which is in the Metropolitan Museum of Art, New York, see Brenk, *Tradition und Neuerung*, pp. 38-43; Frazer, "Iconic Representations," p. 558.

15. Barbara Nolan, *The Gothic Visionary Perspective* (Princeton: Princeton Univ. Press, 1977), p. 4; see also McGinn, *Visions*, pp. 14-27.

16. Wolfgang F. Volbach, *Early Christian Art* (New York: Abrams, n.d.), pl. 151; J. Poeschke, "Schafe und Böcke," *Lexikon der christlichen Ikonographie*, IV, 58-59; Brenk, *Tradition und Neuerung*, pp. 41-43.

17. Frederick van der Meer, *Early Christian Art* (Chicago: Univ. of Chicago Press, 1967), p. 119.

18. Charles M. Radding, "Evolution of Medieval Mentalities: A Cognitive-Structural Approach," *American Historical Review*, 83 (1978), 588.

19. "Ubi sine dubio sententiam suam in nobis impleturus est dominus noster, ut in quo iudicio iudicaverimus, in eo iudicio iudicetur de nobis, et secundum mensuram per quam proximis nostris indulgentiam dederimus remittatur nobis. Qui enim haec implere noluerit, ipse sibi ianuam misericordiae claudit"—*Sancti Caesarii Arelatensis Sermones*, ed. D. Germanus Morin, Corpus Christianorum, Ser. Lat., 103 (Turnhout: Brepols, 1953), p. 174; cited in Herbert Kolb, "Himmliches und erdisches Gericht in Karolingischer Theologie und althochdeutscher Dichtung," *Frühmittelalterlicher Studien*, 5 (1971), 287.

20. Ibid., pp. 284-303.

21. Richard Kenneth Emmerson, *Antichrist in the Middle Ages* (Seattle: Univ. of Washington Press, 1981), pp. 51-52. On illustrated Apocalypses and commentaries see Montague Rhodes James, *The Apocalypse in Art* (London: British Academy, 1931); Wilhelm Neuss, *Die Apokalypse des Hl. Johannes in der altspanischen und altchristlichen Bibelillustration*

(Münster: Aschendorff, 1931), 2 vols.; Richard Kenneth Emmerson and Suzanne Lewis, "Census and Bibliography of Medieval Manuscripts Containing Apocalypse Illustrations, 800-1500," *Traditio*, 40 (1984); 41 (1985); 42 (1986), forthcoming.

22. The Byzantine Last Judgment was also in development during the same period. Although both Eastern and Western Christians were using basically the same texts to represent the same events, they chose different motifs to visualize. Byzantine motifs, including the angels rolling up the heavens, cherubim on wheels of fire, the empty throne (*Hetoimasia*), and the river of fire, seldom appear in Western medieval art except in isolated examples of direct Byzantine influence. On the development of the Byzantine Last Judgment see Brenk, *Tradition und Neuerung*, pp. 77-103.

23. John Beckwith, *Ivory Carvings in Early Medieval England* (London: Harvey Miller and Medcalf, 1972), pl. 1 and catalogue entry 4, pp. 118-19; see also Brenk, pp. 117-20. Don Denny ("The Last Judgment Tympanum at Autun: Its Sources and Meaning," *Speculum*, 57 [1982], 532-47) questions the authenticity of this ivory (p. 536) although he acknowledges that he has not examined it at first hand. There is a wall painting of the Last Judgment from about the same time at Müstair. I have chosen to discuss the ivory instead of the wall painting because illustrations of the ivory can be read more easily; the wall painting is damaged; also its iconography reveals Byzantine influence.

24. Gertrud Schiller, *Ikonographie der christlichen Kunst*, III: *Die Auferstehung Christi* (Gütersloh: Gerd Mohn, 1972), pp. 233-49, Pls. 662-721.

25. This text is not from the Vulgate but an Old Latin variant used by the Fathers. See Beckwith, *Ivory Carvings*, p. 118.

26. Jean Daniélou, *The Angels and Their Mission*, trans. David Heimann (Westminster, Maryland: Christian Classics, 1976), pp. 58-61.

27. Beckwith, *Ivory Carvings*, p. 24.

28. See especially O. B. Hardison, Jr., *Christian Rite and Christian Drama in the Middle Ages* (Baltimore: Johns Hopkins Press, 1965), *passim*. For the impact of Hardison's ideas and subsequent scholarship, see C. Clifford Flanigan, "The Liturgical Drama and its Tradition: A Review of Scholarship 1965-1975," *Research Opportunities in Renaissance Drama*, 18 (1975), 81-102; 19 (1976), 109-36. See also David A. Bjork, "On the Dissemination of *Quem quaeritis* and the *Visitatio Sepulchri* and the Chronology of Their Early Sources," *Comparative Drama*, 14 (1980), 46-69.

29. J. A. Jungmann, "Advent und Voradvent, Uberreste des gall. Advents in der römische Liturgie," *Zeitschrift für katholische Theologie*, 61 (1937), 341-90. On the history of Advent see Peter G. Cobb, "The History of the Liturgical Year," in *The Study of Liturgy*, ed. Cheslyn Jones, Geoffrey Wainwright, and Edward Yarnold (New York: Oxford Univ. Press, 1978), p. 416.

30. C. Clifford Flanigan, "The Roman Rite and the Origins of Liturgical Drama," *University of Toronto Quarterly*, 43 (1974), 263-84.

31. "Quia adventum judicis qui occulte animam rapit praecavens ei poenitendo occurreret, ne inpoenitens periret"; cited by Heisig, "Über den geistesgeschichtlichen Standort," p. 249.

32. For a scholarly edition of text and music as well as a comprehensive review of previous scholarship, see Raffaello Monterosso and D'Arco Silvio Avalle, *Sponsus: Dramma delle Vergine Prudenti e delle Vergine Stolte* (Milan and Naples: Riccardo Ricciardi, 1965). See also Clifford Davidson, "On the Uses of Iconographic Study: The Example of the *Sponsus* from St. Martial of Limoges," *Comparative Drama*, 13 (1979-80), 300-19.

33. "Tanto igitur debet quasi semper veniens metui, quanto a nobis non valet ventura praesciri"—*Moralia*, VII, 45 (Migne, *PL*, LXXV, 792).

34. "Ipse namque bene vigilat qui, cum corpus suum a somno cohibet, cor in pravis desideriis aggravari non permittet, sed mentis oculos ad aspectum veri luminis apertos tenet: vigilat, qui servat operando quod credit, vigilat, qui a se torporis et negligentiae tenebras repellit"; cited by Heisig, p. 249.

35. "Prayer to Christ," *Anselm*, trans. Ward, p. 98.

36. See also Davidson, "On the Uses of Iconographic Study," pp. 312-13.

37. In the apse at Gorze was a Last Judgment of the eighth century that included seraphim, cherubim, the evangelist symbols, and the five wise virgins. Only the *tituli*, written by Alcuin, remain. For a discussion of the composition, see André Grabar in *Cahiers Archéologiques*, 7 (1954), 174.

38. Philippe Ariès, *The Hour of Our Death* (New York: Knopf, 1981), p. 101.

39. C. Clifford Flanigan, "The Liturgical Context of the *Quem Queritis* Trope," *Comparative Drama*, 8 (1974), 48.

40. Cited in Richard Axton, *European Drama of the Early Middle Ages* (London: Hutchinson, 1974), p. 101. Axton favors the Easter Vigil context. As Karl Young observes, however, "The text before us bears no evidence of attachment to the liturgy"; see *The Drama of the Medieval Church*, II, 368.

41. "Modo enim non videtur, et prope est; tunc videbitur, et prope non erit. Necdum in judicio apparuit, et si quaeritur, invenitur. Nam miro modo cum in judicio apparuerit, et videri potest, et non potest inveniri"—*Moralia*, XVIII, 15 (Migne, *PL*, LXXVI, 46).

42. Giles Constable, "Renewal and Reform in Religious Life," in *Renaissance and Renewal in the Twelfth Century*, ed. Robert L. Benson and Giles Constable (Cambridge: Harvard Univ. Press, 1982), p. 46.

43. Peter Brown, "Society and the Supernatural: A Medieval Change," *Daedalus*, 104 (1974), 133.

44. Radding, "Medieval Mentalities," pp. 594-95.

45. *Anselm*, trans. Ward, p. 223.

46. *Life of St. Hugh of Lincoln*, as quoted in A. Caiger-Smith, *English Medieval Mural Paintings* (Oxford: Clarendon Press, 1963), pp. 40-41.

47. "The God of Revelation, enthroned on the rainbow, framed by the mandorla and surrounded by the four beasts, was beyond all question the most important subject treated in Romanesque mural painting, and indeed the same is true of panel painting (frontals), miniature painting, work in precious metals, and carved stone portals"—Otto Demus, *Romanesque Mural Painting* (New York: Abrams, 1970), p. 16. Formally the central figure of Christ in the *Maestas Domini* is related to representations of the Ascension. M. F. Hearn points out that the conflation of Ascension and Second Coming had already begun to take place in the early Christian period (*Romanesque Sculpture: The Revival of Monumental Stone Sculpture in the Eleventh and Twelfth Centuries* [Ithaca: Cornell Univ. Press, 1981], p. 136). The Ascension image included Christ with or without a mandorla flanked by angels and subsidiary figures of the Virgin and Apostles, and two men in white. These two men explain how naturally the themes of Ascension and Second Coming coalesced. According to the Acts of the Apostles 1.11 they referred to the Second Coming: "This Jesus who is taken up from you into heaven, shall so come, as you have seen him going into heaven." Without the subsidiary figures or with the substitution for them of details drawn from the Apocalypse such as the four beasts, the figure of Christ could be interpreted as the *Maestas Domini*. These three themes, the Ascension, Second Coming, and *Maestas Domini*, all signified the triumph of Christ and were thus considered appropriate for painting in the apse of a church, the most prominent and most significant location both because of its proximity to the main altar and its symbolic function as the dome of heaven. Hearn argues (p. 137) that the similarity in form of apse and sculptured portal dictated that the same subject matter as had been traditionally used for apses should be used for portals; he further points to the striking fact that "no reliably dated sculptured tympanum before the third decade of the twelfth century bears any theme not related to this concept."

48. Demus, *Romanesque Mural Painting*, p. 22.

49. Christoph Bernoulli, *Die Skulpturen der Abtei Conques-en-Rouergue* (Basel: Birkhäuser, 1956); Louis Bousquet, *Le jugement dernier de l'église Sainte-Foy de Conques* (Rodez, 1948); Yves Christe, *Les grandes portails romans: Études sur l'iconologie des théophanies romanes* (Geneva, 1969). Don Denny, "The Date of the Conques Last Judgment and Its Compositional Analogues," *Art Bulletin*, 66 (1984), 7-14, argues for a date close to 1150 because "the central register of the tympanum, its most important zone, was derived from a group of English images, in all probability a manuscript cycle closely related to the Winchester Psalter illustrations and, in any case, a work approximately contemporary with the psalter— a work of ca. 1150" (p. 14). Denny's argument here is not entirely con-

vincing. His already-cited article on "The Last Judgment," an analysis of a Last Judgment tympanum contemporary with Conques, emphasizes the Byzantine sources of the Autun tympanum and finds its meaning in trials of ordeal that may have been conducted in front of it.

50. *Anselm*, trans. Ward, p. 175.

51. Ibid., p. 175.

52. Adolf Katzenellenbogen, *Allegories of the Virtues and Vices in Mediaeval Art*, trans. Alan J. P. Crick (1939; rpt. New York: Norton, 1964), p. 18.

53. Gertrud Schiller, *Ikonographie der christlichen Kunst*, IV, Pt. 2: *Maria* (Gütersloh: Gerd Mohn, 1980), 195.

54. *Anselm*, trans. Ward, p. 110.

55. Ibid., p. 138.

56. The story of Lazarus and Dives appears with some frequency near Last Judgment scenes in the pictorial arts (e.g., on the Romanesque porch at Moissac). The story not only provides specific models for blessed and damned (Lazarus a beggar with a dog licking his sores, and Dives the rich man who is "clothed in purple and fine linen; and feasted sumptuously every day"), but also answers a perplexing question: What happens to the soul between the time of death and that of the general resurrection and judgment? St. Luke's Gospel (16.22-23) tells us that Lazarus "was carried by the angels into Abraham's bosom" and that the rich man suffered the torments of hell. Abraham's bosom, according to Tertullian in the *Adversus Marcion*, is a "spatial concept," "for receiving the souls of all peoples . . . which, though not celestial, is above the lower regions, to provide refreshment to the souls of the just until the consummation of all things in the general resurrection"—quoted in T. S. R. Boase, *Death in the Middle Ages* (London: Thames and Hudson, 1972), p. 28.

57. "As the type of all traitors, Judas is of particular importance in connexion with the Last Judgment"—Gertrud Schiller, *Iconography of Christian Art*, trans. Janet Seligman (Greenwich, Conn.: New York Graphic Society, 1971-72), II, 77.

58. In the late twelfth-century Pamplona Bibles there is a whole page depicting the elect seated placidly in rows. This seems to be the accepted interpretation of the text at the top of the page: "That eye hath not seen, nor ear heard, neither hath it entered into the heart of man, what things God hath prepared for them that love him" (I Corinthians 2.9; cf. Isaiah 64.4). For an illustration of this page, see François Bucher, *The Pamplona Bibles* (New Haven: Yale Univ. Press, 1970), facsimile vol., pl. 569.

59. Anselm, *Cur Deus Homo*, in *Basic Writings*, trans. S. N. Deane, 2nd ed. (La Salle, Ill.: Open Court, 1962), pp. 184-85, 244-46; Gustaf Aulén, *Christus Victor: An Historical Study of the Three Main Types of*

the Idea of Atonement, trans. A. G. Herbert (1930; rpt. New York: Mac-millan, 1967). But see also Brian P. McGuire, "God-Man and the Devil in Medieval Theology and Culture," *Cahiers de l'Institut du moyen-âge grec et latin*, 18 (1976), 23, for the argument that the new theology of the Atonement "remained the minority view throughout the Middle Ages."

60. John A. Wilson, *The Culture of Ancient Egypt* [original title: *The Burden of Egypt*] (1951; rpt: Chicago: Univ. of Chicago Press, 1971), p. 119; Mary Phillips Perry, "On the Psychostasis in Christian Art," *Burlington Magazine*, 22 (1912-13), 94.

61. Brenk (*Tradition und Neuerung*, p. 20) observes that this motif is at least typologically strongly related to its Egyptian counterpart ("den ägyptischen zum mindesten typologisch stark verwandt"). Several art historians have assumed that there was a direct adoption of the motif in Coptic Egypt, but Alexander Badawy (*Coptic Art and Architecture: The Christian Egyptians from the Late Antique to the Middle Ages* [Cambridge, Mass.: MIT Press, 1978]) makes no mention of it. See also Perry, "On the Psychostasis in Christian Art," pp. 94-105, 208-18, for further study of the weighing of souls.

62. For a perceptive discussion of the *Ludus de Antichristo* as based in the traditional medieval view of Antichrist see Emmerson, *Antichrist in the Middle Ages*, pp. 166-72. For the text of the play, see Karl Young, *Drama of the Medieval Church*, II, 369-96. See also John Wright's trans-lation with commentary, *The Play of Antichrist* (Toronto: Pontifical In-stitute of Mediaeval Studies, 1967).

63. Young, *Drama of the Medieval Church*, II, 396.

64. Elie Konigson, *L'Espace Théâtral Médiéval* (Paris: Centre Na-tional de la Recherche Scientifique, 1975), p. 37.

65. Axton, *European Drama*, p. 92.

66. Ibid., p. 88.

67. Emmerson, *Antichrist in the Middle Ages*, p. 168.

68. Marie-Dominique Chenu, *Nature, Man, and Society in the Twelfth Century*, ed. and trans. Jerome Taylor and Lester K. Little (Chicago: Univ. of Chicago Press, 1968), p. 201.

69. Axton, *European Drama*, p. 90.

70. Wright, *The Play of Antichrist*, p. 47.

71. Emmerson, *Antichrist in the Middle Ages*, p. 171.

II

"LET US SEEK HIM ALSO": TROPOLOGICAL JUDGMENT IN TWELFTH-CENTURY ART AND DRAMA

Ronald B. Herzman

The explicit theme of judgment grew only hesitantly and belatedly in the art and drama of the eleventh and twelfth centuries, appearing in metaphorical expressions such as the parable of the wise and foolish virgins or in the Antichrist legend as often as in scenes of the Last Judgment itself (see Chapter I, above). I shall further argue that awareness of and concern with judgment also inform presentations in the visual and verbal arts of narrative subjects that, on the surface, have no direct connection with the Last Judgment. Specifically, the Advent and Christmas seasons resonate with overtones of judgment; by the twelfth century, exegetes develop into a commonplace the association between Advent, Christ's first coming, and the day of judgment, his second. In sculpture, drama, and sermon alike, twelfth-century artists and preachers exhort their audiences to perceive the analogy between first and second comings by an affective, psychological, and associative process that renders the events of

Christianity immediate and personally relevant. Viewers or listeners are thus invited to a process of judgment by being asked to consider where they stand. This experience of judgment, here called tropological because it concerns present time rather than eschatological time, is central to the process through which these works of visual and verbal art affect their audiences.

The kind of associative relationship established between Advent and the Last Judgment, in which meditation on one of these events necessarily invites meditation upon the other and presents both events in terms of their meaning for contemporary life, was fundamental to twelfth-century monastic culture. As this chapter will attempt to show, further attention to the Conques tympanum also discussed in Chapter I, above, and additionally attention to a sermon of St. Bernard of Clairvaux will demonstrate the mode of thinking seen here as characteristic of twelfth-century monasticism. This mode will then be used as the basis for an analysis of a dramatic work of art focused on the Advent and Christmas narrative, the Benediktbeuren Christmas play. To be read effectively, these artifacts must be read as documents of monastic culture—that is, they must yield the tropological reading that is inherent in them. A tropological reading of these works will show, for example, how the Magi searching for Christ become models and mediators for the audience in its search for him in their lives. This chapter attempts to see the tropological mode of thinking that permeates the visual and verbal documents of monastic culture as a key to reading the arts in the twelfth century.

The systematic survey of the theme of Last Judgment in the previous chapter has already included some analysis of the great Romanesque tympanum at Conques (fig. 2). That analysis will now be extended to demonstrate that the tympanum at Conques includes elements of monastic spirituality and to show thereby how judgment is treated in a monastic context. Analogies between monastic spirituality and Romanesque art have already received scholarly attention and are beginning to be studied in detail. Jean Leclercq's compelling statement of the relationship between Romanesque art and monastic writings is appropriate here: "Just as the cathedrals of the thirteenth century have been compared to theological summas, monastic writings of the Romanesque period may be likened to the abbey churches of the period: The same simplicity, the same solidity, the same vivacity of biblical imagination."[1] Simplicity, solidity, and vivacity of imagination are all apparent in a tympanum such as that of the monastic church at Conques.

Meditation on the Last Judgment was, of course, frequently an explicit theme in monastic writings; often the audience was asked to picture the event and the audience's relationship to that event so that what is a kind of physical necessity in looking at sculpture—standing in front of the tympanum—has its analogy in monastic writings. Bernard of Clairvaux's pupil, Aelred of Rievaulx, uses just such a metaphor of beholding to describe the process of meditation:

> Turn your eyes to the left of the Judge and gaze upon that wretched multitude. What horror is there, what a stench, what fear . . . dreadful to look upon, their faces distorted, cast down from shame, in confusion because of their body's degradation and nakedness. . . .
> Now turn your eyes to the right and look at those among whom he will place you by glorifying you. What grace is there, what honor, what happiness, what security.[2]

The writer is asking his readers to contemplate judgment as if they were actually at the Last Judgment itself, or as if they were standing before a representation of the judgment in sculpture or painting, as Hugh of Lincoln and King John did when Hugh exhorted John to repent (see Chapter I, above). Aelred's vivid description of the Last Judgment as if it were taking place before him assists his monastic audience to put into practice one of the dictates of the Benedictine Rule: a monk "should think himself guilty of his sins and about to be presented before the dreadful judgment seat of God."[3]

At Conques the viewer is already at the Last Judgment in the obvious sense of being forced to experience this event as though it were happening: an event from Scripture—

Christ's coming in judgment—is immediately present, compelling the viewer into self-examination in terms of that event. The viewer is forced into a relationship with the scenes of the tympanum in other ways as well, for the tympanum connects the important events of salvation history with the seemingly mundane events of present-day history. The great figures of salvation history are presented together with figures whose import and power are specifically local and whose appeal is therefore immediate. The figures of the Virgin, St. Peter, and Charlemagne (who was often treated as a saint in the twelfth century) stand to the right of the impressive central figure of Christ in majesty, with a panel containing Abraham and the souls of the saved who rest in Abraham's bosom directly below. Alongside these figures of universal importance and interest, at the same time the viewer also finds (significantly without a halo) the uncanonized hermit Dadon, the founder of the monastery, and the monk Olderic, builder of the twelfth-century church. Both are persons of local authority. Among the damned, significantly, are three former abbots of the monastery thought to have squandered the wealth of the community and a bishop who was their uncle.[4] Furthermore, the enclosed triangular areas to the right and left of Christ use iconography whose thrust is even more local in its representation of the saved and the damned. St. Foi, patron of the monastery, the saint whose relics helped make Conques an important pilgrimage shrine, is shown on the right asking God's intercession, while on the left a poacher on the monastic grounds receives his just reward in an exactly appropriate inversion: he is roasted on a spit turned by two oversized animals (figs. 4-5).

This juxtaposition of the universal and the local is so familiar from the most well-known medieval depiction of the afterlife, Dante's *Commedia* (wherein figures from universal history exist side by side with figures whose names continue to be recognized only because Dante preserved their identity, such as the local Florentine drunkard Ciacco of Canto VI of the *Inferno*), that we tend to take it for granted without reflecting sufficiently on the debt that Dante undoubtedly owed to the tradition of monastic affective spirituality. At

Conques, the purpose of this juxtaposition is to show that cosmic time and human time are both aspects of the same time. The drama of human history that is consummated at the Last Judgment in no way takes place apart from the viewers, but rather is a drama in which they too are actors. What is presented in stone is not simply an event from salvation history but a focus for describing the entirety of that history; past, present, and future are brought together as its interrelated components.

A thought process that is characteristically monastic underlies the attempt of the tympanum at Conques to relate the meaning of the Last Judgment to the experience of the viewer. Bernard of Clairvaux's twelfth sermon on the Song of Songs will take us deeper into this experiential theology, showing how the attempt of the speaker to recreate for his audience what he himself has experienced is one of the central characteristics of monastic spirituality. This affective spirituality not only links stone and sermon—picture and word—but also will help to locate the relationship between play and audience in the twelfth-century drama. Moreover, the analysis will show how the idea of judgment is implicitly present in Bernard's thought even though it is not explicitly mentioned.

Works such as Bernard's sermon have previously been studied as part of the history of monasticism or of Christian spirituality; the writings of monastic authors in the twelfth century, especially the four great Cistercian authors—Bernard of Clairvaux, William of St. Thierry, Aelred of Rievaulx, and Guerric of Igny—are justly placed among the masterpieces of Christian monastic writing. On the one hand, they draw from the experience of a tradition that reaches back to the desert fathers and continues in an uninterrupted line to their own day. On the other hand, they embody the humanistic and literary achievement of the twelfth-century renaissance. The kind of analysis these works have traditionally received, however, has not paid sufficient attention to their specifically literary qualities, those details of structure and content within which the writer has embodied his vision of the monastic experience.[5] Through the analysis of such detail, the points exemplified in the tympanum at Conques will be refocused and refined.

St. Bernard of Clairvaux's Twelfth Sermon on the Song of Songs, "On the Grace of Loving Kindness," ostensibly glosses the text from the Song of Songs, "Thy name is as oil poured out" (1.2). The sermon is a significant introduction to Bernard's method in that this text is in fact never mentioned; its presence must be inferred from the context and from the expositions of previous sermons.[6] In these previous sermons Bernard gives explications of the breasts of the bride and the bridegroom (Sermon 9) and of the perfumes of these breasts (Sermon 10). In Sermon 10 he says that he will "try to explain the nature of the ointments of which the breasts are redolent."[7] This explanation involves dividing the ointment—the oil of which the breasts are redolent, the oil that is "poured out"—into the "oil of contrition" and the "oil of devotion."[8] A third ointment, that of "loving kindness," Bernard now asserts to be even more important than the other two, making it the subject of his sermon. At the outset, even in defining his subject, Bernard demonstrates one of the characteristics of his sermons and of monastic habits of thought generally: an ease in moving back and forth between the material world and the spiritual world or, perhaps more accurately, the insistence on seeing the interpenetration between the material and the spiritual. Here at the beginning of the sermon a claim is not so much made as taken for granted, namely that a metaphor that describes the name of the beloved—"oil poured out"—retains the physical properties of oil and, then, that this literal oil can suddenly be subdivided into the three spiritual qualities of "contrition," "devotion," and "loving kindness." Only by following similar shifts in their sudden complexity will the reader be able to follow Bernard in his journey; he is trying to establish in his audience the same easy familiarity of movement between material and spiritual worlds that he himself takes for granted.

When St. Bernard defines "loving kindness," he does so indirectly, through its effects:

> Who, in your opinion, is the good man who takes pity
> and lends, who is disposed to compassionate, quick to
> render assistance, who believes that there is more hap-
> piness in giving than in receiving, who easily forgives
> but is not easily angered, who will never seek to be
> avenged, and will in all things take thought for his neigh-
> bor's needs as if they were his own?[9]

Bernard then asks where he might find those who possess such qualities. "There are men of riches in the city of the Lord of hosts. I wonder if some among them possess these ointments."[10] Not surprisingly, his search takes him to Scripture. In looking there for his answer, Bernard allows himself the same kind of freedom in the choice of his subjects that he previously allowed himself with the text of the Song of Songs at the outset of the sermon. He talks of the loving kindness of St. Paul, Job, Joseph, Samuel, and David, presenting these figures from the Old and New Testaments without reference to the order in which they appear in Scripture in what seems at first to be a random association, the order in which each occurs to him. "As invariably happens," he begins, "the first to spring to my mind is that chosen vessel, St. Paul. . . ."[11] For each, Bernard uses the same suggestive imagery that conflates the spiritual and the literal, that sees in anointing something both physical and spiritual. What directs each of these examples to a common center is the relation that each of them has to the thesis he is developing, to the idea of "loving kindness." These examples show an interesting and characteristic way of structuring a "narrative," not through the presentation of a continuous action or series of actions but by the juxtaposition of a series of brief "tableaux"—that is, self-contained descriptions of scriptural references that have the force of short individual scenes. The care in construction and in the use of sophisticated rhetorical forms adds to the evidence showing that the order of these tableaux is in actuality far from random. In creating the fiction that he deals with each one randomly, as it comes to mind, Bernard is enabling his audience to observe the actual process of the search itself, the movement of his own mind as it ranges across the entire span of Scripture.[12] This makes it possible for Bernard to suggest to his audience through this one search an analogue to their common monastic search, that of the soul seeking God. Thus he follows a psychological and associative order at the same time that he maintains a thematic unity.

Bernard turns from his scriptural examples directly to his audience to show exactly how the quality of "loving kindness" can be lived out in their lives too: "A similar influence is achieved by those too who, in the course of this life have been indulgent and charitable, who have made an effort to show kindness to their fellow-men."[13] The ordering of examples even suggests that what is lived out in the lives of the great scriptural figures is to be continued in the lives of those who are his auditors. Bernard describes how these scriptural examples remain alive for his audience:

> All these persons possessed the best ointments and even today diffuse their perfumes through all the churches. . . . Since their purpose was to be of help to everybody they evinced a great humility before all in all that they did, they were beloved by God and men, their good odor a perfume in the memory. Men like these, whatever their number, permeated their own times and today, too, with the best of ointments.[14]

The memory of these men can be preserved for Bernard's audience, then, by the existence of Scripture as a still-living reality, by the liturgy that both commemorates and recreates these scriptural events, by the very sermon that Bernard is giving, and by the lives of all those who in Bernard's time possess the same ointment of "loving kindness." This tropological immediacy, this sense that what has happened in Scripture is still happening in the present, is the core of Bernard's affective spirituality, uniting as it does the movement of universal salvation history—the plan for all mankind beginning in creation and ending in judgment that is the subject of Scripture—with the movement of individual salvation history, the movement of each individual soul in its search for God—the monastic search.

Only when the sermon is near its end does Bernard

66

bring to his audience a text from the Song of Songs, one which can be related to the oil of "loving kindness" that is the subject of the sermon:

> Finally, a few brief words to end the present subject. The man whose speech intoxicates and whose good deeds radiate may take as addressed to himself the words: "Your breasts are better than wine, redolent of the best ointments." Now who is worthy of such a commendation? Which of us can live uprightly and perfectly even for one hour, an hour free from fruitless talk and careless work?[15]

Again Bernard conflates the material and the spiritual, this time to suggest that, although members of his audience may be living out their lives in imitation of the pattern Scripture enacts, for most of them it is an imperfect imitation. Though this perfection is lacking in their individual attempts, it is nonetheless present communally in the Church: "For what she lacks in one member she possesses in another according to the measure of Christ's gift and the plan of the Spirit who distributes to each one just as he chooses." Since it is the Church that must be seen as the perfect continuation of what has been accomplished in Scripture, Bernard's auditors are reminded that they can become more perfect partakers in that unity by uniting themselves to the Church.

Finally, St. Bernard thanks God for allowing this unification:

> Thank you, Lord Jesus, for your kindness in uniting us to the Church you so dearly love, not merely that we may be endowed with the gift of faith, but that like brides we may be one with you in an embrace that is sweet, chaste and eternal, beholding with unveiled faces that glory which is yours in union with the Father and the Holy Spirit for ever and ever. Amen.[16]

The sermon ends, then, with the usual exegesis of the Song of Songs that sees the bridegroom as a figure for Christ and the marriage feast as his unification with his bride—collectively the Church, individually each soul. This exegesis, begun by Origen, was extensively known in the Middle Ages, which may help to explain why it remains understood rather than explicit throughout most of Bernard's commentary.[17] By making it explicit at this point, Bernard is able to bring Sermon 12 to an apt and powerful conclusion. The freedom to range from topic to topic that Bernard sees as the analogue of the soul in its search for God ends in this final consummation. The physical and the spiritual are tied together through the imagery of sexual union, bringing to a definitive conclusion all the ways in which Bernard has been examining this interrelationship throughout the sermon.

At this point it becomes clear that the seeming digressions and the abrupt transitions have been tending toward this conclusion all along. As the sermon comes to a close in the final image of consummation, so also will end the search of the soul that lives according to the oil of "loving kindness," even though life as it is actually being lived may seem like a series of digressions. Thus the sermon, the life of each Christian, and the specifically monastic variation of that life that is Bernard's most immediate concern all come together, and hence can all be seen as different ways of looking at the same journey. What applies to one applies to all: just as the journey of life is never an easy one for the Christian, still less for the Christian living in a monastic community, so also the ability to "read" this sermon is not easy, but rather demands the same kind of vigilance and attentiveness in following the shifting and changing (though ultimately unified) patterns of Bernard's thought that the pilgrimage of the Christian life demands. And conversely, the ability to meditate on the meaning of a Bernardian sermon is the same ability needed to meditate on the spiritual progress of one's life. Such meaning is there, waiting to be embraced, but it is by no means apparent or obvious.

From the close analysis presented above come some important generalizations. The intimate relationship between speaker, subject matter, and audience by means of which the audience is challenged to become participant rather than observer; the complex and intricate way in which the idea of pilgrimage governs Bernard's thoughts; the awareness of and reliance on the exegetical tradition of Scripture—these are the habits of mind that define the monastic sermon. Moreover, by becoming aware of these habits of mind, the reader sees that events that seem casually related to each other are in fact related by means of the common theme toward which they are leading, a theme that is more important than any individual example because it is the end of the intellectual pilgrimage and because the individual examples are means toward that end. No less important for our present purposes, close analysis of the text of Bernard's sermon shows that judgment as a theme is implicitly present here too. At Conques the Last Judgment is made immediately present to the viewer by the figures who mediate between cosmic time and present time. Bernard, on the other hand, forces the immediacy of the present to become subject to the judgment that takes place at the end of time by showing the interconnections between present time and future time. The continuity of all of scriptural history, which for Bernard means the continuity of all history, implies that each moment in the present is a moment of judgment, a moment at which one's actions are to be scrutinized with the same care as they surely will be at the final judgment. Conques literally and Bernard metaphorically but no less forcefully both ask their audience to consider where they stand. Though there are eschatological elements clearly present throughout the Sermons on the Songs of Songs (one example of which may be the oil itself, which, to the reader familiar with Scripture and with Bernard's associative method, might well suggest the parable of judgment of Matthew 25, in which the oil in the lamps of the wise virgins indicates readiness for the Last Judgment [see Chapter I, above]), this judgment is not the explicitly eschatological judgment that is ushered in by the Second Coming. Rather, it might better be termed a tropological judgment, a judgment taking place in the immediacy of the present.

The analysis thus far has emphasized the monastic habits of thought that a sculptural program such as Conques and a sermon such as Bernard's share. It has also suggested that a close relationship between image and text—picture and word—characterizes this monastic milieu. Our understanding of Conques remains incomplete unless we see the extent to which both scriptural and monastic texts inform it. Bernard and Aelred, on the other hand, force the reader to think visually as a means of making the entire sweep of scriptural history present: to imagine the scenes Bernard brings before his audience is to make them present to the mind's eye. This close relationship between text and image will obviously be valuable when we focus on Church drama, a medium in which the relationship between text and image is intimate.

In speaking of the form of the twelfth-century drama as exemplified in the Beauvais *Play of Daniel*, Jerome Taylor observes that such drama is "no play of manners, no dark comedy, no history play, but rather a set of living tableaux, of symbolic moving-pictures, almost like a set of cartoons laid out in a strip, in which each cartoon or picture delivers its message or meaning by selecting and positioning a limited number of exaggerated features and protracting them momentarily before the stylized movement continues."[18] To this valuable insight we can now add what we have learned from an analysis of monastic art, namely that the tableaux—whether in word or stone—are intimately connected to each other, and that such connections can be perceived by their common thematic concerns rather than by chronological linkage. We then have the basis for an aesthetic of twelfth-century drama, a form which, as Taylor rightly suggests, combines word and picture in a unique way. Twelfth-century drama is part of the affective, psychological, associative world of monasticism, the purpose of which is to make the events of Christianity an immediate and continually present aspect of experience.

Examining the Benediktbeuren Christmas play as a document of monastic culture will enable us to bring into sharp focus much that has seemed hazy or blurred in earlier scholarly discussions of twelfth-century drama.[19] Karl Young's attempts to formulate an aesthetic both for this play and for twelfth-century drama generally provide a case in point.[20] Young treats the play with care and affection, trying his best to praise it, and yet is able to do so only with severe reservations. He sees the play as essentially incomplete, at best an example of some fine poetry, but with no real artistic unity. His thesis is that the play's form must be defined by the core of biblical narrative it contains. In outlining the scenes of the play he makes this thesis explicit: "Now begins the real action of the piece, with the Annunciation and the visit to Elisabeth."[21] The "real action" of the piece thus begins with line 235 of a play that is 565 lines long. What then is one to make of the first 234 lines? Young seems to imply that these lines (and all that portion of the play which is not part of the core of biblical narrative) are embellishment either for the sake of narrative continuity or audience interest. The fundamental question for Young thus is this: how is narrative turned into drama? How is the Bible, either in itself or as mediated through the liturgy, transformed into a play to be acted out? Young's perspective guarantees that the method of the Benediktbeuren Nativity play can at best be only partially successful. For him, the twelfth-century drama is typically "A dramatic piece so loosely and casually arranged" that it may "best be regarded not as an attempt towards a closely knit play, but as an episodic religious opera."[22] Such a conclusion follows from his premise, for if one looks at the plays as attempts to transpose biblical narrative directly into stage action, they must necessarily be artistic failures, lacking both unity and coherence.

Biblical material in this play, as in the works of art we have examined, is not drawn directly from biblical narrative, but rather is mediated through monastic culture. The Benediktbeuren Christmas play can be read effectively in much the same way that other documents of monastic culture, whether sermon or stone, can be read. The chronological discrepancies that so bothered Young—the severe distortions in the play of the order of events as they appear in Scripture—are seen to be entirely purposeful from the perspective of monastic spirituality. What links sermon, sculpture, and drama in aesthetic terms is the way that the parts of each form a thematic unity, by attempting to bring the audience into the thematic center of the art work, and by inviting the audience to undertake a journey toward spiritual understanding. In examining the play, therefore, we will use the same methodology as in our examination of the tympanum at Conques and the Bernardian sermon: once again we shall identify the scenes, then suggest the relationship that exists between them, and finally concentrate on the relationship between them as the means of moving toward an an understanding of the thematic unity of the play. To meditate on Advent and on the journey of the Magi is to be aware of the presentness of judgment, especially in view of the many tropological links between the first and second comings.

The Annunciation, the scene which, as we have already indicated, Young sees as the beginning of the "real action" of the play, is followed by the familiar constellation of events surrounding the Incarnation: Visitation, Announcement of the birth of Christ, Journey of the Magi, the Flight into Egypt, and finally the death of Herod. From the Annunciation, in any case, events are presented in their proper chronological order, or at least fairly close to it. Yet even here we still find problems if we look with Young for mimetic biblical presentation, especially since so many familiar biblical scenes and so much action are compressed into the compass of some 300 lines. Some events are announced rather than dramatized, and at times we are abruptly taken from one scene to another. Some events shrink in size and importance, others are telescoped. The play hardly presents the viewer with an accurate dramatic representation of the events as they occur in Scripture, in spite of the approximate chronological fidelity.

The Benediktbeuren Christmas play devotes a great deal of time to the journey, arrival, and departure of the Magi, so much so that to characterize accurately the movement of the play one should describe the Magi as its central focus and the scriptural events surrounding the Incarnation as woven in and out of their journey. The Magi, in fact, occupy the same central position in this play that they occupy in the tympanum at Neuilly-en-Donjon (fig. 6), in which we find another sculptural program requiring the associative monastic kind of "reading" analyzed in this chapter.[23] In the Benediktbeuren Christmas play, as at Neuilly, other events must be seen in relation to the Magi's journey, and it is because of the centrality of this journey that the other events are presented so sketchily. Thus the play moves, for example, from Mary's recital of the Magnificat at the Visitation to simple stage directions announcing the birth of Christ, proclaimed also by the choir, to the appearance of the star, to the Magi, all within the compass of a few short lines (ll. 233ff). To understand this focus, it is necessary not simply to examine the relationship between the Magi and the interwoven scenes, but to go back to the beginning of the play and analyze the lines so casually dismissed by Young.

The subject of this beginning passage is familiar in twelfth-century drama and totally appropriate to what follows: a series of prophecies announcing the birth of Christ, a variation of the so-called *Ordo Prophetarum*.[24] In the Benediktbeuren play, Isaiah, Daniel, the Sybil, Aaron, and Balaam appear in that order, followed by Archisynagogus, a personified abstraction embodying the non-belief of the Jews, who attempts to confute what the prophets have announced. The prophets do not appear in their proper chronological order (a fact that may simply reflect the dramatist's source in the pseudo-Augustinian sermon *Sermo contra Judeos Paganos et Arianos*). After Archisynagogus has railed against the simplemindedness of the prophets and their outrageous claims, a boy bishop announces that a new disputant is ready to answer their challenge. The prophets, retaining their belief in the coming of Christ but yet unable to refute the arguments of Archisynagogus, turn over their authority to no less a figure than the greatest doctor of the Christian church, St. Augustine. The rest of this section, continuing up to the Annunciation, presents the debate with Augustine and the prophets allied against Archisynagogus. The appearance of St. Augustine thus highlights what is true of the prophets themselves, namely that witnesses to the truth of the Incarnation are summoned from widely separate distances of space and time to unite in celebrating the dramatic moment of Christ's birth. To accentuate the diversity even further, historical figures and personified abstractions occupy the same stage together.[25]

We are not watching isolated episodes in the unfolding

73

of salvation history; instead, we are given a vantage point that allows us to see what precedes and follows the events of the Incarnation simultaneously, so that what once took place over the course of time now takes place for the viewer in a juxtaposed dramatic presentation. The viewer is asked to judge between the claims of belief and non-belief and, like one who meditates in front of a Last Judgment tympanum, is given the perspective with which to choose correctly; the arrogance and folly of wrong belief are clear to behold. A Church tradition links the four major prophets of the Old Testament—Isaiah, Daniel, Jeremiah, and Ezekiel—with the four great Latin doctors—SS. Augustine, Jerome, Gregory, and Ambrose; thus it is appropriate that the figure of Augustine, the greatest of these, completes the prophetic line and comes to their aid. What the prophets accomplished in the history of salvation, holding fast to their belief in the coming of Christ despite the ridicule of unbelievers, Augustine has already accomplished by spending his life in the refutation of heresy. All these accomplishments become in turn a model for the viewer, who is continually waging war between belief and unbelief in his own life. In his sermons, St. Bernard of Clairvaux allows himself the freedom to move from one event in the history of salvation to another, to jump rapidly from events in the Old Testament to events in the New and beyond, precisely because each such meditative leap provides a model for what his listeners should be doing to preserve in their present lives an unbroken continuity with these events. The dramatist is able to achieve a similar effect by the simultaneity of his tableaux. What is most important is the virtue of faith, whether exemplified by the prophets, or by Augustine, or indeed by the viewer.

Augustine's first words to Archisynagogus suggest an important direction for the rest of the play. In his hope that the "nation concealed in darkness" will be "converted" when the matter is exposed to them and that the "closed path [clausa semita] of the Scriptures may lie open to them," Augustine employs the metaphor of a journey to describe spiritual understanding. Scripture itself provides the path, and the failure of the Jews as exemplified by Archisynagogus is a failure to undertake a journey toward spiritual understanding. This metaphor, recurring throughout the play, helps to explain the central position of the Magi: their journey, as the monastic commentaries of Peter Damian and Guerric of Igny show,[26] is simultaneously literal and spiritual, a historical seeking-out of the newborn Christ and a contemporary model for the journey of faith of each believer. This language of journey may also explain why Augustine is the chosen spokesman for the claims of belief, since his most important and influential work, *The City of God*, systematically elaborates the idea of belief as a metaphoric journey. Those who are citizens of the City of God are on pilgrimage here on earth. Those who are content with the City of Man remain fixed and static, refusing to undertake their pilgrimage:

> Scripture tells us that Cain founded a city, whereas Abel, as a pilgrim, did not found one. For the City of the saints is up above, although it produces citizens here below, and in their persons the City is on pilgrimage until the time of its kingdom comes. At that time it will assemble all those citizens as they rise again in their bodies; and then they will be given the promised kingdom, where with their Prince, "the king of ages," they will reign, world without end.[27]

This statement from the *City of God* implies also a connection between pilgrimage and judgment, a connection we have similarly found in other documents of monastic spirituality. A major purpose of St. Augustine's refutation of unbelief is to remind Archisynagogus that all his actions are subject to judgment. As countless Advent sermons observe, and as this book has suggested more than once, the first coming of Christ at his nativity is a type of his second coming in judgment. Christians preparing for one should also prepare for the other. By rejecting rather than accepting Augustine's invitation to faith, Archisynagogus invites consequences both now and in the judgment to come. Most tellingly, he mocks the invitation by mocking his own prophetic tradition, failing to understand the Hebrew prophets: "Whenever a virgin will conceive,/ Xanthus River, hasten backwards!/ The wolf will flee from the lamb,/ The flat places will become rough and uneven" (ll. 144-47). He remains closed to his own tradition, alienated from the "opened" meanings of Hebrew scripture. His insistence on what the law teaches and reveals (literally "opens": *lex docet et aperit*) is ironically an insistence on what is closed rather than opened, an attitude that will also characterize the attitude of Herod and his counselors later in the play.

The process by which faith maintains itself in the face of doubt, or overcomes disbelief and heresy, is the subject of the first part of the play which thus prepares the audience for the second (following the break suggested by Young that comes at the Annunciation). The second section expands these concerns to include a still more comprehensive exploration of the meaning of faith. Its major purpose lies not so much in the dramatic recounting of the events themselves—the content of faith, the events of the Incarnation that form the object of belief—as in the recreation of the experience of those who exemplify the first and best model of faith as the events are actually unfolding—i.e., the Magi. Guerric of Igny's description of the journey of the Magi as the journey of faith finds vivid exemplification in the journey dramatized here, since it characteristically begins in doubt, moves to adoration, and returns home with certitude.

The connection between the literal journey of the Magi and the interior journey toward faith it signifies is made continually in the text of the play. The kings at first do not know the meaning of the star. They will know it only after their journey. They express their confusion and perplexity in the very language of the journey they will soon be undertaking. They are perplexed by a *quadrivium*, literally a four-way intersection; they suffer shipwreck of mind and spirit ("*rationis patiens et mentis naufragium*," ll. 246-50). The *cursus* of the star (l. 254), the *quaesti* of the second magus, the taking pleasure in the purpose of the quest, the *una procedamus* of the third magus, asking that they all might go together wherever the star leads—all these underscore the journey as spiritual condition. The second king, when he joins the first, expresses his joy in the meeting:

Now joy sweetly
Adorns my heart;
A great relief has been afforded me
In my journey.
In this matter, about which I am at a loss,
Now I have found a companion
Showing himself to be in doubt
And a partaker of my anxiety. (ll. 278-85).

They are going so that they might make sense out of something that is at first simply perplexing and mysterious.

The journey itself is, of course, not without conflict. The joyful movement of the Magi toward the star ("But since this is a comet,/ May we be anointed with joy,/ Our minds be joyful," ll. 323-25) is interrupted by Herod, who angrily brings Archisynagogus on stage "in colossal pride" to dispute with the Magi. The reappearance of Archisynagogus links the second part of the play with the first; the same antagonist and the same conflict are found in both parts. This linkage is thematic as well as structural since the Magi on their journey toward faith must contend with the same doubts that assailed the prophets and St. Augustine. The chronological impossibility of Archisynagogus' reappearance emphasizes his nature as a personified abstraction, as indeed we would expect from his name and from his first entry on stage. The abstraction points toward the timeless nature of the struggle. Archisynagogus belongs to the time of the prophets, to the time of Augustine, and to the time of the Magi's journey; he lives, one may therefore conclude, whenever the struggle between doubt and faith arises. Just as the figures on the tympana at Conques and Neuilly are all brought together from various places and times to exist on the same sculptural space because they embody aspects of the same coherent idea, the characters in this play inhabit the same dramatic space to form a coherent idea too; in both cases it is a way of embodying the dynamics of faith.

The reappearance of Archisynagogus in the second part of the Benediktbeuren Christmas play also underscores the static nature of unbelief as opposed to the dynamic nature of belief. Archisynagogus, who understands according to the flesh rather than the spirit, who is a citizen of the City of Man rather than a pilgrim to the City of God, can only remain as he is because for him the book of understanding is closed. Herod's desire to find the reason for the Magi's journey leads to a sustained ironic commentary in which his failure to understand the real meaning of the event contrasts with the Magi's movement toward spiritual illumination. When Herod's messengers intercept the kings on their journey, the messengers ask the purpose of the quest, but the very terms in which they put the question already guarantee their failure to understand on any but the most superficial level. The messengers are looking for secrets to be unlocked (*"vel si notum aliquid reserandum noscitis"*), and in one sense this is also the meaning of what the Magi seek: to understand the meaning of the Incarnation is to have the spiritual sense of Scripture unlocked, revealed. That is precisely what happens to the prophecies of the Old Testament presented at the beginning of the play; they are unlocked by their fulfillment in the Incarnation, their hidden meaning revealed. But the kind of locking and unlocking that Herod's messengers want has nothing to do with the spiritual sense of Scripture. Rather, it has to do with the maintenance of court intrigue. These are servants of Herod, whose status lies in the fact that "no secrets of the palace/ are barred to us" (*"Nulla nobis clausa sunt secreta palatii,"* ll. 357-58). Neither Herod, his messengers, nor Archisynagogus will ever be able to understand the inner journey, even though the messengers ironically insist that when he hears the good news Herod will want to follow in their footsteps (ll. 369-75).

Intrigue characterizes a court built on insecurity, as Herod's obviously is. Herod is interested in the new king because he sees in him a threat to his own kingship and is anxious to do what he must to remove this threat. Once again, therefore, his problem can be seen in terms of his spiritual misunderstanding, his failure to see the spiritual nature of Christ's kingship. Archisynagogus, who has assumed the role of spokesman for Herod, addresses the Magi in terms of their kingship: "You are kings, I see,/ Because your costumes say so" (*"Reges estis, video, quod prophetat habitus,"* ll. 417-18). He too, then, judges entirely in terms of externals, and accordingly he points out yet another way in which those whom he represents cannot respond in faith to the coming of Christ. To judge by *habitus* is to fail necessarily to understand the kingship of one whose *habitus* is to be naked in a manger. The figure of Herod therefore allows a sustained contrast between two kinds of kingship, two kinds of secrets, two kinds of searching.

Archisynagogus' advice to Herod about how to handle these kings also brings together outward and inner journeys. The language he uses to describe Herod's perplexity makes this explicit:

> Do not, my lord, become all twisted about
> In the labyrinths of your worries.
> Let the three kings come hither
> Searching for a son. (ll. 409-12)

His worries are described as a double passage, a *bivium*, in which he must not allow himself to become entrapped. After praising the outward journey of the kings, Archisynagogus asks them in effect to reveal the purpose of their inward one. Herod's treacherous and hypocritical speech telling the kings to return to him also implies a connection between inner and outer journey and sustains the irony inherent in his failure to understand the spiritual meaning of their journey. He tells them to go on their journey (and return back to him) so that he too might undertake the same journey to see the king whose rule over the world he cannot doubt to be true. By saying that he wishes to undertake the same physical journey, he implies that he wishes to undertake the same journey of faith, using their journey as a model for his, but this is of course the opposite of what he means. His use of the language of the inner journey (ll. 433ff) is rather an attempt to conceal his true purposes. In fact his "faith," which is to say his idolatrous pride, leads to other sorts of journeys. First, Herod sends his troops out to a journey of destruction and death—the slaughter of the Innocents. Then Herod himself is immediately "gnawed to pieces by worms."

The death of Herod is an emblem of judgment showing the punishment that lack of faith merits. The death of Herod in the Benediktbeuren Christmas play serves the same func-

79

tion as the fate of the damned in the portal at Conques: it is a negative exemplum that reinforces the thematic unity of the entire work. In each, an example of one whose lack of faith has merited such a severe judgment serves as a reminder to the audience that its own actions are at all points subject to judgment as well. Herod is, like Simon Magus in the portal at Neuilly and like Antichrist in the Chester *Coming of Antichrist* (see below, Chapter III), one whose blaspheming actions anticipate in parodic form the second coming of Christ in judgment.[28] Archisynagogus, who plays the role of a false prophet, is an Antichrist figure as well. The Magi, therefore, in their journey to witness the first advent, not only typify the pilgrimage of all Christians and their expectation of the second advent, but also face a cruel tyrant and a false spiritual figure, thereby undergoing persecutions and temptations like those expected to take place at the hands of Antichrist shortly before the Last Judgment. Such allusions to judgment frame the play by powerfully reminding us that the events narrated in it are all subject to the final consummation of Christian history. Within this frame reminding the audience of the judgment to come, moreover, judgment is already taking place in the present. Herod's judgment—his death—occurs during the play; his punishment is still within this world, and it is fittingly tailored to his earthly behavior. He is gnawed by worms now even as he had been gnawed by anxiety at the coming of the new king who is to replace him. For him, revelation brings not salvation but anxiety. Revelation of the truth will do no more for him than confirm his own fears about the security of his reign. Herod says to Archisynagogus:

> You, teacher, disclose
> The writings of the prophets,
> If in them are sayings, handed down
> By the prophets, concerning a boy;
> For truly, when you have
> Revealed to me these things,
> They will show themselves to be
> The hidden fears of my own heart
> [*se monstrabunt proprii cordis abscondita*].
> (ll. 526-33)

For Herod, gnawed by the worms of self-doubt, for Archi-synagogus, confined within the prison of his own literal-mindedness, sin is its punishment, now in the present, just as for the Magi faith and serenity in the face of doubt are their own reward. The Last Judgment will thus eternalize what is already present. The two modes of conduct of belief and disbelief are as clearly distinguished in their effects as are the saved and the damned in a Last Judgment portal, and they present to the audience the same choice.

The conflict between faith and doubt—a conflict that begins with the prophets and Augustine, centers on the jour-ney of the Magi, and is seen by inversion in Herod's refusal to believe—can also be seen to structure the angels' annun-ciation of the birth of Christ to the shepherds and the shep-herds' subsequent journey to adore the Christ child. This event is brought into the movement of the play by adding to the scriptural account an attempt on the part of devils to dissuade the shepherds, using the same kinds of rationalistic arguments that Archisynagogus has used throughout. The language linking outer and inner journey is present in the journey of the shepherds to the manger, reinforcing the par-allel with the journey of the Magi. The guide for the shep-herds' journey is the devotion of their souls: "Let the devotion of your soul/ Direct you thither" ("*sed vos huc dirigat/ mentis devotio,*" ll. 463-64). The angel who offers to lead the shep-herds on the true path warns them not to turn from the path of truth:

> Why do you not heed
> This proclamation of the truth?
> Who is this cunning one
> Turning you from the true path [*vertens vos in devium*]? (ll. 481-84)

The movement of the shepherds toward the manger be-comes, then, another literal movement of faith overcoming doubt, as the devils and the angels take their turn with the shepherds on the way to the Christ child. Doubt ends in adoration and the triumph of faith when they reach the man-ger. This section begins when the Magi leave Herod to continue to follow the star, and ends before the Magi come to offer their gifts to the Christ child, so that once again a chronological re-enactment of the scriptural account gives way to a juxtaposition that is based on thematic appropriateness. Such an interpretation explains, too, why the scene is given in such detail. By means of this juxtaposition, shepherds and Magi arrive to worship together, each at the end of the successful journey of faith.

The "argument" that the shepherd presents to his companion would convince no disbeliever. Indeed it is not an argument that would convince (or even be used by) a doctor in the schools of the high Middle Ages. The shepherd reports:

> At this angelic song
> I draw my breath deeply;
> At this song I have within me
> The joy of lute-playing!
> Let us go forward therefore
> Together to the manger,
> And with bent knees
> Let us adore the son. (ll. 506-13)

As this text makes clear, the shepherd is presenting not an argument for faith but rather an assertion of the experience of it. Likewise, what is being dramatically re-created throughout the play is not proof in any logical or propositional sense, but the process that takes place as one moves toward an acceptance of truth. The process of acceptance or denial applies as well to the actual debates between the prophets or Augustine and Archisynagogus, the Magi and Archisynagogus, and the shepherds and the devil. What are being dramatized are contrasting attitudes of embracing faith or of rejecting it through hardness of heart and spiritual blindness. The arguments—if analyzed as arguments—presented by the prophets, by Augustine, and by the Magi are secondary to the attitude of wonder, of openness, and of acceptance that the speakers employ, and they are secondary also to the consequences of the acceptance or rejection of belief.

The contrast between the two attitudes is well expressed

in an exchange between Augustine and the prophets on the one hand, answered by Archisynagogus and his followers on the other. Augustine and the prophets sing a liturgical exchange:

> The untouched bride brought forth the king of kings,
> A thing to be wondered at,
>> *and so on. Let Archisynagogus say with his*
>> *companions:*
> A thing to be denied!
>> *Again Augustine with his followers:*
> A thing to be wondered at!
>> *Again Archisynagogus with his companions:*
> A thing to be denied!
>> *Let this be done several times.*
>> (ll. 202-06)

To 'wonder,' in the sense in which it is being used here, is a word charged with meaning in a monastic context. It implies the eagerness to ponder the mysteries of faith that is necessary to effective contemplation. By contrast, the denial of Archisynagogus closes the door to a consideration of what might be implied by prophecy. The journey of the Magi and the other journeys embodied in the play recreate the journey of faith, a journey that begins in the awareness of prophecy, is moved by wonder, and ends in adoration.

The play concludes with a journey directly related to the slaughter of the Innocents, the flight of the Holy Family into Egypt. Thus at the end of the play we are forced to deal once more with a scriptural reference that is out of its proper chronological order. In Scripture, the Holy Family is told to flee to Egypt before the slaughter of the Innocents and to return to the land of Israel after the death of Herod. In the play, both the slaughter and the return occur before the flight into Egypt. Once again, thematic necessity overtakes chronological aptness. Mary says in the very last line of the play, "now I will go, do you be my companion" (*"Iam vadam, tu comes esto,"* l. 565). Since an angel has just given instructions to Joseph, these words might be addressed directly to Joseph. Or again, since the stage directions indicate that Mary is to lead out an ass for the journey, they may be addressed to the animal. But these words may also be seen as a climactic direct address to the audience, an appropriate ending for the play because it is the play's most direct invitation to the audience to become participants in a spiritual journey. Mary reminds us that it is a journey of hardship (*"Omnia dura pati"*), but this reminder not to underestimate the hardship of the journey merely confirms what we have already seen in the hardship of the journey of the Magi overcoming the wiles of Herod or of the journey of the shepherds overcoming the temptations of the devil. The associative thought patterns of monastic culture, emphasizing a meditative, experiential theology, inform this play.

The dominant image linking sermon, sculpture, and drama is pilgrimage. In all three the audience is invited to undergo a journey toward understanding analogous to the journey that is the subject of the monastic movement of the soul toward God. If we have read the texts correctly this journey also implies as a correlative emblem the idea of judgment—judgment not primarily expressed in eschatological terms as the event that awaits man at the end of time, but rather what we have called tropological judgment. Such a judgment implies that on any point of the journey one's actions can be frozen, so to speak, and checked to see if they help move one along the right way. At any point in the journey there are always two paths that can be taken. In twelfth-century art and drama, the theme of just judgment provides an awareness that one is at the crossroads at each moment of life. The affective spirituality of the monastic search makes the members of the audience conscious of the presentness of judgment and conscious of their participation in a cosmic drama through carefully wrought, carefully articulated works of art.

NOTES

1. Jean Leclercq, *The Love of Learning and the Desire for God* (New York: Fordham Univ. Press, 1961), p. 306; see also William R. Cook, "Some Analogies between Cluniac Sculpture and Cistercian Writings,"

Récherches de théologie ancienne et médiévale, 31 (1981), 212-17; Erwin Panofsky, *Gothic Architecture and Scholasticism* (Cleveland: World, 1951), *passim*. Additionally see the suggestive remarks of Émile Mâle, *Religious Art in France: The Twelfth Century*, trans. Marthiel Matthews, ed. Harry Bober, Bollingen Ser., 90 (Princeton Univ. Press, 1978), p. 371.

2. Aelred of Rievaulx, *A Rule of Life for a Recluse*, trans. Mary Paul Macpherson, in *The Works of Aelred of Rievaulx*, I: *Treatises, The Pastoral Prayer* (Spenser, Mass.: Cistercian Publications, 1971), p. 99. The same theme is found in the sermons of the two great Anglo-Saxon monastic sermon writers, Aelfric and Wulfstan. The relation between artistic images and religious devotion in the Middle Ages is treated in Sixten Ringbom, "Devotional Images and Imaginative Devotions: Notes on the Place of Art in Late Medieval Private Piety," *Gazette des Beaux Arts*, 73 (1969), 159-70, esp. 163 and n. 40.

3. *The Holy Rule of Our Most Holy Father Benedict* (Trappist, Kentucky: Abbey of Gethsemani, 1942), pp. 75, 77 (chap. 7).

4. *The 12th Century Tympanum of the Church of Conques* (Abbaye St. Michel de Frigolet, 1970), p. 2.

5. John V. Fleming, *An Introduction to the Franciscan Literature of the Middle Ages* (Chicago: Franciscan Herald Press, 1977), attempts a similar relocation with the documents of Franciscan spirituality. His suggestions seem to me to be applicable to medieval spiritual writing in general, and this study is indebted to his analysis. See ibid., pp. 2ff, for a statement of method. Another example of the use of the techniques of literary analysis for texts that have been studied from a different perspective is Robert Alter's excellent study of Hebrew Scripture, *The Art of Biblical Narrative* (New York: Basic Books, 1981). Alter's statements of methodology are also relevant to the analysis presented here.

6. For the significance of this freedom of movement in a monastic context see Leclercq, *Love of Learning*, *passim*. See also Gerhart Ladner, *Ad Imaginem Dei: The Image of Man in Medieval Art* (Latrobe, Pennsylvania: Archabbey Press, 1965), pp. 63-67, for a discussion of the freedom of the will in Bernard.

7. *The Works of Bernard of Clairvaux*, II: *On the Song of Songs*, I, trans. Kilian Walsh (Kalamazoo: Cistercian Publications, 1976), p. 63.

8. See especially Sermon 10, III, 4.

9. *On the Song of Songs*, I, 78. The text continues: "Whoever you may be, if your soul is thus disposed, if you are saturated with the dew of mercy, overflowing with affectionate kindness, making yourself all things to all men yet pricing your deeds like something discarded in order to be ever and everywhere ready to supply to others what they need, in a word, so dead to yourself that you live only for others—if this be you, then you obviously and happily possess the third and best of all ointments and your hands have dripped with liquid myrrh that is utterly enchanting. It will not run dry in times of stress nor evaporate in the heat of perse-

cution; but God will perpetually 'remember all your oblations and find your holocaust acceptable'."

10. Ibid., I, 78.

11. Ibid., I, 78.

12. The rhetorical sophistication of St. Bernard's sermons has been studied by Christine Mohrmann, "Observations sur la langue et le style de saint Bernard," in *S. Bernardi Opera*, II: *Sermones super Cantica Canticorum, 36-86*, ed. J. Leclercq, C. H. Talbot, and H. M. Rochais (Rome: Cistercian Editions, 1958), esp. pp. ix*ff*. See also Jean Leclercq, "Nouveaux aspects littéraires de l'oeuvre de saint Bernard," *Cahiers de civilisation médiévale*, 8 (1965), 299-326. For the relationship between Bernard and the rhetorical culture of the twelfth century, see Jean Leclercq, *Monks and Love in Twelfth-Century France* (Oxford: Oxford Univ. Press, 1979).

13. *On the Song of Songs*, I, 81.

14. Ibid., I, 81.

15. Ibid., I, 86.

16. Ibid., I, 86.

17. Origen, *The Song of Songs: Commentary and Homilies*, trans. R. P. Lawson, Ancient Christian Writers, 26 (Westminster, Md.: Newman Press, 1957), p. 21. See also the introduction to this work for a summary of the image of the Church as the Bride of Christ. For a complete listing of medieval commentaries on the Song of Songs, see A. Cabassut and M. Oliphe-Gaillard, "Cantique des Cantiques: Au moyen age," *Dictionnaire de spiritualité*, II (Paris: Beauchesne, 1953), cols. 101-04. The most comprehensive study of these commentaries is Henri de Lubac, *Exégèse médiévale: Les quatre sens de l'écriture* (Paris: Aubier, 1959-1964), esp. I, pt. 2, 549-86, and *passim*.

18. "Prophetic 'Play' and Symbolist 'Plot' in the Beauvais *Daniel*," *Comparative Drama*, 11 (1977), 201.

19. For the manuscript, see the facsimile edition of the *Carmina Burana*, ed. Bernhard Bischoff (Munich: Prestel Verlag, 1967). Quotations and translations from the play are from David Bevington, ed., *Medieval Drama* (Boston: Houghton Mifflin, 1975), pp. 180-201. For the dating of the drama, see Rosemary Woolf, *The English Mystery Plays* (Berkeley and Los Angeles: Univ. of California Press, 1972), p. 42. Others who have examined the connection between twelfth-century drama and spirituality (although not specifically monastic forms of spirituality) include Taylor, "Prophetic 'Play' and Symbolist 'Plot' in the Beauvais *Daniel*," pp. 191-208; Michael Rudick, "Theme, Structure and Sacred Context in the Benediktbeuren 'Passion' Play," *Speculum*, 47 (1974), 267-86; Kathleen Ashley, "The Fleury *Raising of Lazarus* and Twelfth-Century Currents of Thought," *Comparative Drama*, 15 (1981), 139-58; and Sandro Sticca, "Drama and Spirituality in the Middle Ages," *Medievalia et Humanistica*, n.s. 4 (1973), 84.

20. *The Drama of the Medieval Church* (Oxford: Clarendon Press, 1933). Young's comments on the Christmas play (II, 190ff) must be taken together with his comments on the Benediktbeuren Passion Play (I, 513ff) as part of his implicit theory about twelfth-century drama.

21. Ibid., II, 190.

22. Ibid., I, 536. Young calls the speeches of the Kings "somewhat appalling in their prolixity and pedantry" (II, 193).

23. The tympanum of the church of Mary Magdalene at Neuilly-en-Donjon, 25 kilometers south of Paray-le-Monial, centers on the Adoration of the Magi. Beneath the large star now at rest on the upper edge of the tympanum, the Virgin and Child receive the approaching Magi. Five angels, four blowing trumpets and one holding an open book, surround this scene of adoration, which takes place on the backs of two animals, an ox and a lion. Reading the lintel below the tympanum from left to right, we encounter several seemingly unrelated scenes. First comes the fall of man, wherein Adam has eaten the fruit from the tree of knowledge of good and evil and has turned away from the tree of life. Then, in what is in fact a conflation of two banquet scenes, Mary Magdalene anoints the feet of Jesus and wipes them with her hair; this is immediately conflated with a depiction of the banquet of the Last Supper. The capital flanking the lintel next to the banquet depicts a story from Daniel 14 in which an angel brings the prophet Habakkuk to minister to Daniel in the lion's den. The left hand capital has been more difficult to identify; most recently it has been cogently argued that the scene depicted there is the fall of Simon Magus as told in the apocryphal *Acts of Peter*. For two interpretations of this sculptural ensemble see William R. Cook, "A New Approach to the Tympanum of Neuilly-en-Donjon," *Journal of Medieval History*, 4 (1978), 333-45, and Walter Cahn, "Le tympan de Neuilly-en-Donjon," *Cahiers de civilisation médiévale*, 8 (1965), 351-64.

24. *PL*, XLII, 1117-30.

25. As indeed they do in much medieval (and Renaissance) art. An especially clear example from twelfth-century art is the Deposition in low relief from the Cathedral of Parma.

26. Peter Damian, "Sermon for Epiphany," in *Selected Writings on the Spiritual Life*, trans. Patricia McNulty (London: Faber and Faber, 1959); Guerric of Igny, *Liturgical Sermons*, I, trans. Monks of Mount St. Bernard Abbey (Spenser, Mass.: Cistercian Publications, 1970).

27. *Concerning the City of God Against the Pagans*, trans. Henry Bettenson (Baltimore: Penguin, 1972), p. 596.

28. For the relationship between Herod, Simon Magus, and Antichrist see Richard Kenneth Emmerson, *Antichrist in the Middle Ages* (Seattle: Univ. of Washington Press, 1981), pp. 26-28, 121. Herod's punishment, being "gnawed by worms," is undoubtedly taken from Acts 12.23 where Herod is struck down and eaten by worms "because he had not given the honor to God." But this is yet another way in which chro-

nology is subordinated to thematic consistency, because Herod's crime in Acts is the persecution of the apostles, and in fact the Herod of Acts is not the same Herod who appears in the Gospel account of the Slaughter of the Innocents. For further comment on Herod and twelfth-century drama and art, see Miriam Anne Skey, "The Iconography of Herod in the Fleury Playbook and the Visual Arts," *Comparative Drama*, 17 (1983), 55-78.

III

"NOWE YS COMMON THIS DAYE": ENOCH AND ELIAS, ANTICHRIST, AND THE STRUCTURE OF THE CHESTER CYCLE

Richard Kenneth Emmerson

After staging a long debate between Antichrist and his two righteous opponents—the Old Testament worthies, E-noch and Elias—the Chester *Coming of Antichrist* suddenly introduces the archangel Michael.[1] This traditional herald of doomsday now announces the divine judgment on Antichrist:

> Antechriste, nowe ys common this daye.
> Reigne no lenger nowe thou maye.
> Hee that hath led thee alwaye,
> nowe him thou must goe to. (ll. 625-28)

This just judgment serves as a turning point not only in the career of the great deceiver, but also in the action of the entire play. Up to this moment, Antichrist has risen to power by pretending to be Christ, duping his followers, and over-whelming his opponents. Now he will be punished, while Enoch and Elias, whom he has just killed, will be rewarded.

The play's characters and actions similarly change at this point. Until now, the play has emphasized the conflict between good and evil by portraying human opponents attempting to persuade four kings to follow either Christ or Antichrist, who claims to be Christ. Now the supernatural agents come on stage. For the play's human characters, if not for the audience, the time of decision is past. After Michael damns Antichrist, demons drag him to hell and the archangel leads Enoch and Elias to heaven.

The words of the archangel signal a more profound change in the play's action as well, for now the *Coming of Antichrist* ceases to recapitulate scenes staged earlier in the Chester cycle and begins to foreshadow the final event of the cycle, doomsday. Until Michael's appearance, the play has alluded to particular events and scenes from the life of Christ by portraying the life of the pseudo-Christ. It has also clearly drawn the line between Antichrist and Christ by staging a long disputation between the demonic replacement of Christ and the eschatological representatives of Christ, Enoch and Elias. The divine judgment on Antichrist now shifts the focus from the past to the future, for the play's conclusion is structured to foreshadow the conclusion of the entire Chester cycle, the *Last Judgment* (Play XXIV). It dramatizes for the present what many medieval Christians believed was imminent—doomsday—by staging the just rewards of the types of Christ and the just punishment of the pseudo-Christ.

This particular turning point in the general battle between good and evil that is dramatized throughout the Middle English Corpus Christi plays has received little attention from students of medieval drama. The *Coming of Antichrist* has, it is true, been studied as a reflection of the medieval Antichrist tradition, which it only partly develops.[2] A more promising literary approach is suggested by Rosemary Woolf, who notes that the play "consciously exploits the potentialities" of associating Antichrist with earlier plays in the cycle,[3] but even Woolf and others noting these similarities have not recognized the play's key structural role in the cycle. Part of the difficulty results from the play's comic aspects. The absurdity of Antichrist's sham *imitatio Christi* and the humor of the devilish whining and burlesque action have led critics to minimize the play's significance, to see the play in "farcical" terms as an "antic interlude before the inevitable triumph of righteousness in *The Last Judgment*."[4] But the play's lively comedy should not mislead us. Antichrist's power for evil is formidable, his demonic magic amazingly effective. As the demons state after his death, "Manye a fatt morsell wee had for his sake/ of soules that should have bine saved" (ll. 677-78). His ranting and confused theology may be humorous, but his temptation of the righteous and murder of Christ's messengers would not strike a medieval audience as a farcical interlude in the cycle any more than would the ranting of Herod—a type of Antichrist—after the massacre of the Innocents. The deceitful ploys of Antichrist and his long debate with Enoch and Elias are dire events that Christians expected to take place in the last days and are crucial to the medieval sense of salvation history. The overall dramatic effect of the action, furthermore, is serious, as is the play's purpose in staging for the Chester audience these imminent events. Peter W. Travis, who recently has offered a "moral defense" for the play, rightly stresses how it calls on "nearly all the powers of human discrimination," and how "through these dramatic exercises the viewers should be better prepared to face their future trials and to confront the dramatic image of their own Last Judgment."[5]

A better understanding of the serious meaning of the *Coming of Antichrist* and of its key structural role in the Chester cycle may depend upon a methodology which studies the play in conjunction with other works in the medieval Antichrist tradition.[6] Unfortunately, although Antichrist was apparently the subject of several continental plays in the Middle Ages (e.g., the twelfth-century *Ludus de Antichristo* discussed above in Chapter I, and also the fifteenth-century Corpus Christi play from Künzelsau, both of which develop the Antichrist tradition rather fully and offer helpful analogues for the Chester play[7]), the *Coming of Antichrist* is the only extant Antichrist tradition play in the Middle English cycle drama. Unfortunately, too, the visual arts, which in the later Middle Ages often embodied a cyclical treatment

of Antichrist like that of the cycle plays and which reflect
the same desire to stir the imagination of Christians as they
contemplated the significance of last-day events,[8] are generally lacking for Chester. The relative scarcity of medieval
art from Chester complicates our enterprise and frustrates
attempts to identify specific local art work that may have
been known to the dramatist and his audience. As Sally-Beth
MacLean notes, "although the city is fortunate in the near-
complete preservation of its Whitsun play cycle, it has suffered severe losses in artistic representations of the biblical
or hagiographical stories which were common sources of inspiration for both art and drama in the period."[9] Thus a
search for local medieval art as "source material" for the
Chester *Coming of Antichrist* will be fruitless, and even if
such art were extant it would be difficult at best to show its
influence on the dramatist.

Iconographic analysis will be helpful, nevertheless, in
establishing a more generalized understanding of how artists
portrayed apocalyptic themes for lay (both courtly and popular) as well as religious audiences, and in determining the
sometimes subtle relationships between Christ, Enoch and
Elias, and Antichrist as they appear in developed picture
cycles. Particularly helpful in this iconographic analysis are
three types of medieval books widespread in the later Middle
Ages. The first are the beautifully illuminated Apocalypses
which became especially popular after the mid-thirteenth
century and which emphasize the eschatological dimensions
of Antichrist's career and the preaching of the two prophets.[10] The second grouping of books includes various illuminated manuscripts and early printed books organized
according to typological and symbolic principles that illustrate the biblical story and reflect the ways in which these
apocalyptic figures reverberate throughout salvation history.
The third group consists of the popular late medieval block
books that illustrate a complete *vita Antichristi*. Roughly contemporary with the Chester Whitsuntide plays, these books
reflect the most fully developed artistic treatment of the Antichrist tradition in the fifteenth and early sixteenth centuries.

An analysis of these works of medieval art in conjunction with an awareness of the exegetical tradition and close attention to the dramatic text will highlight two features of the *Coming of Antichrist* not previously noted by scholars which reveal both its significance for Chester's staging of salvation history and its structural role as a major link in the cycle. The first is the close typological and symbolic relationship between Enoch and Elias and Christ. This symbolic association, as well as the witnesses' actual eschatological roles, explains the amount of time given the witnesses and their debate with Antichrist, a section of the play that has particularly bothered critics.[11] The debate between Antichrist and the two witnesses for the allegiance of the four kings, although often confused and sometimes humorous, represents the final conflict between Christ and evil, the last test of mankind, and the final opportunity of mankind to choose right over wrong. The second feature is the way in which the contrast between the just judgment of Enoch and Elias and of Antichrist prefigures the contrast between the saved and the damned at doomsday. Coming after Antichrist's parodic inversion of Christ's life, this prefiguration of the end of time allows the *Coming of Antichrist* to link the earlier plays in the cycle—those concerned with the ministry and passion of Christ—to the *Last Judgment*, in which Christ's final role in the cycle will be that of judge of his creation.

The eschatological role of Enoch and Elias in opposition to Antichrist is evident in the biblical sources of the medieval Antichrist legend. The two witnesses described in Apocalypse 11.3-13, who have miraculous powers and who teach the truth for 1260 days before they are killed by the beast that rises from the abyss, were identified quite early as Enoch and Elias, although occasionally they were identified as Moses and Elias, the two prophets appearing with Christ in the Transfiguration (Mark 9.4-5).[12] Enoch, the righteous patriarch who is described as one who "walked with God" (Genesis 5.22-24) and received special revelation, is an important figure in both early Christian and medieval apocalyptic thought. Exegetical and artistic works, however, generally place greater emphasis on the role of Elias. Certainly some of the miraculous powers of the witnesses resemble the powers of this Old Testament prophet, who was able to call up fire against his enemies (4 Kings [AV: 2 Kings] 1.10; 3 Kings [AV: 1 Kings] 18.37-38) and also prevent rain (3 Kings [AV: 1 Kings] 17.1). The expectation of the return of the prophet Elias is also biblical. Based upon the prophecy of Malachi 4.5-6, the expectation clearly continued to be influential in New Testament times (Mark 6.15, 8.28, 9.11-13). That the witnesses are to be the messengers of God in opposition to the beast, the opponent of God who is identified quite clearly throughout medieval exegesis as Antichrist, becomes an important characteristic of the medieval tradition that is based on scriptural support.[13]

The medieval interpretation of Apocalypse 11 particularly emphasizes the conflict between the two representatives of Christ and Antichrist. This emphasis is evident in a wide spectrum of medieval literature and art.[14] Even some of the earliest illustrations of Apocalypse 11 interpreted the witnesses as Enoch and Elias and the beast as Antichrist. Many of the Spanish illuminated Apocalypses, following the commentary of Beatus of Liebana (d. 798), portray not a beast but a human figure who kills two men dressed in simple robes. The well-known Saint-Sever Apocalypse (mid-eleventh century) is an early example of a pictorial tradition popular throughout the Middle Ages. It shows a regal figure (inscribed as Antichrist) wielding a huge sword and decapitating the two men of God (inscribed as Enoch and Elias).[15] This tradition is similarly reflected in the Chester play. Having lost the allegiance of the kings, Antichrist gives up the claim of spiritual "might" based on his pseudo-miracles and turns to cruder tactics:

> A, false faytures, turne you nowe?
> You shall be slayne, I make avowe;
> and those traytors that so turned you,
> I shall make them unfayne,
> that all other by verey sight
> shall knowe that I am most of might,
> for with this sword nowe wyll I feight,
> for all you shall be slayne. (ll. 617-24)

The rubrics here read: "Tunc Antechristus occidet Enock et Heliam et omnes reges conversos cum gladio et redibit ad cathedram; cum dicat Michaell cum gladio in dextera sua." In other words, Antichrist's murder of the two prophets immediately precedes the dramatic turning point of the play, visualized on stage when the sword of homicide symbolizing Antichrist's claim of earthly power is replaced by the sword of judgment in Michael's right hand.

Enoch and Elias are important in medieval tradition not only as opponents of Antichrist, but also as representatives of Christ. Such a dual role is quite evident, for example, in the Anglo-French illuminated Apocalypses that flourished from the mid-thirteenth century and influenced the early block-book Apocalypses of the fifteenth century. In one particular grouping, as represented by the Cloisters Apocalypse, these beautiful picture cycles concentrate upon the conflict between the witnesses and Antichrist by portraying four scenes illustrating Apocalypse 11.3-14.[16] The first two scenes show the witnesses working miracles and then being attacked by the beast. The following two scenes picture the particular characteristics associating them with Christ. In the first, the spirit in the form of doves enters the dead witnesses, who, to the amazement of their enemies, stand (fig. 7). One of the witnesses points heavenward and looks into a cloud at an angel who, like Michael in the *Coming of Antichrist*, has called the witnesses. In the last scene, they rise into heaven while on earth an earthquake destroys a city. The illustrations clearly portray not only the marvelous power of the witnesses and their defeat by the beast, but also their resurrection and ascension, two supernatural events that help establish their close relationship to Christ.

This relationship is suggested by the biblical sources and explicitly developed in medieval picture cycles. To begin with, the term translated "witness," the Greek *martus*, is first applied, as John M. Court points out, to Christ in Apocalypse 1.5 and 3.14.[17] The term refers there and elsewhere in early Christian sources to a person who witnesses not only by word, but also through his death. Christ, whose passion is the prototype of all Christian martyrdom, testifies to his

95

righteousness as the witnesses do to theirs when killed by the beast. Thus the suffering of the witnesses, interpreted usually as the deaths of Enoch and Elias at the hands of Antichrist, associates them with the first *martus*, Christ. This association is further underscored by biblical suggestions that particularly connect Elias with Christ. As a forerunner of the Messiah, Elias was expected to suffer as Christ would suffer.[18] Since in medieval exegesis the discussion of one witness usually led to discussion of the other, it is not surprising that many of the biblical suggestions connecting Christ with Elias were expanded to connect Christ to Enoch. Even some early manuscript illustrations portrayed Enoch and Elias alongside the Crucifixion of Christ. For example, the two Carolingian Apocalypses of Paris and Valenciennes, which devote only one full folio each to Chapter 11, portray two scenes significantly related.[19] The first, placed at the top of each folio, shows Enoch and Elias standing to the left of a crucified Christ. Clearly the artist conceives of their martyrdom as a reenactment of the passion of Christ. The lower scene on each folio is also of interest, for here the artist has chosen to portray the angel that blows the seventh trumpet (Apocalypse 11.15). According to Bede and much medieval exegesis, the seventh trumpet signals the end of the world and introduces the Sabbath age.[20] Thus this early Apocalypse illustration already mirrors not only the close relationship established in Scripture between the witnesses and judgment but also the ties linking Enoch and Elias to Christ.

The *Coming of Antichrist* carefully develops medieval tradition concerning the two witnesses (based primarily on Apocalypse 11.3-13). These two Old Testament prophets, protected in the Earthly Paradise until the end of the world, first preach against Antichrist (ll. 253-512), next convert those who have hearkened to Antichrist by proving the apparent miracles to be false (ll. 513-616), and then are killed by the tyrant (ll. 617-24). As the medieval audience would expect from the tradition and as the Expositor explained in the preceding play, the witnesses are finally resurrected and led to Heaven (699-722).[21] Furthermore, expectations concerning the two witnesses are developed elsewhere in the Chester cycle, in two separate plays preceding the stage appearance of Enoch and Elias. In the *Prophets of Antichrist*, which more properly should be titled "Prophets Before the Day of Doom"[22] since it really introduces the entire eschatological grouping that concludes the cycle, the Expositor notes that Antichrist will kill Enoch and Elias "in middest of the holye cyttye/ where Christ was nayled on a tree" (XXII.206-07). As in the Carolingian Apocalypses, the Expositor specifically relates the suffering of the two witnesses to Christ's passion. Continuing his interpretation of the apocalyptic prophecies, the Expositor notes that "after three dayes and halfe one" the witnesses, like Christ, "shall ryse" (XXII.209-10). Later the Expositor once again explains that Antichrist will kill Enoch and Elias, who until then have not died, but who "to paradyce through Goddes postee/ were ravished both, and there shalbee/ ever tyll the daye doe come" (XXII.250-52).

The belief that the two prophets await Antichrist in the Earthly Paradise is staged even earlier in the cycle, in the *Harrowing of Hell*. This pageant, which in the sixteenth century quite appropriately concluded the second day of performance,[23] holds a particularly important place in the Chester cycle for both theological and dramatic reasons. Theologically, it portrays the "second Adam" releasing the "first Adam" (and other righteous souls) from the prison of hell (XVII.193-228) by defeating Satan and his army of demons. Immediately following the Passion, in other words, Christ is proven victorious. The pageant further portrays "Latro," the good thief crucified with Christ (XVII.255-72), as well as "Mulier," the alewife who remains in hell (XVII.277-336).[24] The good thief, now in the Earthly Paradise, exemplifies the saved repentant sinner, whereas the alewife, in hell and married to its denizens, represents the damned beyond mercy.[25] These two characters thus prepare the audience for the radical division of good and evil at doomsday. The play similarly has an important structural role. It links the beginning of time dramatized in the *Fall of Lucifer* and *Adam and Eve*, which began the first day of the cycle, to the *Passion* (XVIa.309-24), which as the turning point of salvation history dominated the second day of acting after the division of the Chester play into three segments to be presented on the three days following Whitsunday.[26] It also foreshadows the eschatological plays concluding history, the cycle itself, and the third day of acting by staging the thief and the woman, who more than any other characters in the entire cycle resemble the allegorical figures of the *Last Judgment*.

What is more significant for our purposes is that, alone of all the Harrowing of Hell plays in the extant Middle English Corpus Christi cycles, the Chester *Harrowing* brings Enoch and Elias on stage.[27] As major figures from the Old Testament, they are here connected to Adam (at the beginning of human history), Christ (at the crucifixion), and Michael (at the end of time). Here, as in the conclusion of the *Coming of Antichrist*, Michael leads the saved to heaven. The saved are, to be sure, the souls recently released from hell, not the two witnesses, and yet Enoch and Elias are present as well. They are introduced when Adam, startled to see anyone in the Garden of Eden, questions them and wonders in particular "what manner of men bene yee" who "dead come not to hell as wee,/ sythen all men dampned were?" (XVII.229-32). The question is particularly relevant because, like the recently released Adam and David, the patriarch and the prophet represent the ages of natural law and Mosaic law; under the strictures of the "old law," they should have been brought to hell. Up to this point in the play (and salvation history), furthermore, the only other "man" to die and not be damned is Jesus, and he has just released Adam by coming to hell. The connection between the two and the Savior is implicit. Even the differences, moreover, are significant. Christ, as the *Last Judgment* makes clear (XXIV.357-436), establishes his eschatological role by the very means of his death. The two worthies here preparing for their eschatological roles have not yet died (XVII.245-46); nonetheless, as Elias explains to Adam, in the last days Antichrist will slay them in the "holye cittye;/ but sekerly, within dayes three/ and a halfe, we shall ryse" (XVII.250-52). The Chester *Harrowing* thus connects Enoch and Elias not only to both Antichrist and Michael, but also to Christ in his passion and victory over death and the powers of evil.

In the Chester cycle, therefore, the figures of Enoch and Elias are polysemous. Their relationship to Christ is especially complex and not limited to their eschatological function as the two witnesses of the Apocalypse. A look at medieval exegesis and the biblical picture cycles reflecting salvation history will suggest other ways in which these Old Testament figures anticipate through their actions events from the life and ministry of Christ. The popular *Biblia Pauperum*, biblical illustrations that flourished in the fourteenth and fifteenth centuries both as manuscript codices and as early block books, perhaps approximate the dramatic cycles as closely as is possible for a static art form. Like the Corpus Christi plays, they were intended as basic primers of Christian doctrine for popular audiences, both lay and religious.[28] Although ranging from the creation to doomsday, like the plays they focus primarily on the life of Christ. These Bibles are arranged chronologically, following the events of Christ's life from birth to his ascension and then, like the cycle plays, they picture Pentecost and finally the judgment day.[29] Each event is surrounded by illustrations drawn from the Old Testament that typologically foreshadow the life of Christ, thus providing visual examples of the multiplicity of ways in which figures from various epochs of salvation history reappear and are reinterpreted in later events.

Enoch and Elias often appear in the *Biblia Pauperum* as types of Christ. Perhaps their most important typological function is based on their having been taken up without dying (Genesis 5.24; 4 Kings [*AV*: 2 Kings] 2.11-13). The significance of this event is exemplified in one group of the picture Bibles, which represent the Ascension of Christ in the very center of the page (fig. 8).[30] The Virgin and the disciples of Christ kneel around the Mount of Olives, which is clearly marked with two footprints, while directly above the hillside Christ's feet disappear into a cloud. The scene to the left of the page then shows Enoch in a landscape setting reaching up to the sky where Christ, appearing from a cloud, takes him up. The scene on the right, meanwhile, illustrates the second type of Christ's Ascension: Elias, sitting in a chariot and ascending to the clouds above, while Elisha remains kneeling on the ground. Elisha here is symbolically identified with the apostles whom Christ leaves behind to continue his ministry. Similarly arranged typological portrayals of both Enoch and Elias on each side of Christ's Ascension are included in the earlier manuscript versions of the *Biblia Pauperum* as well.[31]

In addition to their portrayal of Elias with Enoch as types of Christ in his Ascension, the *Biblia Pauperum* portray Elias as a type of Christ in four other scenes. Enoch receives less attention in these typologically arranged picture Bibles, probably because he appears only briefly in the genealogies of Genesis 5. In contrast, Elias figures prominently throughout the Old Testament books of 3-4 Kings (*AV*: 1-2 Kings), where—as miracle worker, chief of the prophets, and outspoken opponent of the religious and political powers of his day—for medieval exegetes he clearly prefigures Christ. One of the most widely illustrated scenes interprets Christ's raising of Lazarus from the dead (John 11.17-44) as an antitype of Elias' raising of the son of the widow of Zarephath (3 Kings [*AV*: 1 Kings] 17.17-23).[32] The scene illustrated in the center of the page shows Christ as he calls Lazarus from a coffin. To the left, Elias and the widow pray for the dead boy. Elias here becomes a type of Christ through his ability to raise the dead, a powerful miracle that Antichrist will pretend to accomplish in the Chester play in order to prove his claim to be Christ. The *Biblia Pauperum* also suggest that Elias' miracle is a type of Christ's Passion, another event that Antichrist attempts to imitate. The portrayal of Christ's carrying the cross to Calvary is illustrated typologically not only by the standard Old Testament type—Isaac's carrying a bundle of wood toward the hillside where Abraham has been instructed to sacrifice him—but also by Elias' meeting the widow at the gates of Zarephath.[33] The illustration arranges the wood collected by the widow (3 Kings [*AV*: 1 Kings] 17.10) in the form of a cross, illustrating in a not unusual way how explicit typological symbolism influenced the artistic visualization of the Old Testament.[34] A third

100

scene that interprets Elias as a type of Christ once again involves an event that Antichrist falsely re-enacts for his deceitful purposes in the *Coming of Antichrist*: Pentecost. The *Biblia Pauperum* (see fig. 9) compare Christ's sending of the Holy Spirit onto the faithful apostles with Elias' calling fire down from heaven on the altar of the Lord established on Mount Carmel (3 Kings [*AV*: 1 Kings] 18.38). According to medieval tradition, Antichrist's deceitful claims to be Christ are impressive because he is able to imitate (however falsely) the miraculous elements in the life of Christ: his ability to raise the dead, his own death and resurrection, his rising to heaven, and his sending of the Holy Spirit.[35] To understand the symbolic energy of the two witnesses in the *Coming of Antichrist*, we must realize that the events blasphemously parodied by Antichrist are, according to the *Biblia Pauperum* and medieval exegesis, properly typified by Enoch and especially Elias.

The final scene in which the *Biblia Pauperum* interpret Elias as prefiguring Christ is of particular significance because it represents a common theme illustrated in much medieval art: the confrontation between the righteous, who will suffer for their faithfulness to God, and a powerful, wicked ruler, who is closely allied to the powers of evil. The Bibles develop this theme around a central scene portraying the falsely accused Christ standing before Pilate. The Roman ruler washes his hands after passing the sentence that will lead to Christ's death (Matthew 27.24-25). The scene to the left portrays the Old Testament type of this event, Elias confronting Jezebel (3 Kings [*AV*: 1 Kings] 19.1-3).[36] The prophet threatened by Jezebel (whose role in medieval exegesis is roughly comparable to that of the Whore of Babylon, a symbol of Antichrist) exemplifies the righteous man of God in opposition to the wicked ruler. The same theme is suggested in an earlier typological arrangement specified in the *Pictor in Carmine*, the thirteenth-century treatise outlining appropriate biblical typology for artists wishing to illustrate the life of Christ.[37] Here the flight of the holy family from the rage of Herod is typified by the flight of Elias from Ahab. By his opposition to Jezebel and Ahab, therefore, Elias specifically prefigures Christ threatened by Pilate and Herod and represents the righteous before the wicked ruler. The Chester cycle, it should be noted, repeatedly stages this same theme. In *Balaam and Balaack*, even the unwilling prophet Balaam steadfastly blesses Israel (V.280-319) before the wicked king Balak, considered in medieval exegesis to be a type of Antichrist. In the *Magi* (Play VIII), the Three Kings confront Herod the Great, yet another prefiguration of Antichrist. In the *Slaughter of the Innocents*, Herod vows to kill Christ (X.21-24), and subsequently goes to his death in a scene vividly resembling the death of Antichrist, for devils drag Herod to hell and describe his punishment (X.434-57). The *Trial and Flagellation* (Play XVI) also portrays Christ's confrontation with Pilate, Cayphas, and a later Herod (Antipas).

Although the *Biblia Pauperum* provide the best examples of picture cycles that can appropriately be compared to the late medieval cycle plays, other cyclical art from the high Middle Ages similarly explores the typological significance of the two witnesses. For example, the Moralized Bibles, painted (in contrast to the "poor man's Bibles") for wealthy patrons, are helpful because of their encyclopedic scope in reconstructing the Christocentric associations of Enoch and especially Elias. Some of these Bibles, in their complete editions, include more than 5000 biblical and symbolic illustrations. Painted in roundels arranged in columns, usually eight scenes to a folio side, the illustrations are accompanied by short passages of text from Scripture and standard commentaries.[38] Instead of first illustrating the life of Christ and then suggesting Old Testament prefigurations, these lavish Bibles illustrate the Old Testament text and introduce the New Testament event as a typological fulfillment. For example, the Bodleian *Bible Moralisée* (Oxford, Bodleian MS. 270b) interprets 4 Kings [*AV*: 2 Kings] 2.11-13 in two roundels, the first portraying Elias taken up in a cart, the second Christ rising into a cloud. The explanatory text makes the point directly: "Elias significat Christum."[39] The same Bible makes similar connections in its four sets of roundels illustrating 3 Kings (*AV*: 1 Kings) 17 (see fig. 10). The first set (on the upper left) illustrates Elias being fed by the ravens at Kerith, where the prophet hides from Ahab. According to the gloss, the seclusion of the prophet prefigures the veiling of Christ's divinity in humanity, while the bread prefigures the Corpus Christi that sustains the Church. The next two sets of illustrations (on the lower left and upper right) develop ecclesiological interpretations, whereby the prophet's ministry to the woman of Zarephath (3 Kings [*AV*: 1 Kings] 17.10-17) prefigures Christ's care for Ecclesia. The fourth set of roundels (on the lower right) boldly equates Elias and Christ. In the top roundel of this fourth set, Elias, while looking heavenward at Christ, lifts the arms of the widow's dead child (3 Kings [*AV*: 1 Kings] 17.21) in order to restore him to life. The gloss for the accompanying illustration, the Crucifixion, states: "Helias qui extendit se super puerum significat iesum christum qui extendit se in cruce."[40]

Many other examples develop similar interpretations of Enoch and Elias, but the foregoing should be sufficient to show that their significance in medieval exegesis, art, and drama is the result not only of their eschatological but also of their Christocentric associations. To summarize, these associations are centered on the life of Christ and extend into the past and the future. The Old Testament prophet Elias is a type of Christ in his ability to raise the dead; he is linked to Christ's passion through the symbolism of the cross; and, along with Enoch, he prefigures the Ascension. Other events from the life of Elias not only relate him to Christ but also identify him as one of the witnesses of the last days. His manipulation of supernatural fire, evident when he called fire onto the altar on Mount Carmel, serves both as a type of Pentecost and as a link between Elias and the witnesses who use fire against their enemies. In his opposition to Jezebel and Ahab, he prefigures Jesus standing before Pilate and fleeing from Herod, exemplifies the faithful in opposition to the wicked ruler, and foreshadows his eschatological role when, with Enoch, he challenges Antichrist. Finally, as the witnesses of the last days, Enoch and Elias are associated with Christ. They re-enact the death of Christ by which he becomes the prototypical *martus* or witness, and, in their own restoration to life and ascension to heaven, recapitulate the central doctrines of Christian belief establishing Christ's divinity—i.e., the Resurrection and Ascension.

Although these symbolic resonances may not all be at work in the Chester cycle, Enoch and Elias are clearly more than mere spokesmen for the Christian faith in their long disputation with Antichrist. As they explain when first entering, they have been set aside and protected in paradise through the "privitie" (l. 257) of God for this very moment. Through their affiliation with Jesus, as Enoch explains, they gain their power; by him they certify their mission, and for him they act as soteriological agents:

> To doe him downe wee shall assaye
> through might of Jesu, borne of a maye,
> by right and reason, as you shall saye,
> and that you shall well here.
> And for that cause hither were we sent
> by Jesus Christe omnypotent,
> and that you shall not all be shent.
> Hee bought you all full deare.

> Be gladd, therefore, and make good cheare,
> and I doe reede as I you leere,
> for wee be commen in good maneere
> to save you everychone. (ll. 325-36)

Antichrist's hostile and brutal reaction to the witnesses inadvertently supports these associations. For example, at the beginning of the play Antichrist accuses Jesus of "falsehood" and "fantasye," and claims that Jesus was "slayne through vertue of my sond" (l. 31). Then he threatens to hang Enoch "and that lurdayne that standes thee bye" (l. 374), whom he accuses of falseness and flattery. His short exchange with the Doctor is equally revealing, since it resembles an earlier exchange between the Doctor and Herod— the cycle's tyrannical prefiguration of Antichrist. In *The Slaughter of the Innocents*, the Doctor advises Herod to "deeme" all the children of Israel "for to be dead" in order "to catch that lyther swayne" (X.126, 128), the newborn Jesus. Faced with a similar challenge to Antichrist's authority, now not by the Christ-child but by his latter-day representatives, the Doctor in the *Coming of Antichrist* similarly advises his master to curse the two witnesses:

> For those whom thou blesses, they shall well speede,
> and those whom thou cursest, they are but deade.
> This ys my counsell and my reade,
> yonder heretikes for to spill. (ll. 436-39)

After further debate, Antichrist finally slays Enoch and Elias "in Jerusalem" as the *Prophets of Antichrist* anticipated (XXII.243). Significantly, it is this act of murder—the martyrdom of the two witnesses representing the first *martus*—that brings on the just condemnation of Antichrist. Just as the crucifixion of Jesus is the ultimate sacrilegious deed of Satan, so the murder of Enoch and Elias is Antichrist's final act as Satan's agent. The death of Christ results in the destruction of the power of Satan and the loss of his hellish booty, when in the *Harrowing of Hell* Michael leads the righteous to heaven; similarly, the death of the two witnesses after the conversion of the kings leads immediately to Michael's judgment and Antichrist's destruction.

The special relationship between Christ and the two witnesses is paralleled in the play (and throughout medieval tradition) by the similarly close relationship existing between Satan and Antichrist, who is not merely the last great figure of evil but nearly identical to the devil. He is, according to the two witnesses, "the devyll," "this devylls lymme," "the devylls owne nurrye!" (ll. 299, 313, 354). Although, unlike the fourteenth-century Old French play, the *Jour du Jugement*, the *Coming of Antichrist* does not stage the actual conception and birth of Antichrist, he has "the devylls power . . . within" (ll. 287-88) and, according to Michael (ll. 633-36), his life is so imbued with evil that he is essentially the devil incarnate.[41] That he effectively gains control of a Christian society is the result of his devilish power and his blasphemous re-creation of Christ's life. Thus the *Coming of Antichrist* stages not so much a debate between spokesmen of varying powers as a contest between claimants to Christ's ministry in the last days, both sides staking their claims on their real or conjured associations with the key events of

Christ's life. As is typical of much medieval teaching concerning the last days, the Chester cycle has given ample warning of the great deceit of Antichrist by earlier outlining his career of evil and explaining the role of the two witnesses both in the *Harrowing of Hell* and the *Prophets of Antichrist*. The problem in the *Coming of Antichrist*, as in human experience, is that previous teachings and past warnings are not especially effective in a crisis. The prophets' dependence on the word seems feeble in comparison to Antichrist's immediate and imaginative visual *imitatio Christi*. As is often the case in medieval tradition, Antichrist's claim seems at first to be the most trustworthy.

In representing the blasphemous pronouncements and supernatural tricks of the pseudo-Christ, the play captures on stage the same sense of fear and wonder so effectively pictured in later medieval art illustrating Antichrist. Although at first only portraying Antichrist as symbolized by the creatures of Revelation, the illuminated Apocalypses did introduce in the thirteenth century a short cycle of Antichrist pictures which was later greatly expanded in the fifteenth-century block books devoted entirely to surveying Antichrist's life. An early example is the Apocalypse of the Pierpont Morgan Library, an Anglo-French manuscript illustrating Antichrist's life in five scenes. In the first Enoch and Elias approach a royal Antichrist, who is seated on a throne in the fashion often associated with illustrations of Herod and other tyrants.[42] The scene clearly represents the opposition of the witnesses to Antichrist, who, in the second scene, directs his henchmen to kill them. The final three scenes then follow exegetical interpretations of 2 Thessalonians 2.3-11. In these scenes Antichrist successively displays his supernatural power by working strange marvels (e.g., turning trees upside down), calls his disciples into the temple where he is worshipped, and at last is destroyed by the "spirit of Christ's mouth," which among other things represents Michael's destruction of Antichrist.[43] Finally, devils drag him to hell. All these events are frequently portrayed in medieval art and are given prominence in the Chester play (ll. 81-96, 169-92, 625-86).

Perhaps best exemplifying the visual treatment of Anti-

christ's life, as well as the widespread popularity of the eschatological expectations in the later Middle Ages, are the
fifteenth-century block-book *vitae Antichristi*.[44] These early
printed books, which illustrate the major components of the
Chester *Coming of Antichrist*, portray Antichrist as a parodic
Christ, emphasize the role of Enoch and Elias, and set all
events in their eschatological context. One Antichrist book,
for example, includes sixty-two woodcuts chronologically illustrating scenes from the conception of Antichrist to his
death and thereafter the events leading to doomsday.[45] Of
the forty-six scenes detailing the career of Antichrist, four
portray his supernatural wonders, including the flowering
upside-down tree and the raising of the dead; six portray the
teaching of Antichrist's "new law"; three illustrate the
preaching of Enoch and Elias against Antichrist; and two
show the death of the witnesses and their resurrection through
the power of an angel. Significantly, these two scenes are
juxtaposed with two other scenes illustrating Antichrist's own
pretended death and resurrection, thus underscoring the distinction between the true representatives of Christ and the
parodic acts of the pseudo-Christ. The fake resurrection of
Antichrist is followed, as it is in the *Coming of Antichrist*,
by the pseudo-Pentecost.[46] The next three scenes show Antichrist gathering his followers on the Mount of Olives in a
parody of Christ's Ascension. While attempting to rise to
heaven with the help of devils, he is struck down by angels
and then carried to hell. A following illustration portrays
Enoch and Elias converting those deceived by Antichrist.
The next fifteen illustrations portray the Fifteen Signs of
Doomsday, which are described in the *Prophets of Antichrist*.[47] The block book then concludes, as does the Chester
cycle, with the Last Judgment.

The *Coming of Antichrist* is structured in three sections,
each developing a particular theme. The first two sections,
which have received most attention in this essay, are roughly
equal in length (ll. 1-252, 253-624). In the first section, Antichrist makes his claim as the true Christ in contrast to "Jesu,"
whom he labels false. Thematically, the play suggests the
vulnerability of mankind—represented by the conversion of

107

the four kings—to such bold pronouncements, especially when the pronouncements are reinforced by wonders. Structurally, the section looks to the past and re-creates (with some important variations) several scenes recently staged in the cycle. In the second section, Enoch and Elias (representing Christ) reply to Antichrist's challenge. Here the audience, aware of the warnings previously expounded by the Expositor in the *Prophets of Antichrist*, has an advantage over the four kings, who must judge between the disputants on the sole basis of the merits of the rival claims; nevertheless, the four kings are ultimately convinced by the witnesses and die martyrs, acting thereby as *exempla* for the audience. Thematically, the section also emphasizes the importance of conversion even in the last days and, while not minimizing the danger of the pretender, concludes by staging the moral victory of the Church over Antichrist.[48]

Structurally, the play is here balanced between past and future, for, although Enoch and Elias are symbolically closely related to Christ's life, they do not re-create the past on stage nor do they warn of the future, although they do curse Antichrist to hell. The play's much shorter third section (ll. 625-722), which now demands attention, is introduced by Michael's pronouncement on Antichrist, "Nowe ys common this daye." Thematically, it serves as a warning to all those unwilling to follow the object lesson of the four kings. Structurally, it prefigures the *Last Judgment* by staging the just judgment and rewards of both Antichrist and the two witnesses.

The prefigural quality of the play's concluding section is reflected in its pattern of death, resurrection, and judgment. Earlier, Antichrist has pretended to die and to be resurrected. Now, after the deaths of Enoch and Elias, St. Michael announces the judgment of God on Antichrist, first accusing him and then condemning him to hell:

> Thou hase ever served Sathanas
> and had his power in everye place.
> Therefore thou gettes nowe no grace.
> With him thou must gonne. (ll. 641-44)

Conversely, Michael brings the two witnesses killed by Antichrist back to life and takes them to their just reward in heaven:

> Enock and Helye, come you anon.
> My lord wyll that you with mee gonne
> to heaven-blysse, both blood and bone,
> evermore there to bee.
> You have binne longe, for you bynne wyse,
> dwellinge in yearthly paradyce;
> but to heaven, where himselfe ys,
> nowe shall you goe with mee. (ll. 715-22)

By introducing the basic pattern of death, resurrection, and just judgment, the play's conclusion contrasts the two witnesses and the pseudo-Christ, particularly emphasizing the distinct rewards of the opponents. Antichrist, who has falsely imitated the life of Christ by pretending to die and be resurrected, is punished in hell to remain with his master. In contrast, Enoch and Elias, who like Christ truly suffered death and tasted the joys of resurrection, join their lord in heaven.

This contrast is further underscored visually by the pattern of rising and falling action that characterizes judgment scenes in art and drama and that becomes particularly prominent in the conclusion of the *Coming of Antichrist*. Demons cart off Antichrist, probably carrying him down from the stage into hell's mouth, as the rubric in the Peniarth manuscript suggests: "Tunc ibunt demones ad infernum cum animam Antechristi" (Appendix IIB, after l. 702). This falling action contrasts with the rising action of the two righteous, who ascend toward heaven, perhaps imitating the rise of Christ staged in the *Ascension* (see Play XX, rubric after l. 104). Michael specifically states that he takes them to heaven, and the play's concluding rubric notes, "Tunc abducens eos ad coelos" (after l. 722). This visual contrast on stage strongly resembles that of a thirteenth-century Apocalypse now in Paris.[49] One scene of this Apocalypse, conflating earlier illustrations, portrays both the death of Antichrist and the ascension of the witnesses. In the center of the illustration, Antichrist, seated on his royal throne, is destroyed by "the

spirit of [Christ's] mouth" (2 Thessalonians 2.8). Reaching
down from a cloud, Christ holds a mask-like object from
which fire falls onto Antichrist's head. As in Chester, two
devils pull and poke him into hell. The right side of the
illustration concurrently represents Enoch and Elias as they
rise in a cloud to their heavenly reward.

With the ascension of the witnesses, the *Coming of Antichrist* ends and is followed by the *Last Judgment*. This play,
which concludes the Chester cycle, not only develops at
much greater length the basic pattern of judgment developed
in the concluding section of the *Coming of Antichrist*, but
also resembles in its characters and speeches that preceding
play. After opening with a statement of Deus concerning the
necessity of judgment, the *Last Judgment* stages the general
resurrection of the dead, the division of the righteous from
evil, the taking of the righteous to their just reward in heaven,
and the dispatching of the damned to hell. Although Antichrist and Enoch and Elias do not appear, angels and demons
once again play key roles in directing the action; the other
characters at doomsday in some important ways similarly
resemble the major figures of the Antichrist play. The saved,
for example, like the four kings in the *Coming of Antichrist*,
are all repentant sinners. Furthermore, the words of praise
spoken by the righteous bring to mind the comments of the
two witnesses after their resurrection. Enoch, alluding to the
general resurrection before doomsday and extolling the power
of God, rejoices as follows:

> A, lord, that all shall leade
> and both deeme the quycke and deade!
> That reverence thee, thou on them reade
> and them through right releaved.
> I was deade and right here slayne,
> but through thy might, lord, and thy mayne
> thou hast me reased up agayne.
> Thee will I love and leeve. (ll. 699-706)

Similarly, the first resurrected in the *Last Judgment*, the
Papa Salvatus, refers to judgment and God's power over
death:

> A, lord, mercye nowe aske wee,
> that dyed for us on the roode-tree.
> Hit ys three hundreth yeares and three
> synce I was put in grave.
> Nowe through thy might and thy postye
> thy beames blast hath raysed mee—
> I, flesh and blood as I nowe see—
> my judgment for to have. (XXIV.41-48)

These passages tend to associate the witnesses with those joyful persons saved at doomsday, another important symbolic tie already suggested as early as Bede's *Explanatio Apocalypsis*.[50]

In the same way the remorse of the damned recalls Antichrist's complaint at the conclusion of the *Coming of Antichrist*. After being condemned by Michael, Antichrist states:

> Alas, alas, where ys my power?
> Alas, my wytt ys in a weare.
> Nowe bodye and soule both in feare
> and all goeth to the devyll. (ll. 649-52)

The Papa Damnatus, a false spiritual leader like Antichrist and the opposite of the Papa Salvatus quoted above, is the first of the resurrected evil figures to speak:

> Alas, alas, alas, alas!
> Nowe am I worse then ever I was.
> My bodye agayne the soule hasse
> that longe hase benne in hell.
> Together the bee—nowe ys noe grace—
> fyled to bee before thy face,
> and after my death here in this place
> in payne ever to dwell. (XXIV.173-80)

Whereas Enoch and Elias are associated with the Papa Salvatus, Antichrist clearly in his language resembles the Papa Damnatus. Similarly, the demons argue that both leaders of evil (along with the other damned) ought to be delivered to them, since through their lives they have chosen hell over heaven (ll. 661-74; XXIV.517-32). Finally, both the pseudo-Christ and the evil vicar of Christ are beyond grace. Michael insists on this point in his condemnation of Antichrist (l. 643), and Christ, after his awesome display of the wounds of the cross, explains that even if "my sweete mother deare/ and all the sayntes that ever were/ prayed for you right nowe here" (XXIV.613-15) there would still be no grace for the damned.

In staging the reward of the two witnesses and the punishment of Antichrist as prefiguring the just judgment of all mankind at doomsday, the *Coming of Antichrist* reflects a late medieval development of the Antichrist tradition. Although in earlier medieval thought the death of Antichrist was understood in a general eschatological sense to be a sign of the end of the world, not until the later Middle Ages did art and literature particularly emphasize the close relationship between Antichrist and doomsday. The twelfth-century *Ludus de Antichristo*, for example, does not stage the events following the end of Antichrist's career. In such later plays as the Perugia *Doomsday* (c. 1320-40), the *Jour du Jugement* (c. 1330), and the Künzelsau Corpus Christi cycle (c. 1479), on the other hand, the death of Antichrist leads directly to doomsday.[51] Similarly, art in the later Middle Ages particularly emphasizes the punishment of Antichrist and links this punishment to doomsday, even in non-Apocalypse illustrations. For example, the British Library Moralized Bible interprets the death of Herod (Acts 12.21-23) as typifying the death of Antichrist, in contrast to the glorification of the elect which is to be "in iudicio."[52] Generally, as in the *Coming of Antichrist*, this connection is based on interpretations of Apocalypse 11.15-18 which, following the reward of the two witnesses, describes the sounding of the seventh trumpet, the establishment of Christ's rule, and the judgment of the dead.

The great Moralized Bibles of the high Middle Ages illustrate the explicit relationship between doomsday and the major events concluding the eleventh chapter of the Apocalypse: the resurrection and ascension of Enoch and Elias, the fall of Antichrist, the victory of Christ, and judgment. For example, the British Library Bible (fig. 11) portrays in eight roundels four key texts with symbolic interpretations.[53]

The first pair of roundels (on the upper left) illustrates Apocalypse 11.11, the miraculous resurrection of the witnesses.
The representation of the "letter" of the biblical text shows
doves breathing life into Enoch and Elias, who are watched
by a group of people. The accompanying roundel, illustrating
the "spirit" of the text, shows Christ in glory above in a
cloud, while below on earth the general resurrection and the
division of the righteous from the evil takes place. An angel,
pointing upward, directs those on Christ's right who are
saved, whereas a devil pulls those on Christ's left to their
destruction. The second pair of roundels (on the lower left)
illustrates the ascension of the two witnesses in full view of
their enemies (Apocalypse 11.12), interpreting the event as
representing the general resurrection and specifically the
glorification of the righteous. The third pair of roundels (on
the upper right) next illustrates the earthquake that accompanies the ascension of the witnesses (Apocalypse 11.13).
This cataclysmic event signifies the damnation of evil. The
literal illustration shows the collapse of a city, thereby alluding to the tenth part of the city destroyed after the ascension
of the witnesses. The symbolic illustration shows the separation of the damned from the saved, its gloss explaining that
the tenth part of the city represents the damnation of those
who are known as Christians but who deny Christ by their
works. These first three sets of roundels, therefore, closely
relate the resurrection and ascension of the witnesses of
Apocalypse 11 to the general resurrection at doomsday and
the salvation of the righteous and damnation of the evil. The
last set of roundels (painted on the folio's lower right) then
emphasizes the relationship of these events to Antichrist.
Interpreting the blowing of the seventh trumpet (Apocalypse
11.15), the first scene shows an angel on the right sounding
a trumpet. The second finally pictures a scene in heaven,
where Christ crowns the Virgin (representing Ecclesia). The
explanatory gloss to the left of the illustration notes that the
seventh trumpet signifies the joy of the church "post des-
tructionem antichristi."

It is important to note that although the medieval tradition closely links Antichrist to the Last Judgment, he is

not destroyed at doomsday but, as in the Chester cycle, shortly before.[54] The block-book *vitae Antichristi* make this point quite evident. After portraying the death and resurrection of the two witnesses and the pseudo-death and resurrection of Antichrist, these fifteenth-century books contrast the just reward of Enoch and Elias with the punishment of the pseudo-Christ. Antichrist is shown falling from the heavens after having attempted to imitate Christ's Ascension, a scene popular in later medieval art and probably influenced by the iconography of the fall of Simon Magus.[55] After rising with the help of devils, Antichrist has been struck down by the angels of God. Two demons then jab and poke at him, while a third pulls him by a chain into a gaping hell's mouth (fig. 12). The following illustration, in contrast to Antichrist's hellish destiny, portrays Enoch and Elias preaching true Christianity to all those earlier deceived by Antichrist. Although they are not shown ascending to heaven, they are evidently saved. The block books finally illustrate the Fifteen Signs of Doomsday, including the general resurrection of the dead, and finally the Last Judgment.

An English book contemporary with the revision and development of the Chester plays from a single-day Corpus Christi play to a Whitsuntide cycle exemplifies the continuing vivacity of the Antichrist tradition in the sixteenth century. Like much late medieval art and literature, the *Byrthe and Lyfe of the Moost False and Deceytfull Antechryst* reflects popular yet serious concern with Antichrist who is now closely linked with doomsday.[56] Although of minor artistic value in comparison to the earlier block-book *vitae*, this early printed book serves as a useful visual analogue to the concluding plays of the Chester cycle because it includes most elements of the late medieval understanding of the tradition. Published by Wynkyn de Worde around 1528, the *Byrthe and Lyfe* testified to the continuing popularity of the Antichrist tradition in England right up to the Reformation. Intended for a growing reading public wishing serious books in the vernacular, it includes both an English text detailing the life of Antichrist and also accompanying woodcuts. These show Enoch and Elias killed by Antichrist, their resurrection,

Antichrist's own pretended death and resurrection, his attempted ascension to heaven, and his destiny in hell. The book concludes by describing how Enoch and Elias preach to those deceived by Antichrist and notes that "whan Antechryst shall be slayne & brought to helle body and soule," then the Fifteen Signs will follow. The last woodcut illustrates a traditional Last Judgment with the resurrection of the dead. Thus the general arrangement of the *Byrthe and Lyfe* includes the key events of the eschatological plays of the Chester cycle, the plays differing in only one detail: the Fifteen Signs are described in the *Prophets of Antichrist* preceding the stage appearance of Antichrist rather than after the death of Antichrist and immediately before doomsday. In view of the fact that the *Prophets* is really an introduction to both the *Coming of Antichrist* and the *Last Judgment* and that it is not so much an acting out of the events of the last days as it is a sermon on Christian eschatology, the change is not surprising. Furthermore, this one change in the order of events is dramatically effective. As a result, the *Last Judgment* follows immediately after the staging of the punishment of Antichrist and the reward of Enoch and Elias, thus allowing the conclusion of the *Coming of Antichrist* to prefigure explicitly the general resurrection and just judgment of mankind at doomsday.

Although the nineteenth-century evolutionary model tracing the gradual "secularization" of medieval drama has been generally rejected, scholars still tend to see the dialogue, comedy, and even the crudeness of late medieval drama as a realistic rejection of symbolism and religious meaning. Yet late medieval drama shares with late medieval art a "symbolic naturalism," in which even the everyday action has symbolic overtones. John V. Fleming has recently urged that in an analysis of the highly naturalistic painting of St. Francis by Giovanni Bellini (now in the Frick Collection), the "working hypothesis should be that every pictorial item in the painting is 'guilty' of symbolic intention unless the unequivocal innocence of its self-simulation is demonstrable—and not, as various connoisseurs would have it, the other way around."[57] Surely scholars should approach the late medieval cycle plays with similar, although more cautious, assumptions. In the case of the Chester *Coming of Antichrist*, rather than emphasizing the surprise and comic originality of the play, condemning its long disputation, or assuming that it is a farcical interlude in the cycle, critics should concentrate on the play's manipulation of the tradition. They should explore the significance of its characters and the highly patterned treatment of specific scenes. In such an investigation, comparative analysis of medieval drama and art is particularly helpful. Although just one among many critical approaches to the Middle English cycle plays, comparative analysis highlights popular traditions influencing medieval culture and helps visualize the multifaceted symbolic overtones of religious drama. Combined with a knowledge of medieval exegesis and close attention to the extant texts, the study of the iconography of Antichrist as developed in the later Middle Ages and set forth in a contemporary book such as the *Byrthe and Lyfe of Antechryst* can teach us much about the concluding plays of the Chester cycle. Such study reveals the cycle's profound treatment of the biblical texts basic to the exegetical tradition and the symbolic significance of its major characters. It explains the prominence given Enoch and Elias, helps us appreciate the ultimate seriousness of Antichrist's parodic *imitatio Christi*, and reveals the important role played by the *Coming of Antichrist* in the structure of the cycle.

NOTES

1. *The Chester Mystery Cycle*, ed. R. M. Lumiansky and David Mills, EETS, s.s. 3 (1974). Subsequent references to the Chester cycle are to this edition and will appear in the text of this chapter.

2. Linus Lucken, *Antichrist and the Prophets of Antichrist in the Chester Cycle* (Washington, D.C.: Catholic Univ. of America Press, 1940).

3. Rosemary Woolf, *The English Mystery Plays* (Berkeley and Los Angeles: Univ. of California Press, 1972), p. 294.

4. Leslie Howard Martin, "Comic Eschatology in the Chester *Coming of Antichrist*," *Comparative Drama*, 5 (1971), 163-75.

5. Travis, *Dramatic Design in the Chester Cycle* (Chicago: Univ. of Chicago Press, 1982), p. 235.

6. On the Antichrist tradition, see Richard Kenneth Emmerson, *Antichrist in the Middle Ages: A Study of Medieval Apocalypticism, Art, and Literature* (Seattle: Univ. of Washington Press, 1981), especially pp. 163-87.

7. See Klaus Aichele, *Das Antichristdrama des Mittelalters, der Reformation und Gegenreformation* (The Hague: Martinus Nijhoff, 1974).

8. On the relationship between the visual arts and drama, see Clifford Davidson, *Drama and Art* (Kalamazoo: The Medieval Institute, 1977), especially chap. I.

9. *Chester Art: A Subject List of Extant and Lost Art Including Items Relevant to Early Drama*, EDAM, Reference Series, 3 (Kalamazoo: Medieval Institute Publications, 1982), p. 1. The list does not include a single work relevant to the Antichrist tradition.

10. For a description of these manuscripts, see Richard Kenneth Emmerson and Suzanne Lewis, "Census and Bibliography of Medieval Manuscripts Containing Apocalypse Illustrations, 800-1500," *Traditio*, 40 (1984), 41 (1985), 42 (1986), forthcoming.

11. See John Wright, *The Play of Antichrist* (Toronto: Pontifical Institute of Mediaeval Studies, 1967), p. 63. Travis, on the other hand, defends the disputation as epitomizing "the entire play's disputatious nature" (p. 233).

12. On Enoch and Elias as the two witnesses, see Emmerson, *Antichrist in the Middle Ages*, pp. 95-101.

13. See the discussion of the two witnesses in John M. Court, *Myth and History in the Book of Revelation* (London: SPCK, 1979), pp. 82-105.

14. Medieval Apocalypses particularly emphasize the role of Enoch and Elias. See Emmerson, *Antichrist in the Middle Ages*, pp. 136-40.

15. Paris, Bibliothèque Nationale, lat. 8878, fol. 155; Emmerson and Lewis, "Census," no. 25. See Emmerson, *Antichrist in the Middle Ages*, fig. 7.

16. Metropolitan Museum of Art, Cloisters collection; Emmerson and Lewis, "Census," no. 86. For a facsimile, see Florens Deuchler, Jeffrey M. Hoffeld, and Helmut Nickel, *Cloisters Apocalypse* (New York: Metropolitan Museum of Art, 1971), fols. 17^v-19^r.

17. Court, *Myth and History*, p. 89.

18. Ibid., p. 94.

19. Paris, Bibl. Nat., lat. 1132, and Valenciennes, Bibl. Mun. MS. 99; Emmerson and Lewis, "Census," nos. 5, 7. See H. A. Omont, *Manuscrits illustrés de l'Apocalypse aux ixe et xe siècles*, Bulletin de la Société française de reproductions de manuscrits (Paris, 1922), pp. 69, 79.

20. Bede, *Explanatio Apocalypsis* (Migne, *PL*, XCIII, 165): "Sex

tubae priores saeculi praesentis aetatibus comparatae varios bellorum Ecclesiae denuntiavere concursus. Septima vero, Sabbati aeterni nuntia, victoriam tantum et imperium veri regis indicat."

21. Travis, *Dramatic Design*, pp. 230-33, overemphasizes surprise and the unexpected in the play's action, which from the appearance of Antichrist to the resurrection of the witnesses closely parallels the well-known apocalyptic tradition. He is right, however, to stress its dramatic quality.

22. For this title, see the "Early Banns" (1539-40) and the list in "Rogers' Breviary" (1609), in Lawrence M. Clopper, ed., *Chester*, Records of Early English Drama (Toronto: Univ. of Toronto Press, 1979), pp. 32, 251.

23. Ibid., pp. 32, 251.

24. On the alewife, see R. M. Lumiansky, "Comedy and Theme in the Chester *Harrowing of Hell*," *Tulane Studies in English*, 10 (1960), 5-12.

25. Although the transition into this final scene is admittedly awkward, the alewife can be justified on dramatic and thematic grounds, whereas the "textual surgery" suggested by Travis (pp. 67-68) is based on the unsubstantiated argument that the alewife is a later Protestant addition.

26. On the development of the Chester cycle, see especially Lawrence M. Clopper, "The History and Development of the Chester Cycle," *Modern Philology*, 75 (1978), 219-46. Most recently the distributing of the Chester plays into three days of playing during Whitsun week has been reviewed by R. M. Lumiansky and David Mills in *The Chester Mystery Cycle: Essays and Documents* (Chapel Hill: Univ. of North Carolina Press, 1983), pp. 176-92.

27. The *Cornish Ordinalia* "Resurrection," however, stages Adam's questioning of the two witnesses during the Harrowing; see Markham Harris, trans., *the Cornish Ordinalia* (Washington, D.C.: Catholic Univ. of America Press, 1969), pp. 184-86.

28. See, for example, Gerhard Schmidt, *Die Armenbibeln des XIV Jahrhunderts* (Graz: Hermann Böhlaus, 1959).

29. One fourteenth-century manuscript (Weimar, Zentralbibliothek Fol. Max. 4; Emmerson and Lewis, "Census," no. 145) combines a *Biblia Pauperum* with an illustrated Apocalypse. See *Biblia Pauperum, Apocalypsis: The Weimar Manuscript* (New York: Hacker Art Books, 1978).

30. See Elisabeth Soltesz, ed., *Biblia Pauperum: Faksimileausgabe der vierzigblättigen Armenbibel-Blockbuches in der Bibliothek der Erzdiozese Esztergom* (Hanau: Werner Dausien, 1967), pl. 34.

31. See Schmidt, *Armenbibeln*, pls. 29b, 36b.

32. See Soltesz, *Biblia Pauperum*, pl. 11; Schmidt, *Armenbibeln*, pls. 4, 51, 11b.

33. See Soltesz, *Biblia Pauperum*, pl. 24; Schmidt, *Armenbibeln*, pls. 2, 21a, 21b, 28a, 30a, 30b, 30c.

34. For similar typological symbolism on the St.-Bertin Cross, see John V. Fleming, *From Bonaventure to Bellini: An Essay in Franciscan Exegesis* (Princeton: Princeton Univ. Press, 1982), pp. 120-21, fig. 28.

35. See Emmerson, *Antichrist in the Middle Ages*, pp. 92-94, 132-34.

36. See Soltesz, *Biblia Pauperum*, pl. 22; Schmidt, *Armenbibeln*, pls. 3a, 3b.

37. See M. R. James, "Pictor in Carmine," *Archaeologia*, 94 (1950), 153.

38. Several Moralized Bibles include extensive Apocalypse cycles portraying Antichrist; see Emmerson and Lewis, "Census and Bibliography," nos. 153-58.

39. Alexandre de Laborde, *Bible Moralisée, Consèrvé á Oxford, Paris et Londres* (Paris: Société française de reproductions de manuscrits a peintures, 1911-27), I, pl. 174.

40. See Laborde, *Bible Moralisée*, I, pl. 168; all abbreviations in the gloss are expanded.

41. See also Emmerson, *Antichrist in the Middle Ages*, pp. 81-83; on the *Jour du Jugement*, see pp. 173-74.

42. Pierpont Morgan Library, MS. M.524, fols. 6^v-7^v. This Apocalypse follows the interpretations of Berengaudus, *Expositio super septem visiones libri Apocalypsis* (Migne, *PL*, XVII, 843-1058).

43. See Emmerson, *Antichrist in the Middle Ages*, pp. 102-03; see also ibid., figs. 4-5.

44. See H. T. Musper, ed., *Der Antichrist und die fünfzehn Zeichen* (Munich: Prestel Verlag, 1970); and Kurt Pfister, ed., *Das Puch von dem Entkrist* (Leipzig: Insel-Verlag, 1925).

45. *Der Antichrist und die fünfzehn Zeichen vor dem Jüngsten Gericht*, a facsimile of the Strassburg block book published in 1480 (Hamburg: Friedrich Wittig, 1979).

46. For a similar scene from *Das Puch von dem Entkrist*, see Emmerson, *Antichrist in the Middle Ages*, fig. 9.

47. The Fifteen Signs portrayed in the block book differ in some details from those described in the play. For the signs, see William Heist, *The Fifteen Signs Before Doomsday* (East Lansing: Michigan State College Press, 1952). See also Clifford Davidson, "The End of the World in Medieval Drama and Art," *Michigan Academician*, 5 (1972), 257-61.

48. Although Travis, *Dramatic Design*, p. 234, argues that truth triumphs only with the appearance of Michael, the victory is really won by Enoch and Elias with the conversion of the four kings, even in the face of martyrdom.

49. Bibliothèque Nationale MS. fr. 403, fol. 18^r; Emmerson and Lewis, "Census," no. 107. See Emmerson, *Antichrist in the Middle Ages*, fig. 10.

50. Migne, *PL*, XCIII, 164.

51. See Emmerson, *Antichrist in the Middle Ages*, pp. 164-65, 172-80.

52. British Library MS. Harley 1527, fol. 70^v; Emmerson and Lewis, "Census," no. 154. See Laborde, *Bible Moralisée*, III, pl. 541.

53. MS. Harley 1527, fol. 132^v. See Laborde, *Bible Moralisée*, IV, pl. 603.

54. See Emmerson, *Antichrist in the Middle Ages*, pp. 101-06, 141-44.

55. See Richard K. Emmerson and Ronald B. Herzman, "Antichrist, Simon Magus, and Dante's *Inferno* XIX," *Traditio*, 36 (1980), 376-82.

56. *Byrthe and Lyfe of Antechryst* (London: Wynkyn de Worde [c.1528]).

57. Fleming, *From Bonaventure to Bellini*, p. 146.

IV

"ALLE THIS WAS TOKEN DOMYSDAY TO DREDE": VISUAL SIGNS OF LAST JUDGMENT IN THE CORPUS CHRISTI CYCLES AND IN LATE GOTHIC ART

Pamela Sheingorn and David Bevington

The Last Judgment serves a vital structural function in all of the extant English Corpus Christi cycles, one similar to the function of *The Coming of Antichrist* in the Chester cycle as examined in the previous chapter. The Last Judgment is, as V. A. Kolve notes, an essential part of the "protocycle" of episodes common to all the cycles, beginning with the Creation and including the Fall of Lucifer, the Fall of Man, Cain and Abel, Noah's Flood, Abraham and Isaac, Moses, Christ's Advent and Baptism, the Temptation in the Wilderness, the Raising of Lazarus, the Passion sequence, the Harrowing of Hell, and the Resurrection.[1] It is a climactic moment of recapitulation and of completion. It is a moment of reversal and discovery, for the souls of the saved and of the damned both learn what it is they have done to merit salvation or damnation and are parted everlastingly onto the right and left sides of God. The Judgment thus recapitulates and fulfills the earlier reversal and discovery in which the devil is foiled in his plot to destroy mankind and learns that Christ is truly God. The Judgment Day both completes the cosmic frame of the play in ending all time and God's creation and makes an accounting of the individual life of each Christian.

In the Corpus Christi cycles, the Judgment is also the final scene of a long and complex play; it functions as in many a later Renaissance play to bind together seemingly unrelated episodes, to resolve the plot or plots, and above all to pronounce a verdict on the characters and thereby to interpret the moral significance of what the audience has seen. The great reward bestowed on the virtuous and the endless suffering awarded to the vicious are a necessary completion not only of this episode but of the cycle's earliest events; not until now are the sons of Adam finally vindicated and the heirs of Cain eternally punished. Adam's soul was freed from Limbo in the Harrowing of Hell, in an anticipation of his endless bliss, but not until the Judgment is that bliss perpetually assured.

The concern of this chapter is with the cycles' visual means of illustrating this dramatic function of completion or closure. Viewed as a text for the theater, the Judgment is very much the final scene of a play, not unlike that of Shakespeare's *Measure for Measure*, for example, in which numerous figures are summoned to judgment before a duke who resumes his own princely identity in order to test his subjects' intents, expose corruption, judge, and forgive. Chapter VI, below, will deal with ways in which this image of judgment is transformed in post-Reformation England into something that is secular as well as spiritual; here we are interested in a dramatic expression of judgment that is still fully in harmony with the pictorial arts of the medieval church. What is fascinating is that the devices and images used in the Corpus Christi Judgment serve an essentially dramatic function in the cycle play as a whole, and yet resemble so closely those devices and images found in painting and sculpture. Recapitulation, organizing principles of symmetry and anti-

thetical contrast, the use of symbolic stage structures and
scaffolding, hieratic ordering of figures, the rhetorical pairing
of virtue and vice and of the generic and the particular, con-
trastive imagery of the idealized and the particular—all these
are carefully suited to the dramaturgic and theatrical needs
of the cycle play as a whole, and yet find their counterparts
in sister art forms that do not operate through speech and
action, and would seem at first glance to have no need for
the closure that belongs to a dramatic action told through
narrative in time and space.

An examination of the analogy between art and drama
ought therefore to illuminate some differences in the means
employed by medieval art forms in presenting a particular
subject, but such an examination can also discover essential
similarities. The arts borrow one another's methods: the pictorial arts make extensive use of narrative techniques far
more commonly than in more recent art, whereas drama is
pictorial to a degree that we find hard to imagine today.

The narrative tendency of medieval art can be seen in
the sequences of illustrations that appear in medieval manuscripts, culminating in the Last Judgment in a way that invites the artist to conceive of that scene as recapitulatory
and organized to allude to what has come before. The great
Romanesque tympana discussed above in Chapters I and II
usually form part of a complex scheme that covers the entire
façade of a church. Similarly, the Last Judgment belongs to
an entire program of decoration that dominates the interior
of many English Gothic churches. As E. W. Tristram writes,
"The Doom, with the Seven Deadly Sins, and the Seven
Corporal Works of Mercy, all allied subjects, are more often
found after c. 1350 than any others, except perhaps figures
of Saints."[2] At least seventy-eight examples of paintings of
the Doom still survive in England (see figs. 13-14).[3] These
Dooms are usually located above the arch separating the
nave, the space of the laity, from the choir or chancel, the
space of the clergy. A congregation facing the altar from the
nave must then behold a huge painting of Doomsday on the
arch that frames the chancel. The decorative scheme of the
surrounding nave interior commonly treats, in wall painting

and painted glass, Old Testament history, the life of Christ or Mary, or lives of the saints. These events of human history are all seen in relation to the final day of reckoning and in visual juxtapositions that emphasize typological relationships and the pattern of God's interventions on earth or provide models of behavior for earthly men. The beholder is invited to "read" the pictures he sees in narrative sequence and to view the Judgment itself as a closure.

Conversely, the symbolic theater for which the Corpus Christi cycles were written encourages the dramatist to cast his presentation in the form of a cosmically significant picture, one in which spatial arrangements and properties have spiritualized meanings akin to those depicted in the pictorial arts. Our interest is not so much in asking which art form influenced the other—indeed, the very degree of proximity argues the likelihood of mutuality—as in the insight afforded concerning the nature of genre. Medieval drama differs from the other visual arts in many particulars, but it shares with them the appeal to the visual mode of perception by means of which all the visual arts enhance both narrative and iconic content through carefully chosen principles of composition.

One of the most striking features of the Last Judgment in the pictorial arts is its bilateral symmetry about a central axis formed by the frontal judging Christ. The symmetry is not quite a mirrored reflection but rather a repetition of pose or gesture or balance either of likes or opposites. Thus in Rogier van der Weyden's Last Judgment the four angels who display the Instruments of the Passion reflect each others' poses (fig. 15). Each holds a different instrument; the large column of the flagellation is balanced by the cross on the opposite side. The heavenly court is similarly balanced: the Virgin Mary and John the Baptist, the two intercessors, sit at opposite ends of the rainbow; behind each are six apostles, their poses and garments carefully varied to avoid an overly static presentation; and behind them are figures who have been identified as the patron and his family. Trumpeting angels are almost always disposed symmetrically about Christ, as they are in a fifteenth-century Book of Hours from York, the Bolton Hours (fig. 13); and the sun and the moon flank

Christ, as in the large Doom from the late fifteenth century painted on the chancel arch in the Church of St. Thomas of Canterbury, Salisbury (fig. 14). The Psychostasis or Weighing of Souls extends the central axis downwards in van der Weyden's painting, the placement of the two pans of the balance scale reiterating Christ's gestures of welcome and condemnation directly above. The notion of antithetical contrast replaces that of mirrored symmetry in the lower levels of the composition: the pious elect are opposed to the howling damned; St. Peter, an angel, and Abraham are opposed to demons; gates or doors are opposed to a voracious monster's mouth; the Gothic architecture of paradise is opposed to cauldrons of sinners boiling in hell's fire. Spectators are reminded, both in the pictorial arts and in the scenes of judgment from the Creation to Doom cycles, that no middle way is possible in the separation of the blessed from the damned.

Coexisting, to a certain degree in tension, with this symmetrical arrangement is the hieratic principle of organization that results in a triangular composition. The hierarchy is clearly ordered, from God, Ruler of the Universe, at the apex, to his heavenly court, including the intercessors, to earth where the dead are resurrected and judged, and finally to paradise and hell. Frequently in English painting Christ dominates by reason of the very large scale to which he is drawn; his hierarchical function, rather than his humanity, is made visually central. His position, seated on the arch of a rainbow, places him at the top of a triangle completed by paradise and hell, so that Christ, paradise, and hell are spatially positioned at the three points of that most stable of geometric figures. Such a composition has a practical function as well, for it nicely fills the arched shape of the wall separating nave from chancel.

At the same time, however, a pull toward vertical movement creates tension and threatens to destabilize the lowest band of the composition. Although paradise and hell form a balanced pair to Christ's right and left, with the eternally elect on one side corresponding to the eternally damned on the other, paradise and hell are vertically differentiated in terms of the soul's ultimate destiny: the elect rise to enter paradise whereas the damned are thrust down into hell. Such a vertical conception of salvation and damnation is common in both biblical language and popular mythology. Most artists, following the major compositional tradition, adopt the symmetrical pattern that stresses horizontal balancing of right and left, but they are also able to imply vertical movement. In van der Weyden's painting, for example, the blessed ascend steps to the Gothic paradise with its steeply pointed arches and pinnacles, whereas on the opposite side the huddled and crouched figures of reprobation are about to fall into the zone of hell. Similarly, in the Bolton Hours a welcoming St. Peter stands on a ramp that slopes upward to the gates of paradise, whereas the hell mouth open in the opposite corner of the page allows the possibility of downward motion only.

Not all representations of the Last Judgment in the pictorial arts are organized in this pattern of dominant horizontal symmetry. In their well-known painting of the Last Judgment, Hubert and Jan van Eyck break with tradition and exploit to the full the vertical dimension of their subject (fig. 16). Placing their vividly detailed hell below the zone of paradise with the shadow of death creating an immense gulf between them, the van Eycks realize a logical hieratic arrangement of great power. Their choice necessarily destroys, however, the balanced horizontal symmetry of the traditional composition. In the same vein, the Doom on the chancel arch of the Church of St. Thomas of Canterbury, Salisbury, reflects influence from the van Eycks or one of their followers. To either side of Christ appears an elaborate architecture of paradise, forming a heavenly zone appropriately inhabited by angels and apostles. Below, in the narrowing spandrels of the arch, the dead rise from their tombs. Rising motion brings those on Christ's right to the gates of paradise, whereas those on his left are immediately captured by devils and dragged downward toward hell mouth. Corpus Christi drama of Judgment makes use of symmetry with intent similar to that of the pictorial arts. The arrangement is most formal in Chester where, as all the dead arise from their sepulchers, the speeches proceed in turns: Papa Salvatus, Imperator Salvatus, Rex Salvatus, and Regina Salvata deliver nearly equal speeches of four or five eight-line stanzas, followed by Papa Damnatus, Imperator Damnatus, Rex Damnatus, and Regina Damnata, each with four stanzas. Even when the dramatist unsymmetrically adds the lamentations of Justiciarius Damnatus and Mercator Damnatus to swell the ranks of the damned, he does so with four-stanza speeches for each. Only when this elaborately repeated testimonial is complete ("*Finitis lamentationibus mortuorum*") does Christ descend to the scene of judgment.[4] At the climactic moment of judgment, Christ first addresses the saved and is answered by them in a series of four-line speeches; once they have been led away to bliss by a choir of singing angels, the devils come forward to accuse the wicked, "this pope myne" and "This kinge and queene" (ll. 517, 541), whose speeches are again confined to four lines each. Following the deportation of these sinners to hell by the demons, the four evangelists come before the audience to bear witness and interpret what has been seen in an orderly succession of four eight-line stanzas, one for each speaker.

A major component of symmetry is the balancing of right and left. In the Towneley Judgment, the angel with sword ("*cum gladio*"), resembling the central figure of Michael in the van Eyck painting, orders the souls to "stand not togeder, parte in two! . . . On his right hand ye good shall go,/ the way till heuen he shall you wys;/ ye wykid saules ye weynd hym fro,/ on his left hande as none of his" (ll. 74-80). The stage directions are no less explicit in describing Christ's symbolic movement to right and left: "*Tunc vertens se ad bonos, dicit illis*," then, turning to the good souls, he says to them that they are the "blissid barnes on my right hande" (ll. 433-34). The wicked he condemns as "ye cursid catyfs of kames kyn" (l. 474). He bids his chosen children "commes to me" while the cursed are commanded "from me ye fle" (ll. 524-28). The York text is basically identical in these particulars, and has Christ speak of "Mi blissid childre on my right hande" (l. 277), though this version does not include the actual stage direction of turning toward them.

In both York and Towneley, Christ is answered by a symmetrical number of speeches from right and left, though York assigns four-line speeches to each of two speakers whereas Towneley divides the same sequence into two-line speeches assigned to four speakers on each side.

The Seven Works of Mercy and their opposite sins provide material for symmetrical presentation in the Judgment plays. The text found basically alike in Towneley and York is typical. Christ praises the good souls on his right hand for having fed him when he was hungry, slaked his thirst, clothed his nakedness, and the like, prompting the good souls to ask in succession how it was that they aided Christ without knowing him directly, and yielding the answer that they did these things to Christ when they aided the least of God's creatures. To the wicked, in an address of comparable length, Christ offers his reproaches for their churlishness, hears their protestations of ignorance, and replies that "To the lest of myne when ye oght dyd,/ to me ye dyd the self and same" (Towneley, ll. 522-23). In Chester, Christ similarly condemns the wicked because "When I was hungrye and thyrstie both,/ and naked was, you would not mee clothe" (ll. 621-22).

Symmetry is not the only spatial convention through which Corpus Christi drama of Judgment makes use of a rich variety of devices and images found also in the other visual arts. As in the paintings already examined, vertical movement is no less essential. It is another visual metaphor through which the final scene of judgment serves the entire cycle and its need for reversal, discovery, and closure. As in painting, vertical movement introduces action into the more static symmetrical dimension, thereby creating a tension between movement and stasis or between verticality and horizontal balancing of opposites. In the pictorial arts all vertical movement in the same composition tends to be perceived as occurring simultaneously; drama can show its vertical movement in chronological progression.

Enabled thus to reveal its visual images of motion in a narrative structure indicating the passage of time, Corpus Christi drama of Judgment displays a sequence of vertical movements expressive of dramatic conflict and resolution.

Typically, God in heaven announces his intention to judge mankind and sends his angels down to earth to proclaim a summons; the souls, both good and wicked, arise from the dead; God descends as Christ to earth (or just above it) where he reminds his listeners of his Passion, and pronounces judgment; angels lead off the saved to heaven with song, while demons herd their victims into hell with jibes and torturings. At last we are left with hymns of praise to God or with the witnessing of the four evangelists.

The climactic moment of descent is Christ's coming to earth as judge. "Till erthe nowe will I wende," says Christ in the York (and Towneley) version, "Miselue to sitte in magesté./ To deme my domes I woll descende" (ll. 179-81). The N-town fragment commences at this point with the stage direction, "*Ihesu descendente cum Michaele et Gabriele Archangelis.*" The emphasis on vertical movement is conscious and repeated. Whether performed on pageant wagons or on scaffolds and platea, this event in the theater makes literal use of downward movement, from an upper acting station representing heaven into the world of humanity that is about to end for ever. The actor who before presented God is now visibly his Son, with cross and crown of thorns, descending for one last time into human history.[5]

Rising to meet this downward movement are the souls of all those who must be judged. "Svrgite! All men Aryse/ venite Ad judicium," begins the first speech of the N-town fragment. The stage direction following the angels' speech is graphic: "*Omnes resurgentes subtus terram clamauit* ha aa. ha aa. ha aa. *Deinde surgentes dicat* ha aa etcetera." The description of the souls as underneath the earth, "*subtus terram,*" suggests that they arise from sepulchers. In Chester, at the sound of the angels' trumpets the stage direction specifies that "*omnes mortui de sepulchris surgent,*" openly indicating the need for stage structures resembling sepulchers (l. 40). Christ descends to these souls on earth, where he takes his seat of judgment: "I schall sitte you betwene," he announces to his disciples in the York version (l. 215), and the stage direction specifies the symbolic function of his throne: "*Hic ad sedem iudicii cum cantu angelorum.*" In

Towneley, a wicked soul who has been summoned by "yonde horne" wonders what he shall say when Christ "sittys in his trone" (ll. 42, 52). The Chester stage direction is the most vivid, and most interested in exploiting whatever vertical effects the pageant wagon or stage may make possible: following the lament of the dead, Christ descends *"quasi in nube, si fieri poterit,"* in a cloud, if this can be arranged, *"quia, secundum doctoris opiniones, in aere prope terram judicabit Filius Dei,"* because, in the opinion of learned men, the Son of God will pronounce judgment in the air near to the earth (l. 356). At Chester, then, if staging permits, Christ is to descend from heaven to earth but still remain above those he judges. The list of stage properties for the Last Judgment play at York includes "A cloud & ij peces of Rainbow of tymber," suggesting that the vertical hieratic ordering is to be achieved as it was in the pictorial arts, with Christ seated on a rainbow.[6] In all the cycles, Christ's judgment seat must have been elevated.

The final crucial movement of the play, the separation of the saved from the damned, makes use of the spatial separation between heaven and hell, with earth in between. Even if performed under some circumstances in the "round," with platea and scaffolds, the contrast between heaven and hell is vertical, for Christ is enthroned above while the devils thrust their victims down into the lowest level of hell with its hellmouth. The N-town cycle suggests the upward movement of the blessed as they are invited by St. Peter to enter the gates of heaven:

> The gatys of hevyn I opyn this tyde
> Now welcome dere bretheryn to hevyn i-wys
> Com on and sytt on goddys right syde
> Where myrthe and melody nevyr may mys. (ll. 53-56)

The blessed move forward to accept his invitation on their knees: "On kne we crepe we gon we glyde" (l. 57). In all the cycles, their entry into bliss is accompanied by songs of thanksgiving. Conversely, in Towneley the wicked are herded off to hell by jesting devils like work animals. Thus the result of the vertical movements that characterize the play's action is a world in which the final and eternal order is one of symmetrical balance. The final stage picture recapitulates the events of the play and resembles a living tableau of a Doomsday painting.

In England, both the pictorial arts and drama prefer to treat spatial depth in a non-illusionistic fashion, restricting activity to a shallow space that spreads out in front of the viewer but does not recede into depth. English painting, despite strong influence from the Low Countries in the fifteenth century, adopted only certain aspects of the new Flemish style with its emphasis on illusionism and realism.[7] The Last Judgment painted by the van Eycks successfully exploits the new ability to convey the illusion of depth in space to present the Last Judgment as, in Erwin Panofsky's phrase, a "cosmic catastrophe."[8] These artists' ability to portray limitless space gives new meaning to the universality of Christian eschatology. In English painting, details might be realistically rendered and individual forms illusionistically modeled, as in the nude figure of one of the elect turning to enter the gate of paradise in the painting from the chancel arch at Wenhaston (fig. 17);[9] nevertheless, as Margaret Rickert observes, "with . . . [the] concept of deep space the medieval English artist was not in sympathy."[10] Thus the innovations of the van Eycks, who could paint a vast space that actually seems to contain the universe, were less congenial to English painters than the symbolic space of van der Weyden's Last Judgment, a painting which is, in Panofsky's words, "frankly medieval."[11]

English cycle drama is by its nature similar in its use of symbolic space, combining as it does the illusionistically satisfying spectacle of live actors in costume with an absence of verisimilar scenic effects. Spatial relationships among the actors, and use of properties like thrones and regalia, need to rely on a symbolic language of associations to be correctly interpreted by the audience. These stage devices define their own function and sense of locale instead of relying on a painted scenic environment to frame the action in plausible and realistic terms.

Within the symbolic space of painting or stage, a limited number of individual figures must represent the numberless legions of human beings and immortal personages present at this great scene of final judgment. The Wenhaston painting depicts only five saved souls and not many more of the damned, and yet no viewer can doubt that the judgment is intended to be as universal as that of the van Eycks. Similarly in the medieval drama, a limited number of actors must stand for a vastly larger group. This is true to an extent of all drama, but never more so than in depictions of the Last Judgment to which are summoned all mankind, the heavenly host, and the denizens of hell. The speakers especially must be limited in number, for practical reasons. In the Towneley Judgment four damned souls speak on behalf of an infinite number. The York version uses only two souls on each side to similar effect. Chester's cast of speakers is restricted to a pope, emperor, king, and queen on each side of the great division, as well as a damned judge and a merchant. Three angels, two apostles, and three devils speak in the York Judgment. The N-town fragment does not specify the number of actors, but refers instead to "*Omnes resurgentes,*" to "*Omnes animae resurgentes,*" to "*Omnes salvati*" and "*Animae dampnandum,*" and the like; in addition, there are three devils who speak. However much the scene of judgment in all the cycles calls for a cast no less large than that of the Passion sequence, the "all and sum" who take part can at best be only symbolically represented.

Two distinct emphases, on the individual and on the mass of humanity, characterize two different types of Last Judgment in the pictorial arts of the late Middle Ages. Works intended for a large or general audience are comprehensive, universal in their inclusiveness. Those commissioned by a wealthy patron for a private chapel or luxury manuscript sometimes refer primarily or exclusively to one individual. Books of hours, which enabled the reader to follow the monastic offices in his or her private devotions, were often richly decorated and created for specific patrons. Morality drama, with its presentation of an everyman or "mankind" figure, offers ways of exhibiting on stage the story of individual salvation that bears certain resemblances to individual judgment in the pictorial arts. The Creation to Doom cycle drama, on the other hand, is by its all-encompassing design less attuned to the fate of any specific named individual. It does possess, however, a capacity for presenting dramatis personae who are at once generic and individualized, as in comprehensive paintings of judgment. In paintings and in plays alike we are presented with individual after individual in a potentially limitless series of satiric or homiletic vignettes. Virtually all paintings show us churchmen among the saved and among the damned, their mitres and vestments pointedly visible. No less in evidence is the armor of noble warriors. All the various estates are present. Among the damned, money bags identify usurers or misers. Crowns or coronets signal rulers or members of the aristocracy. Finery of dress is indicative of decadent splendor at court, now reaping its just reward. The broad spectrum of society is an essential part of the panoramic inclusiveness of the painting.

Portraiture in the Corpus Christi plays of Judgment, at once generic and particularized, makes extensive use of visual devices like those found in painting. Although the speech prefixes usually specify only *"2 Malus," "Prima Anima bona,"* or at most (in Chester) *"Rex damnatus"* and *"Regina salvata,"* the details we learn about each are piquantly varied. Especially in the Towneley Judgment, for which the Wakefield Master has evidently provided stanzas depicting the worldly follies of those now entering torment, the satiric vignettes are as vivid as those recorded on canvas by Hieronimus Bosch. As the demons look over their register of sinful deeds, they find a plenteous supply:

> Of Wraggers and wrears/ a bag full of brefes,
> Of carpars and cryars/ of mychers and thefes,
> Of lurdans and lyars/ that no man lefys,
> Of flytars, of flyars/ and renderars of reffys.
>
> (ll. 143-46)

Here the emphasis is on those who cheat, lie, and abuse the legal system with their bags full of briefs, quarrelers, fugi-

133

tives from justice, receivers of stolen goods. The demon insists that they are "Of alkin astates" (l. 148), from every social rank. Tutivillus, a fellow devil, adds testimonial as to their great number: he has brought souls into the devils' hands, he says, "Mo than ten thowsand/ in an howre of a day" (l. 216).

Rich costuming and lavish expense are a favorite target of Tutivillus' satire and additionally are a source of vivid particularization in the portraiture. He describes a typical dandy, a man of "Gay gere and witles," one who is "As prowde as pennyles," accoutered in "hemmyd shoyn," with fancy imported weapon at his side, his sleeves striped with ornament, and his long hair hanging to his shoulder (ll. 235-43). Tutivillus' portrait of a court lady is as unsparing; with her "kelles" or nets and her pins she can "make it full prowde," and she paints with cosmetics shamelessly. Her headgear is so elaborate that she seems "hornyd like a kowe," and she wears a side gaiter "furrid with a cat skyn." She is a creature "Of prankyd gownes & shulders vp set," that is, of elaborately decorated gowns and padded shoulders that are sewn and stuffed with moss and wool padding inside (ll. 260-88). Another practitioner of pride displays himself in "A kodpese like a pokett," a codpiece shaped like a pocket, and his "luddokkys" or buttocks are all too plainly visible (ll. 311-14). Still other members of this profane congregation include a whole "menee" or throng of "kyrkchaterars," those who chatter in church, "barganars and okerars" (usurers), and "lufars of symonee," "rowners" or scandalmongers, "Ianettys of the stewys" or whorehouse wenches and their customers, "extorcyonars," dicers and other gamblers, forgers of deeds, and still more (ll. 296-98, 350-65).

Along with symmetry, hieratic ordering, non-illusionistic rendering of space, and a portraiture that is at once personalized and generic, another principle that the pictorial and dramatic arts of the Middle Ages share in common is recapitulation. The scene of Judgment, in which the elect are separated from the damned, recalls other events of judgment in sacred history, from the banishment of Adam and Eve from paradise and the deluge to Christ's harrowing of hell. Just as Christ's birth had adumbrated his second coming, that great eschatological event sums up all human history even as it brings the story to the most final of ends.

Both Chester and York (the other two cycles are textually imperfect here) begin with recapitulatory speeches by God in heaven. As at other turning points in the cycle, including the Creation, Noah's Flood, the Advent, and the Passion sequence, recapitulation sets the action at hand in the context of the totality of sacred history, and thus underscores the essential structure of the Corpus Christi cycle as a single play. In York, God recalls his motives in creating the world and mankind in his own likeness, his disappointment at the sinfulness of the human race, and his sending his own son "Till erthe" to be sacrificed and to harrow hell, and finally his sorrowful resolution that he must now "sende" his angels to earth for a day of judgment. Both Chester and York make clear that it is God the father who speaks, in heaven; when he descends to earth he will do so as Christ, with cross, crown of thorn, and other tokens of his human suffering.

The pictorial arts seek to express the same idea of closure of sacred history through the principle of recapitulation. Although of necessity they must do so without the verbal methods discussed thus far, medieval artists had learned, as part of developing methods of recording narrative content, to summarize a sequence of events in one scene by using symbols, gestures, and placement of figures to recapitulate, much as drama had also learned to recapitulate. Thus representations of the Last Judgment in the pictorial arts contain the sun and the moon not only to state the finality of judgment, when the sun and the moon will be extinguished, but also to recall the creation. Adam and Eve kneeling at either side of Christ refer to the fall of man and to Christ as the Second Adam. The intercessors, Mary and John the Baptist (in some cases, by analogy to the Crucifixion, replaced by John the Evangelist), as well as the àpostles, recall Christ's life on earth, while the *Arma Christi* and five wounds recall his passion, crucifixion, and resurrection. The saints in paradise, and Peter at its gates, summarize the history of the

Church. Antichrist is sometimes shown seated in hell in Byzantine or Byzantine-influenced Last Judgments, a placement that speaks not only of his true nature as a manifestation
of the devil, but also refers, as indicated in the previous
chapter, to his whole history as a deceiver and a parodic
Christ. By thus recapitulating the events that will take place
immediately before the judgment, Antichrist both warns
against false gods and rehearses the signs of approaching
doom. In the pictorial arts all of this recapitulatory history
can be read from the imagery, but is, of course, subordinated
to the central subject of final judgment; in the drama, visual
recapitulation reminds the audience of God's introductory
speech, so that the relationship of judgment to all prior history remains present in mind throughout the Judgment play.

Whereas the drama can introduce recapitulation both
verbally and visually, and thus make richer use of this principle than the other visual arts, the temporally linear nature
of drama hinders it from introducing analogues to, or metaphors of, the central subject as effectively as in the other
visual arts. Thus earlier chapters have examined the relationship of the parables of the wise and foolish virgins and
of Lazarus and the rich man to the Last Judgment; the story
of the wise and foolish virgins teaches the lesson of preparedness, while that of Lazarus and the rich man teaches charity and promises that each person will receive what he
deserves according to his conduct in this earthly life. In the
pictorial arts each of these subjects can be juxtaposed to or
integrated within a central image of Doomsday; Lazarus and
the wise virgins are related to the paradise side of the composition, the rich man and the foolish virgins to the hell side,
where they impart their resonances of meaning to the main
theme. Although a German Corpus Christi cycle from Künzelsau moves from the story of the wise and foolish virgins
into the life of Antichrist and the events of the Last Judgment,[12] the English cycles prefer not to mix levels of abstraction by combining metaphorical and literal levels of
meaning in the same play. Even in the German cycle, the
juxtaposition cannot be as immediate or as visual as in the
pictorial arts.

Although both recapitulatory history and metaphoric analogue can be read in painted or carved Last Judgments, the pictorial arts can achieve sequential narrative similar to drama essentially only through a series of distinct compositions. In one comprehensive image, the artist must rely on several aids, one of which is a viewer thoroughly familiar with the content of the narrative. Such a viewer in the medieval Christian world could read a sequence of events in one static image, so that, for example, from the first sight of the angels and the bone-chilling blast of their trumpets to the raucous cacophany of monstrous demons with sinners in tow, he could reconstruct for himself a narrative text. Other narrative devices, including gesture and organization into bands or registers, have been discussed above in Chapter I. At the same time, a successful work of art must also impart memorable images that will be retained in the mind of the viewer, so that the artist must consider both the logic of the narrative and the visual impact of each image that makes up the narrative.

One striking and memorable image found at the very core of the Last Judgment narrative is the Psychostasis or Weighing of Souls. As Chapter I demonstrates, this weighing of a naked soul on a balance scale signifies the measuring of an individual's good deeds against his sins. Sometimes, indeed, the two sides of the scales are labeled *"peccata"* and *"virtutes."* As an isolated image, the Psychostasis encapsulates the events of Doomsday and, because one person is weighed at a time, it focuses the import of those events on one individual. In comprehensive Last Judgment paintings and sculptures, the Psychostasis usually stands in a central location, with groups of people waiting in fearful anguish for the moment of reckoning, and others, having been judged, either rejoicing or howling in anguish.

For obvious reasons, this arresting visual image does not appear in Last Judgment plays. On the stage a giant balance scale would be cumbersome and probably unreliable as a stage property. Nor could it actually weigh many people without the scene's becoming repetitive and boring. Further, the hieratic differentiation of the pictorial arts in which, even in the realistic rendition of van der Weyden, the angel charged with the weighing looms much larger than the tiny insignificant humans, is not realizable on the stage, and without it much of the scene's effectiveness would be lost.

In place of the Psychostasis, the stage uses the dialogue from Matthew 25 of the Acts of Mercy. Thus in the plays both the judgment and the separation of saved from damned rely more on verbal content than is possible in the pictorial arts. Christ's direct address, with its repetition in the negative, effectively informs the audience of his great intent. The symmetry of the staging is also essential to the scene's design, but it works in concert with a dialogue that is also symmetrical. The language offers specific motivation and justification for rewards and punishments. The wicked know that they deserve to be damned:

> On good deede in God his sight
> nowe have I not to shewe.
> (Chester, ll. 259-60)

The audience can tolerate and perhaps even delight in the torments of the damned, having heard them condemn themselves in describing their wicked lives:

> Bot oft tymes maide we sacrifice
> to sathanas when othere can slepe.
> (Towneley, ll. 23-24)

Such motivation is only implicit in the pictorial arts, where at most we are shown symbols of individual sins such as the moneybags of the miser.

Still other reasons explain artists' preference for the Psychostasis over the Works of Mercy in comprehensive Last Judgment scenes, and these reasons further illuminate differences between capabilities of art and drama. Pictorial artists of the medieval period were not indifferent to the appeal of the Works of Mercy. Indeed, given that it was the duty of the parish priest to provide instruction to his congregation in, among other subjects, the Corporal Works of Mercy and the Deadly Sins, it is not surprising that these subjects were painted on the walls of parish churches.[13] They appear in the form of a tree, a wheel, or a group of scenes, organized in relation to a personification such as Mercy or Grace, a blessing angel, or a blessing Christ. In some cases an angel weighing souls or a judging Christ appears above the Works of Mercy to make their eschatological meaning absolutely clear, but the subject was not really suited to the comprehensive Last Judgment itself and does not occur there. The Acts of Mercy were, after all, a practical guide for everyday conduct. Although their importance for future salvation was not to be forgotten, on Doomsday itself the time to practice them was inescapably past. The resurrected souls could therefore not be shown performing them.

We see, then, various ways in which some devices on the stage would not have been effective in the visual arts, and vice versa. Each device is best suited to the medium in which, in fact, we find it. At the same time, a reading of Corpus Christi plays of Judgment in visual terms yields extensive and detailed resemblances in both iconography and compositional methods between dramatic conventions and those found in the pictorial arts. Such resemblances are a powerful argument that iconography and its visual presentation in both art and drama correspond to ideas on the subject held by the typical medieval viewer. This fundamental correspondence can be further illustrated by examining ways in which the pictorial arts and drama approach the rendition of the central figure, Christ.

In the pictorial arts Christ is triumphant in his judgment, idealized, no longer suffering the torment of his Passion, and yet the implements of that Passion are evident all around him in the symmetrically presented *Arma Christi*. He opens his hands in a gesture that is at once the judgment and the showing of his wounds. He is robed and crowned as a King, and yet his side is visible where he was stabbed by the spear, and his feet are visible with their wounds. The viewer is reminded of the Passion that is no longer gruesomely portrayed and yet is timelessly essential to human salvation. Angels blow trumpets to emphasize that Christ has come again to earth not to suffer but to judge.

All these tokens of the Passion and judgment are preserved in the Judgment plays, where they serve in effect as
hand properties and appurtenances. In the Chester cycle,
God instructs his angels, as he prepares to descend to earth:

> Shewe you my crosse appertlye here,
> crowne of thorne, sponge and speare,
> and nayles to them that wanted nere
> to come to this anoye;
> and what weede for them I weare,
> upon my bodye nowe I beare. (ll. 17-22)

Once he has descended in a cloud and is enthroned, if possible, in the air above the earth, the angels are to stand beside
him "*cum cruce, corona spinea, lancea, et instrumentis aliis,*"
and are to display them as in traditional paintings of the Last
Judgment: "*ipsa demonstrant*" (l. 356). The Chester play even
provides for the blood to flow afresh from Christ's side as a
sign of salvation: "see my blood freshe owt flee/ that I bleede
on roode-tree/ for your salvatyon" (ll. 426-28). The stage
direction makes clear that this is no mere figure of speech:
"*Tunc emittet sanguinem de latere eius.*" One of the damned
souls in the Towneley Judgment, seeing Christ sitting "in his
trone," laments that it is a doleful case "To se his Woundys
bledande" (ll. 52-53).

Nevertheless, this stage action is no verisimilar rendition of the Passion. When God announces in heaven, as he
does in the York and Towneley versions, "This body will I
bere with me" in the descent to earth (ll. 182, 186), he appears to require a costume change that is more symbolic
than realistic. Perhaps he dons a shirt such as that listed in
a Mercers' Pageant document in the York records for 1433:
"Array for god that ys to say a Sirke [i.e., a shirt] Wounded."[14]
The instruments of the Passion are visible to remind the
audience of Christ's sacrifice for them, not to re-enact it:
"Behalde, mankynde, this ilke is I,/ That for the[e] suffered
swilke mischeue" (York, ll. 265-66; cf. Towneley, ll. 422-23).
When Christ spreads apart his hands and shows them his
wounds, "*Tunc expandit manus suas et ostendit eis vulnera
sua,*" the vision is commemorative and recapitulatory: "Here

may ye see my woundes wide,/ The whilke I tholed for youre mysdede" (York, ll. 245-46; cf. Towneley, ll. 402-03). In this drama, as in the medieval pictorial arts, Christ is God who became man, idealized and serene but exhorting those who would be saved to remember his Passion. The trumpet calls that are so important a part of the sound effects in every cycle similarly remind the audience that Christ comes as judge, that he "callys vs to the dome" (Towneley, l. 3).

Stage presentations of both heaven and hell seem to use iconography found also in the pictorial arts. For example, in the Judgment from the N-town cycle, Christ says to the blessed, "Come hedyr to me to myn hygh hall" (l. 42), implying an architectural structure with Gothic arches and pinnacles perhaps like that in the Bolton Hours or the Salisbury painting. St. Peter, instructed by Christ to escort the blessed, greets them with words that imply his possession of the keys of eternal bliss as well as the presence of the locked gates that the keys will open:

> The gatys of hevyn I opyn this tyde
> Now welcome dere bretheryn to hevyn i-wys
> Com on and sytt on goddys ryght syde
> Where myrthe and melody nevyr may mys. (ll. 53-56)

The blessed are to sit in heaven, perhaps in neat rows as in pictorial presentations of the Judgment discussed in Chapter I, and will be entertained with heavenly music that may be produced by choirs of angels with instruments such as are seen frequently in representations of heaven.

The iconography of hell, in drama as in the pictorial arts, makes use of downward vertical movement, of a hell mouth, and of grotesque diabolical torturers. Hell and the entrance to it are on an acting level below that representing middle earth. "Therfor to hell I shall you synke," proclaims Christ to the damned in the Towneley Judgment (l. 488). The damned must enter hell not unwillingly or with a gentle welcome, like the blessed as they approach paradise, but like herded animals. The devil's words in Chester, "I have them tyed upon a rowe" (l. 547), find their exact parallel in the

Salisbury painting. A "helle mouthe" is listed in the properties of the Mercers' Judgment play at York in 1433, and the image of hell as a monster that swallows sinners lies behind the devil's lines in Chester, "Judged you be to my bellye/ there endles sorrowe ys and noye" (ll. 657-58).

The relationship between artwork and audience is particularly complex when the subject matter is the Last Judgment. The audience cannot empathize, to the point of identification, with Christ in the Last Judgment, as in devotional images so popular in the late Middle Ages such as the Pietà and the Man of Sorrows. At the time of the judgment Christ's bleeding wounds are a sign of his once human nature, put on like a shirt for the purposes of this play, but his suffering is past as is his patience with mankind.

In order for the subject to be effective, the audience must experience it as an accurate vision of the closure of history, and yet must remember that all individual Christians in the audience have time still to repent—unlike their counterparts who are being judged in the play or painting. Thus a theatrical audience cannot, as Rosemary Woolf correctly perceives, identify with the crowd standing before Christ's judgment in the way that the audience was able to do in earlier episodes of the cycle.[15] The audience's members may alternately "try on" roles of damned and saved but must finally see themselves, uneasily, in the middle ground with choices still to make. Nevertheless, the audience's personal concern in such a weighty matter of eternal judgment is necessarily direct and unavoidable; Woolf is not entirely justified in saying that "at the Last Judgment Christ addresses characters on the stage, and the audience is outside the play." The audience's concern is engaged at the very start of the Last Judgment play, before the judgment has begun, a moment which the audience can still experience as contemporary time. As God declares in the York text:

> Men seis the worlde but vanité,
> Yitt will no manne beware therby;
> Ilke a day ther mirroure may thei se,
> Yitt thynke thei noght that thei schall dye. (ll. 49-52)

This familiar *memento mori* theme is addressed to the audience watching the play, not the dead waiting to be resurrected. In Chester, too, God reminds the audience that "It ys full youre syns I beheight/ to make a reckoninge of the right" (ll. 9-10). And he appears to refer directly to the town and surrounding countryside when he says of his Second Coming, "The most stowtest this sight shall steare/ that standeth by streete or stye" (ll. 23-24). Thereupon, without pause, the events of Doomsday begin to unfold and the audience is carried with the action from contemporary time into eschatological time.

The pictorial arts make this transition by different means—a painting of the Last Judgment on the chancel arch exists within contemporary time, while presenting to us a vision of the closure of time—but the essential process of involving the viewer in futurity is much the same. A painting must be energized by a preacher who can convince members of the congregation of its relevance to their own lives, or by individual contemplation. The crucial part of the viewing experience, whether for painting or for drama, is that contemporary time be perceived as continuously linked with eschatological time. Use of contemporary costume helps create such a link. So does inclusive language linking the actor and the spectators, as when in the Chester play Christ bids those who are before him, "Behould nowe, all men! Looke on mee" (l. 425). The spectator of painting or play is invited, in fact exhorted, to reflect on himself as a member of the limitless congregation of human beings awaiting final judgment. The viewer sees a sublime recapitulatory moment at the end of time when the distinctions between substance and spirit vanish. The souls of those who are to be judged must come to judgment in the flesh: "Rise and fecche youre flessh that was youre feere . . . Body and sawle with you ye bring" (York, ll. 86, 91). God himself is there in the body he wore among men. The moment of putting on the garment of flesh thus borrows from theatrical metaphor and thereupon expresses itself visibly in a way suited alike to the medium of drama and of other visual arts. The picture, that is to say, whether in the theater or in pigment or in stone, is itself only a sign of what the viewer must acknowledge to be within himself and in the cosmos. Drama and painting alike deal in tangible images, vivid, particularized, grotesque at times, sensually pleasing; but the duty of the willing viewer is to translate these tactile and audible images created out of costume and speech or paint and brush into idealized form beyond the realm of human imperfection. Time in Judgment art similarly partakes of the intersection of the timeless with time. The viewer sees himself and his own present in the framework of his own inevitable death and of the Second Coming. The didactic force of drama or painting urges both an attention to daily conduct and an acceptance of the infinite and unknowable will of God. As even a demon can recognize in the Towneley Judgment, "Alle this was token/ domysday to drede" (1. 197).

NOTES

1. V. A. Kolve, *The Play Called Corpus Christi* (Stanford: Stanford Univ. Press, 1966), pp. 57-100.

2. E. W. Tristram, *English Wall Painting of the Fourteenth Century* (London: Routledge and Kegan Paul, 1955), pp. 19-20.

3. A. Caiger-Smith, *English Medieval Mural Paintings* (Oxford: Clarendon Press, 1963), p. 33.

4. All quotations from the cycle plays in this chapter are taken from the following editions: K. S. Block, ed., *Ludus Coventriae, or the Plaie Called Corpus Christi*, EETS, e.s. 120 (1922; rpt. London, 1960), cited here as N-town; George England and Alfred W. Pollard, eds., *The Towneley Plays*, EETS, e.s. 71 (London, 1897); Richard Beadle, ed., *The York Plays* (London: Edward Arnold, 1982); R. M. Lumiansky and David Mills, eds., *The Chester Mystery Cycle*, EETS, s.s. 3 (London, 1974). In quotations from these texts, runic letters such as the thorn have been replaced for convenience by their modern equivalents. On a deliberate asymmetry in the Wakefield Master's revision of the York Judgment— and its consequent resemblance to Bosch's triptych of the Last Judgment in the Vienna Academy of Fine Arts—replacing the Giotto-like symmetry of the York version, see Jeffrey Helterman, *Symbolic Action in the Plays of the Wakefield Master* (Athens: Univ. of Georgia Press, 1981), pp. 3-7.

5. See Lynette R. Muir, "The Trinity in Medieval Drama," *Com-*

parative Drama, 10 (1976), 116-29, for a historical survey of ways of impersonating God in medieval plays.

6. For a transcription and discussion of this very interesting list, see Alexandra F. Johnston and Margaret Dorrell, "The Doomsday Pageant of the York Mercers, 1433," *Leeds Studies in English*, n.s. 5 (1971), 29-34; the list is also transcribed in Alexandra Johnston and Margaret Dorrell Rogerson, *York*, Records of Early English Drama (Toronto: Univ. of Toronto Press, 1979), I, 55-56.

7. "The interest in realistically rendered detail and its organization in an essentially decorative compositional scheme was the particular phase of the new style which the English artist could understand best"— Margaret Rickert, *Painting in Britain: The Middle Ages*, 2nd ed. (Harmondsworth: Penguin, 1965), p. 198. The implications for drama of this limited acceptance of the new style need further exploration.

8. Erwin Panofsky, *Early Netherlandish Painting* (1953; rpt. New York: Harper and Row, 1971), I, 269.

9. See also Charles E. Keyser, "On a Panel Painting of the Doom Discovered in 1892, in Wenhaston Church, Suffolk," *Archaeologia*, 54 (1894), 119-30.

10. Rickert, *Painting in Britain*, p. 198.

11. Panofsky, *Early Netherlandish Painting*, I, 269.

12. Peter K. Liebenow, ed., *Das Künzelsauer Fronleichnamspiel* (Berlin: Walter de Gruyter, 1969).

13. Caiger-Smith, *English Medieval Mural Paintings*, pp. 53-55.

14. Johnston and Rogerson, *York*, I, 55.

15. Rosemary Woolf, *The English Mystery Plays* (Berkeley and Los Angeles: Univ. of California Press, 1972), p. 299.

V

"MAN, THINKE ON THINE ENDINGE DAY": STAGE PICTURES OF JUST JUDGMENT IN *THE CASTLE OF PERSEVERANCE*

David Bevington

> To save you fro sinninge,
> Evyr at the beginninge
> Thinke on youre last endinge!
> (ll. 3646-48)[1]

This concluding statement to the audience by God the Father, sitting in judgment on his heavenly throne, underscores the importance of just judgment throughout *The Castle of Perseverance*. The play is usually regarded as a "full-scale morality," dramatizing by means of abstractions the whole life of man: his birth, his fall into sin, his recovery to virtue, his relapse into the covetousness of old age, his death-bed plea for mercy, the debate of his body and soul, and his trial among the four daughters of God before their Father's throne.[2] As such, the play appears to have several different "plots": the Psychomachia or soul-struggle, the Seven Ages

147

of Man, the Coming of Death, the Debate of Body and Soul, and the Debate of the Four Daughters of God. Such large scope is indeed essential to the play's panoramic inclusiveness, but its seemingly diverse parts should not blind us to a particular emphasis on judgment and on Last Things that is adumbrated in the play's earliest lines and is a means of drawing together the different "plots" of which the play is constructed.

Elsewhere in medieval literature as well we find evidence of a profound connection between just judgment and the various "plots" of the morality play. The Psychomachia, or battle of the Virtues and Vices for the soul of man, has eschatological overtones of doomsday wherever it appears. In the romance by Huon de Méry called *Tournoiement de l'Antecrist* (1234-37), for example, we find the Psychomachia tradition combined with apocalyptic symbols. In Langland's fourteenth-century *Piers Plowman*, where the four daughters of God also play a prominent role, Antichrist appears as a leader of the Vices. The connection between the morality play of *Everyman* and the parable of the talents, noted by V. A. Kolve, depends upon eschatological interpretation; in the *Speculum humanae salvationis* (1324) and elsewhere, the parable is seen as a prefiguration of doomsday in much the same way that the parable of the foolish and wise virgins and the writing on the wall at Balshazzar's feast also anticipate the final judgment.[3]

The visual arts of the same period reflect a similar development. Increasingly, the Last Judgment is seen as a subject of meditation, one in which the viewer is to reflect on his spiritual condition. As a result, morality themes such as the Weighing of Souls and the seven Deadly Sins gain prominence in eschatological wall paintings of churches and the like. A Doom panel at Gloucester, for example, bears the inscription, "In all thy works remember thy last," while at Trotton in Sussex a late fourteenth-century mural on the west wall of the nave combines the scene of Christ's judgment with symbolic representations of the Seven Deadly Sins and the Works of Mercy.[4] Woodcut illustrations of the fifteenth century visualize the connection between final judgment and the Coming of Death, as in a scene of Last Judgment from Syon, near Isleworth in England, prominently featuring a skeletal Death aiming his dart at the human figure who is about to be judged (fig. 18). A late continental woodcut by Jörg Breu the Younger, entitled *The Last Judgment with the Ages of Man and Death*, 1540, unites in one composition the Second Coming with seven generic portraits of the life of Man from infancy to old age.[5] The imminence of death and judgment in *The Castle of Perseverance*, then, is thematically in accord with developments in late medieval art and literature generally. Final judgment has become, for the individual Christian, a matter of personal reflection for which the morality play offers an instructive and poignant model.

This essay will attempt to analyze the ways in which the issue of just judgment in *The Castle of Perseverance* builds toward the climactic final scene of debate and judgment concerning man's soul, and will do so in terms of stage picture: that is, of theatrical images presented to the audience through which homiletic metaphors of spiritual conflict and of divine justice are physically manifested in the theater. The play's aims are essentially similar to those of the judgment pageants in the Corpus Christi cycles examined in the previous chapter, and yet, because the audience is asked to identify more closely with a single representative protagonist than in the more heterogeneous scenes of the cycles, a different kind of visual symbolism is required. The argument here will be that the dramatist's method of construction, in this early and influential morality, is to search out costuming effects, gestures, props, structures, and spatial arrangements that will express metaphorical truths in visual and audible form much as *exempla* illustrate the medieval sermon or as iconic details express meaning in eschatological painting and sculpture. Stagecraft arises directly as a process of finding dramaturgical equivalents for spiritual metaphors found in biblical and liturgical texts and pictorially presented in art. This is not to reduce the play itself to mere illustration of texts, but to suggest that its stagecraft is an integral part of a visual tradition in medieval religious art. The stage images given such iconographical importance are plentifully available in the visual arts of the period, where they fulfill comparably symbolic functions.

"Man, thinke on thin[e] endinge day/ Whanne thou schalt be closyd under clay!" warns the Good Angel as the recently-born Mankind considers going to play with the World. "*Homo, memento finis, et in aeternum non peccabis*" (ll. 407-10a). The overwhelming issue that defines what course Mankind should choose is that of God's ultimate judgment of his conduct. This is so for the audience as well as the protagonist, since the Mankind figure is representative of that audience. "Every man in himself forsothe he may it finde," explains one of the Vexillators who speak the Banns, "Whou Mankinde into this werld born is ful bare/ And bare schal beried be at his [l]ast ende" (ll. 15-17). It is because Mankind speaks "at his laste ende" of mercy that the Good Angel can beg that "of mercy schal he nowth misse" (ll. 122-23).

The trial of Mankind's soul conducted by the four daughters of God is patently an image of that "dredful domysday" (l. 3545) on which, as God says, "To me schal they geve acompt at my digne des" when "Mihel his horn blowith at my dred dom" (ll. 3616-17). God's triumphant function in this play is to "deme this case" and to announce "What that his jugement schal be" (ll. 3219-27). He saves Mankind, who seems to represent the whole erring human race, and yet his great act of judgment is, like the Last Judgment of which it is a type, a parting of the goats from the sheep. People that do good in this world, he proclaims, shall be "heynyd" (l. 3638), that is, exalted in bliss,

> And they that evil do, they schul to helle-lake
> In bitter balys to be brent: my jugement it is.
> (ll. 3639-40)

Man's life on earth is but a preparation for last judgment, and *The Castle of Perseverance*, by dramatizing that life, is concerned first and last with judgment.

In his task of visualizing the judgment of Mankind, the dramatist of *The Castle of Perseverance* faced a central artistic problem for which Corpus Christi drama of judgment provided an imperfect model: that of illustrating in concrete dramatic forms the abstractions of allegory.[6] He had to begin not with a biblical narrative, complete with characters, plot, and the like, but with a proposition such as that enunciated in the later morality play of *Mankind* (ll. 227-28): "ther is ever a batell betwix the soull and the body: *Vita hominis est militia super terram*" (Job 7.1). How does one visualize a battle between the soul and the body? The word "battle" suggests, of course, a military metaphor, but the process required to develop this homiletic proposition into narrative or dramatic form depends necessarily on finding concrete shapes for a figure of speech that is by its nature rhetorical and abstract. The artist must invent character and story that will convincingly represent the substance of the proposition contained in the metaphor. To be sure, the artist has access to the work of others before him who have given corporeal substance to similar abstract ideas, beginning no later than the fourth century with Prudentius' long and influential allegorical poem, the *Psychomachia*. The battle of the Virtues and Vices presented in that poem came in time to enjoy a rich iconographic tradition. The process of visualizing allegory may seem evident enough when we survey the great allegories of the later Middle Ages. Still, earlier evidence suggests that visual artists found the concretizing of metaphor to be sufficiently different from biblical illustration as to constitute a novel and puzzling task.

Early efforts at visualization of metaphor can be seen in graphic illustrations of the figurative language of the Psalms, especially in the illustrated psalters of the ninth century such as the Carolingian Utrecht Psalter and the Stuttgart Psalter. The artists' uncertainty and inexperience can be seen in the occasionally amusing naivete of their literalizations, as when the Utrecht illustrator of verse 43.23, "Arise, why sleepest thou, O Lord?" (44.23 in the English King James or Authorized Version), shows God in a curtained bed with angels in attendance, or, to depict verse 84.3 (85.2 in *AV*), "thou hast covered all their sins," shows two angels spreading a large drapery over a group of people.

Even though such literalizations betray the artists' difficulty in deciding how and when to visualize a figure of speech, we perceive that the artists are drawn to serious themes. Since many of the psalms were interpreted by the Church Fathers in an eschatological context, the concretized metaphors in the illustrations are often those of Last Judgment. The subject, because of its awesomely unknown dimensions, invites imaginative and figurative interpretation. To visualize the ninth verse of Psalm 6 (6.8 in *AV*), "Depart from me, all ye workers of iniquity," for example, the Stuttgart illustrator shows Christ in the center with a sheep on his right marked with a cross, and a goat on his left. The hand of God appears in the heavens above the sheep, while a devil above the goat wings toward hell. Christ turns up his thumb for the sheep, and down for the goat. The eschatological reading of this verse derives from St. Augustine. In the Utrecht Psalter, this same verse is accompanied by a picture of four devils tormenting the damned in a fiery pit filled with serpents. Psalm 9.5 (9.4), "thou hast sat on the throne, who judgest justice," is similarly rendered as a judgment icon in the Stuttgart Psalter, in accordance with the interpretation of St. Augustine and Cassiodorus. A sitting Christ with scales confronts the souls of those who are to be judged; behind Christ, an angel bears a scroll with the word *equitas*, while St. Peter stands on Christ's left bearing a cross-staff.[7] Among other eschatological verses are 10.5-6 (11.5), 47.2, 4-6 (48.1-5), 81.1-3 (82.1-3), and of course 84.11 (85.10), where Righteousness and Peace are seen kissing each other (fig. 19) while Mercy and Truth meet.

The Utrecht Psalter was copied in England during the Romanesque period,[8] and thus, despite its lack of coherent narrative structure, established a model for the concretizing of spiritual metaphor in a way that paralleled the illustrating of narrative biblical event. F. P. Pickering and James Marrow have shown how visualizations of the Old Testament, and especially of the Psalms, contributed to the development of New Testament narrative art; metaphors from diverse parts of the Old Testament, especially the Psalms, were combined to produce a narrative full of realistic detail derived from

concretized metaphor, and that narrative was then illustrated.[9] A similar process also made possible the kind of
allegorical narrative on which *The Castle of Perseverance*
depends.

For its particular metaphoric propositions of a battle
between soul and body and the trial of Man before his su-
preme judge, *The Castle of Perseverance* is indebted not only
to the tradition of the illustrated psalters but also to didactic
poems of military conflict, including the *Psychomachia* of
Prudentius already mentioned, Guillaume de Deguileville's
Pèlinerage de l'âme (fourteenth century), and Grosseteste's
Le Chasteau d'Amour (d. 1253). The verbal images of conflict and judgment in these poems were graphically represented in the visual arts as well, as for example in a marginal
illustration of the Castle of Love showing a large central
fortification defended by female personifications against male
attackers (fig. 20).[10] Eschatological drama of the twelfth century, including the Tegernsee *Antichrist* and the *Sponsus* play
discussed above in Chapter I, offered practical dramatic examples of pictorial arrangements on stage based upon metaphors of debate and confrontation.

No doubt the Corpus Christi drama of Last Judgment
(as explored in the previous chapter) provided still another
contemporary model for staging a scene of judgment, with
its hieratic ordering, symmetries, balance, vertical and horizontal movement, and the like. We will see that the dramaturgy of *The Castle of Perseverance* indeed resembles that
of Corpus Christi judgment in many particulars. Nonhistor-
ical setting and abstract characterization oblige the Corpus
Christi dramatist, like the morality dramatist, to seek out
forms that are eschatological. The Last Judgment pageants
from the cycles are distinctly more like morality dramas than
are the earlier dramatizations of events taking place in historical time and involving historical personages. Still, even
if the event portrayed takes place in apocalyptic rather than
historical time, the scene of final judgment is based on narrative scriptural account. Its pictures are necessarily those
of its story; the concrete and particularized forms of the
narrative are already provided in Scripture. In morality

drama, conversely, the pictures derive from figures of speech: Man's life is a battle, or a journey, or a fall and recovery.

Narrative in allegorical drama is an extended working out of one or more figures of speech; characterization is a means of illustrating abstract qualities encountered in such an invented narrative; properties must likewise illustrate some proposition related to man's battle with vice and virtue. Stage setting and spatial arrangement show with a particular vividness the origin of the allegorical plot in figures of speech: because the stage must show the battle for the soul of Man, it centers its action on a castle in a way that the Corpus Christi cycles do not. Everything in allegorical drama depends upon the proposition or propositions to be figuratively illustrated.

The rhetorical concern of the *Castle* dramatist with illustrating proposition can be seen in the numerous biblical texts incorporated into the manuscript. Although they are seemingly not (in most cases at least) lines to be spoken by the actors, these biblical citations are a telling reflection of the play's interest in argument. The "story" of *The Castle of Perseverance* cannot be summarized in any narrative account from Scripture, but it can be fairly well represented in the proposition, based upon Ecclesiasticus 7.40, "*Homo, memento finis*" ("Man, think on thine ending day"). The play's plot, and the focus of the action on the centrally located castle, is equally well crystallized in the text from Matthew 10.22 quoted at line 1705a, "*Qui perseveraverit usque in finem, hic salvus erit*" ("he that shall persevere unto the end, he shall be saved"). Other such texts point to ironies and inversion in the action of the play, whereby the mighty shall be put down from their seats and the meek raised up.[11] Some citations detail the metaphors through which the individual Vices and Virtues are visualized. When Chastity douses the "fowle hete" of Lechery with water, for example, the text includes a prayer to the Virgin Mary to quench carnal lusts ("*Mater et Virgo, exstingue carnales concupiscentias*," ll. 2303a, 2388). Stage action simply literalizes this metaphor.[12] When World deserts Mankind, a number of citations state the proposition that takes visible form on stage:

"*Mundus transit, et concupiscentia eius*" ("the world passeth away, and the concupiscence thereof," 1 John 2.17), and so on.[13]

Most centrally, perhaps, the debate of the four daughters of God gives to the entire play its moment of *peripeteia* when the stage action literalizes the well-known lines from Psalm 84.11 (85.10), "*Misericordia et Veritas obviaverunt sibi; Justitia et Pax osculatae sunt*" ("Mercy and Truth have met each other: Justice [*AV*: Righteousness] and Peace have kissed," 1. 3521a). This is not to argue, to be sure, that the dramatist need have gone to the Psalms as his source. The iconographic tradition of this greeting and kiss was highly developed by the early fourteenth century. What is apparent is that the play's turning action depends on the visualization of a metaphor, one that is familiar in the art of the period. The whole ending of the play too, with God's judgment and the ascent of the four daughters to his throne accompanying the soul of Mankind, presents through symbolic gesture the substance of a series of interrelated propositions: "*Justitias Dominus justitia dilexit*" ("The Lord of righteousness has loved righteous deeds," 1. 3382a; see Psalm 10.8 [11.8]), and so on.[14] Even if, as Jacob Bennett has argued, the scene of the four daughters of God is a late addition to the play text, the crucial reversal of the action must have involved a similar iconic literalization of a metaphor, perhaps one in which the blessed Virgin Mary alone interceded before God on behalf of the soul of Man.[15] A provençal French judgment play of the fifteenth century, *Lo Jutgamen General*, shows Mary reconciling the debate of Justice and Mercy, and elsewhere in medieval art and drama Mary is associated with the kiss of Righteousness and Peace.[16] In any case, then, a visualization of the metaphoric embrace of Psalm 84 provides a central image for the climactic action of *The Castle of Perseverance*.

In the absence of a narrative biblical source, the visualizing of figures of speech must serve allegorical drama not only as plot line but as principle of organization. In *The Castle of Perseverance*, the metaphorical image of the kiss has a recapitulatory function necessary to a play that serves, like Corpus Christi judgment drama, to sum up all human endeavor at the time of final reckoning before God's throne. From the time of St. Bernard onward, as Gordon Kipling has indicated, allegorical expressions of Psalm 84 depicting the meeting of the four daughters of God were used in homilies of Advent to draw a connection between the first and second comings.[17] The visual similarities of the embrace explicitly link the Annunciation and the Visitation of Mary by Elizabeth to the reconciliation of the four daughters of God.[18] Advent theology and liturgy lent themselves to this connection; in medieval Christianity, as we have seen on several occasions, Advent was a time of moral reminders and apocalyptic warnings when the Christian community was taught to express gratitude for God's grace on the one hand and fearful anticipation of his judgment on the other. The liturgy of Advent celebrated both the Incarnation and the Last Judgment. The funeral office enjoyed close ties with Advent; the twelfth-century sequence *Dies Irae*, now part of the burial Mass, was composed originally for the first Sunday in Advent. In his similar drawing together of Advent and Doomsday through stage picture, the dramatist of *The Castle of Perseverance* uses visualized allegory to achieve the kind of recapitulation based in the Corpus Christi cycle plays on narrative biblical material.

The function of proposition, enunciated as homiletic figurative speech, is thus all-embracing. Narrative content is absent until it is supplied by way of metaphor cast in the form of dramatic action and speech. Metaphor becomes at once the story and its abstract meaning, since the story is basically nothing more than the literalization of the meaning. This dual rhetorical function can be illustrated by telling the "story" of *The Castle of Perseverance*, not as plot summary but in terms of the metaphors it chooses as its vehicle for becoming dramatic and stageworthy. We find that we can tell the entire story in metaphors that are the commonplaces of life as spiritual combat or journey, and yet simultaneously in this play are the stuff of what the actors say and do. Thus: Man is born naked into this world. He is presented with a spiritual choice between good and evil counsel, one sent from heaven and one from hell. Not knowing at first which way to turn, he betakes him to the world and its pleasures. Dwelling there and serving the world, he is caught on folly's hook. He takes lechery and gluttony as his companions, among other sinful acquaintances. Raised up by folly, since fools prosper for a time in this world, he is arrayed in the world's wealth and allows himself to be guided by false reputation. He adopts covetousness as his mentor. Only when he feels the prick of conscience does he betake himself to penance and confession, and finds absolution for having followed evil. Taught to flee filth by the counsel of humility, patience, charity, and other virtues, he is content to dwell in perseverance. He does penance with his body, and with the aid of virtuous counsel he repudiates sinful doing and quenches lust. In old age, nonetheless, he once again hearkens to covetousness and turns to vice, descending into iniquity, no longer led by virtue. His avarice is unsatiable. When death comes to him and pierces him to the heart with death's lance, Mankind knows not who will inherit his wealth, and so dies pleading for God's mercy. His soul is taken to hell and is tortured, but on his behalf mercy and peace contend with justice and truth before God's throne until Mankind's soul is saved and escorted upward to heaven, to sit on God's right hand.

The expressions here are recognizable as figures of speech. Mankind does not know which way to turn, he allows himself to be guided, he is content to dwell, he falls and is raised up. In this play, such figures also take the form of literal and precise actions on stage. Gestures of turning, leading, striking, and the like are everywhere apparent in the text as visualizations of choice and conflict. Quenching of lust is a physical action requiring water. The prick of conscience and death's dart are stage properties. Mankind's nakedness is not simply a manner of speaking, but a costume using tights, and the hoariness of his old age is conveyed by white hair and beard. Falling and rising are at once spiritual metaphors and indicators of spatial movement between platea and scaffolds. Companionship bespeaks grouping of characters in the theater. The contrast between right and left hand is throughout a sign (as it is in judgment drama and art generally) of the binary opposition with which this play moves toward its final tableau of judgment, separating the saved from the damned.

We might begin a more detailed analysis of such theatrical signs with costuming, since it is so immediately visible and relates so closely to characterization. The most observable effects are those signaling the Ages of Man, as the protagonist of *The Castle of Perseverance* moves from infancy to old age. In accord with his resolution to use "propyrtes" as a visual means of bringing his play to life (l. 132), the dramatist presents us with a *Humanum Genus* whose nakedness and frailty are repeatedly stressed in his opening lines. "Ful feynt and febyl I fare you beforn," he confesses to the audience; "I am nakyd of lim and lende" (ll. 278-79). His costume (probably of tights, as in the Norwich Creation with its inventory of "hoses of apis skinns"),[19] is a conventional form of representing nakedness, as when Adam and Eve are ashamed of their nakedness in the York *Fall of Man*, and is unmistakable to the audience: "Nakyd I am, as ye may se" (l. 285). Mankind speaks of a "sely crisme" (chrisom or baptismal headcloth) on his head (l. 294). The nakedness is representative not only of his infancy but of his original condition and of his need to follow the example of Christ, who, as the Good Angel explains, refused to "coveit werldys goode," choosing rather to remain "All in povert" with his "meynye" or disciples while he was here on earth (ll. 350-52). The visual arts commonly portray Adam and Eve as naked, as for example in the Terrestrial Paradise of *Les Très Riches Heures of Jean, Duke of Berry*.[20]

When the protagonist of *The Castle of Perseverance*, still "but yonge," longs to "be riche in gret aray" (ll. 377, 423), his turning away from virtuous counsel and simple dress is thus a forsaking of Christ's example. "He schal sittyn in sendel softe," Pleasure assures the Bad Angel, and Folly promises Mankind "Thou schalt be clad in clothys newe" (ll. 554, 564). This promise of a symbolic change of costuming is literally effected in the theater, as we can see from the description of Mankind when he next appears; his companions observe that he is now "in welthys wonde" and "In robys rive" (ll. 625, 699), bound "in bryth besauntys" or gold coins, as a sign of his depraved reliance on worldly wealth. Such worldly arrogance and splendid array are typical also in fourteenth-century English wall paintings of the Three Living and Three Dead, a morality subject in which three insolent young worldlings, often seen hunting with hawks and other paraphernalia, encounter three cadavers as a reminder of the judgment to come.[21]

Later in *The Castle of Perseverance*, when Mankind is "sexty winter hold" (l. 417), the signs of advancing age are visually apparent: we are told that his hair waxes "al hore," his back begins "to bowe and bende," he can do no more than "crulle and crepe," and he is "arayed in a sloppe" or loose gown appropriate to age (ll. 2482-91), like the old man in Bosch's *Death of the Miser* (fig. 21). Comparison may also be made with "The Deathbed of Richard Whittington" (1430).[22] Despite the lack of actual stage directions here about costuming, these visual characterizations of costume suitable to the various ages of humankind are plainly aimed at actor and producer as well as the audience, and they accord with the evidence we do have in the staging diagram concerning the symbolic costuming of the four daughters of God. The text also does not tell us precisely what costume changes are effected when Mankind goes to confession and enters the Castle of Perseverance, but suitable changes at these junctures are plainly implied. This use of costume to mark stages of a spiritual journey anticipates that of sixteenth-century morality drama as well, where its omnipresence is amply documented by stage directions.[23]

The alterations in Mankind's state of mind and soul are also signaled by the garments of those who contend for his wavering allegiance. The binary opposition that extends throughout the play must begin visually with the Good and Bad Angels accompanying Mankind at his first entry, for one angel "cam fro hevene trone" (l. 317) and is presumably accoutered like other angels on the scaffold of heaven, whereas the Bad Angel is at last thrust down into hell, and clearly his costuming associates him with the scaffold of hell and its inhabitants. The Deadly Sins are presented in opulent finery, jewels, and other tokens of extravagant luxury, though Satan is also blackened like the Bad Angel: he sits, he tells us, "in draf as a drake," that is, in filth like a dragon, and calls himself "Belial the blake" (ll. 197-99). He instructs Mankind to affect "longe crakows" or pointed and curved toes on his shoes, and to "Jagge" or frill his clothing in every manner possible (ll. 1059-60). He attacks Meekness in her castle "With robys rounde, rayed ful ryth," that is, fully arrayed in flowing robes and in sumptuous gowns (ll. 2072-73).

Some details in these descriptions may be owing to alliteration, but cumulatively their evidence is plainly in favor of decadent sumptuousness for the Deadly Sins. Flesh tells the audience that with "tapitys of tafata," silken tapestry, he decorates the towers of his scaffold (l. 239). A similar attention to rich hangings and ornamented pavilions can be found, for example, in Bosch's depiction of Lechery in his Prado *Tabletop of the Seven Deadly Sins and the Four Last Things*, where several pairs of lovers disport themselves in a tent, well provided with dainties to eat and drink, musical instruments, and a fool to entertain them. An English illustration in the visual arts can be found in the depiction of the Seven Deadly Sins at Trotton, Sussex, where for example the portrait of Avaritia shows a man seated before an open chest.[24] Death is, as we would expect, arrayed in *The Castle of Perseverance* as in the visual arts in "carful clothys," an ominous shroud in which Mankind will be caught (l. 2797).

Conversely, the Virtues are clothed in garments that betoken simplicity and modesty. The ladies who help Mankind defend himself in the castle are "lovely in lace" (l. 2548), tastefully dressed, in pointed contrast to the "robys rounde" and "Grete gounse" (ll. 2072-73) of Pride and his company. Their simple but attractive dress accords with their sisterhood: they are the "sevene sisterys swete" (l. 2047), and are also called "maidyns" and "ladys" (ll. 1764, 1806). The Deadly Sins refer to the Virtues disparagingly, but in words that nonetheless acknowledge their womanliness, as "olde trat," "wenchys," "moderys," and "bicchys" (ll. 1578, 1728-31, 1884). In their feminine character and sisterly relationship they anticipate the four daughters of God, who, according to the stage design for the play, are arrayed in mantles colored to symbolize their grouping into two opposed pairs: Mercy and Peace in white and black, Truth and Righteousness in green and red.[25] The Virtues of the play are thus predominantly female characters, though their femininity is also travestied in Lechery, "dowter so dere" to Flesh (l. 999). *

Most of the Deadly Sins and other tempters are not only masculine but aggressively so, boisterous, arrogant, loud. Their masculinity and worldly power are insisted upon in the forms of address used: World, Flesh, and Devil are "tho kingys thre" (l. 1720), Sloth is Flesh's "swete sone" (l. 251), Pride, Wrath, and Envy are "dukys dowty" (l. 902), Lust-Liking and Folly are "Comly knytis of renoun" (l. 470), and the like. The paradoxical triumph of feminine over masculine in the siege of the castle prepares the way for the play's climactic scene of judgment in which the four daughters of God are reconciled to peace and mercy. (The accent on femininity would be no less if, in the original version, it was the Virgin Mary who interceded before God on behalf of mankind.) Striking oppositions in costume help visualize the process of conflict and resolution in this play.

An analogy in the visual arts, from French painting in the time of Jean de Berry, shows the seven Virtues and the Seven Deadly Sins in violent combat; as Millard Meiss observes, "the Virtues, all female, wield sticks as they turn on the Sins, all male."[26] Indeed, as Goffredo Rosati notes, the Virtues and Vices are almost always paired in iconographical tradition, in battle or in counterbalancing positions in a visual scheme, rather than appearing alone.[27] A fine twelfth-century representation of the Psychomachia, with opposing Virtues and Vices, appears on the portal of St.-Pierre-de-la-Tour, Aulney-de-Saintonge.[28] Rosamond Tuve illustrates, in her study of the allegory of Vices and Virtues, how the Virtues are traditionally seen as feminine, and how they are identified by visual attributes: Prudence bears a sieve to betoken circumspection, Fortitude a tower as a sign of her impregnable constancy, Temperance a clock as a sign of

161

moderation, and Justice her sword and balance.[29] These are the Cardinal or Aristotelian Virtues, subsumed into Christian iconography and combined with the theological Virtues, Faith, Hope, and Charity, to make up the number of seven. The attributes found in illustrations of the Virtues vary considerably in the medieval period; earlier, in Carolingian times, Prudence was often associated with a book indicating knowledge of Scripture, and Temperance with a torch.[30] The lists of the Virtues vary also. That of *The Castle of Perseverance* conceptualizes them as *remedia* for the Deadly Sins,[31] and accordingly the hand properties by which they are identified differ from earlier attributes. Nonetheless, the association of each Virtue with appropriate visual signs provides the dramatist with a ready-made inventory of symbolic properties whose meaning would be familiar to the audience. The Vices, as Adolf Katzenellenbogen demonstrates, were originally feminine, like the Virtues, and modeled on figures in Roman classical art; but in the eleventh and twelfth centuries they became particularized into more contemporary human types, such as the miser representing avarice, and most such types were male.[32] Hence the preponderance of male versus female abstractions representing vice and virtue by the time of *The Castle of Perseverance*.

Stage properties, like costume changes, mark the epochs in the career of Mankind as he oscillates from good to evil, and give concrete theatrical form to conventional homiletic metaphor. The prick of conscience and death's dart are enough alike to juxtapose visually two critical moments in the life of the protagonist. They are also familiar in the visual arts, on the one hand in the popular iconographic tradition of the Virtues crucifying Christ and thrusting him through the side with a spear in order to obtain for mankind the benefits of his grace,[33] and on the other hand in representations of the Dance of Death, of Ars Moriendi, and the coming of Death to Mankind or Everyman (see figs. 18 & 21). *The Castle of Perseverance* reflects the duality of grace and death in the image of the thrusting spear. Penitence comes to the worldly and insolent Mankind "With point of penaunce," with "launce" or "spete of spere" or "spud [dag-

ger] of sorwe swote" in order to "reche to thine hert rote"
and thus bestow on Mankind a healing drop from the foun-
tain of mercy (ll. 1377-1400). Penitence knows that he can
bring Mankind to repentance and thus to Christ's bliss "If
sorwe of hert lache [prick] him with launce" (l. 1419). Cor-
respondingly, Death later comes to Mankind "With this
launce," to "reche" with "this point" to "thine herte rote"
(ll. 2807-42). The gesture and phrasing are nearly identical,
and the resemblance to Christ's being pierced in the side by
the spear of the blind Longeus (Longinus) can hardly be
accidental, though it is also partly ironic. Man dies to sin
and the world in imitation, conscious or unconscious, of
Christ.

A number of stage properties characterize the battle between virtue and vice by visualizing the abstract qualities
that aid or subvert Mankind. Some employ the elemental
conflict of fire and water as a means of expressing the burning or quenching of lust. Gluttony goes to battle "With a
faget on min[e] hond, for to settyn on a fire" (l. 1961). The
point is that gluttony "fuels" lust, as we say in conventional
homiletic expression, by inflaming appetite; a longing for
dainty fare soon passes into desire for sexual pleasure. Armed
with a "wrethe of the wode," or twisted firebrand of wood
(l. 1962), and determined to "makyn a smeke [smoke]/
Ageyns this castle," he attacks Abstinence with "a faget in
min[e] necke," that is, on his shoulder (ll. 2248-52). Lechery
too boasts that she can "make a fer in Mans towte/ That
launcith up as any leye," as we have seen (ll. 2289-90). She
is repelled by Chastity's undertaking to "qwenche that fowle
hete" (l. 2303), pouring on water until Lechery is "drenchyd"
(l. 2388). Covetousness is spoken of elsewhere as a compul-
sion which no man may ever "Qwenche" (l. 2765); conversely, God assures Mankind that his mercy is "sinne-
quenchand" (l. 3603). Sloth proposes to "delve with a spade"
in order to empty the "diche" surrounding the castle of its
"watyr of grace" (ll. 2326-29); he "makith this dike drye,/
To puttyn Mankinde to distresse" (ll. 2352-53). Slothful behavior, in other words, dries up the sources of grace for mankind
by depriving man of his ability to perform good works. Wrath

proclaims to Patience that he is to "brenne" her "with wild fere," in token of the consuming nature of rage (l. 2115). Visual analogues to this symbolic opposition of fire and water can be found as early as Carolingian times, when Temperance often bore as her attributes a torch and a jug full of water from which she poured, thereby illustrating (for example) the text of Julianus Pomerius, "Ignem libidinosae voluptatis extinguit."[34]

Fire in these images is related to the conflagration and smoke of hell-fire, visible at the devil's scaffold where, as the Bad Angel informs Mankind, he shall "brenne . . . In picke and ter"—i.e., in pitch and tar (ll. 3076-78). Fire is thus an explicit visualization throughout the play of one of the consequences of divine judgment, as it is also in Corpus Christi and other medieval drama and in the visual arts; we may compare, for example, the staging plan for the Valenciennes Passion Play (fig. 22), in which fire and smoke issue from structures representing hell and hell mouth on the far right of the picture.[35] The conflict of fire and water is between two of the four basic elements, an appropriate action in a theatrical arena representing the whole divine universe. The contest between earth and air is also evident in references to the platea as "grounde" and the scaffolds as "on lofte" or in "yon hey place" (ll. 1078, 1145, 3217).

Other stage properties used to identify their owners visually include Folly's hook for Mankind anticipating the hooks in hell for Mankind's soul (ll. 512, 3066), Backbiter's letter box filled with "letterys of defamacioun" (l. 671), and the jewels and gold bestowed on Mankind by Covetousness (ll. 743, 2726). Devils with hooks are a familiar feature of Last Judgment art, as indicated in Chapter I, above. Such identifying features are not, technically speaking, visual attributes like the key used to identify St. Peter or the lily the Virgin Mary in medieval iconography, since attributes of this sort were sufficient to identify a figure outside any narrative context, whereas the identifying features in *The Castle of Perseverance* depend on a specific narrative situation. They are similar, however, in their use of iconographic tradition found in Last Judgment art. Moneybags and gold, conventional visual signs of miserliness, are traceable back to depictions of the story of Dives and Lazarus in which the sinner is shown with his moneybags in hell.[36] Money and moneybags are ubiquitous in depictions of Avarice, in manuscript illuminations,[37] in sculptured renditions of the Deadly Sins found in the lower story pillars of the Ducal Palace at Venice, c. 1350,[38] in Bosch's Prado *Tabletop of the Seven Deadly Sins*,[39] or in Jan van Eyck's diptych of the Last Judgment.[40]

Many stage properties of conflict are appropriately military. Mankind, we are told, is "Wel armyd with vertus" (l. 54), and in this play the familiar set phrase bespeaks a metaphor that is far from dead. Banners repeatedly proclaim the identities of the attacking parties as they besiege the Castle of Perseverance (ll. 1879, 2083). Belial orders his followers to "Sprede my penon upon a prene"—that is, spread his banner on a standard (l. 1903). Pride is bidden to "put out thy penon of raggys and of rowte," his ensign of rags and riot, symbolic of prodigality and disorder (l. 1973). The Bad Angel, acting as "herawd," boasts that he bears about the "brodde" or scutcheon of Belial (ll. 1969-71). In their turn, the ladies are also provided with banners: "Ageyns thy baner of pride and bost/ A baner of meknes and mercy/ I putte ageyns Pride," declares Meekness (ll. 2082-84). Shields too are borne on both sides. Belial commands his retinue to "Schapith now youre scheldys schene," prepare your shining shields (l. 1905), whereas the seven sisters undertake "Mankind for to schilde and schete/ Fro dedly sinne and schamely schot" (ll. 2049-50), and Envy swears that he will strike Charity a grievous blow "Thy targe for to tere" (l. 2155). The metaphor of shielding is essential to the concept of the Castle of Perseverance, with its walls of stone able to withstand a siege, and elsewhere the virtuous friends of Mankind speak of their function to "schelde" him from hell-fire and "schelve" him from deadly sin (ll. 1457, 2575, 3211).

The weapons of this play tend to accentuate the contrast between virtue and vice which is also generally female versus male, and thereby anticipate the final judgment scene in which mercy triumphs over justice. The Deadly Sins are provided with "schaftys" which they are to shiver "Scharply on scheldys" (l. 1952). The sister Virtues, preparing the castle for siege, expect to receive "schamely schot" (l. 2050). Wrath explicitly declares his intention to pelt Patience "With stiffe stonys that I have here." He also has a bow, with which to sling at her "many a vire," or cross-bow bolt (ll. 2111-12). Envy is similarly armed, for he proclaims he "schal schetyn [let fly] to this castel town/ A ful fowle defamacion—/ Therfore this bowe I bere" (ll. 2157-59). His bow is at once a stage property and a symbolic accouterment, like all these weapons; the bow of Envy will shoot forth defamation. Other emblematic weapons of masculine aggression, as we have seen, include fire and smoke. Visual analogues to this kind of weaponry abound in the iconographical tradition of Death armed with a bow and arrow.[41]

The ladies, conversely, are armed with flowers or with quenching water, and the great Christian paradox of *Deposuit potentes de sede* is manifested on stage by the comic incongruity of burly men wincing in pain and cowardly humiliation at the wounds they have received from such passive weapons of grace. "I weyle and wepe, with wondys wete," howls Pride, "I am betyn in the hed" (ll. 2202-03). Envy sobs that "With faire rosys" Charity "min[e] hed gan breke" (l. 2211).

Trumpets sound repeatedly, not only during the battle, as when Belial orders the "Clariouns" to "cryith up at a krake [loudly],/ And blowe your brode baggys [bagpipes]," or when Flesh orders them to "Late blastys blowe" (ll. 2197-98, 2377, 1898), but earlier when the stage direction "*Trumpe up*" announces the gathering of Pleasure, Folly, the Bad Angel, and Mankind at the World's scaffold (ll. 574, 646). "*Music*" too accompanies the successes of the Deadly Sins in winning Mankind to their side (l. 455); later, as though in response, the sister Virtues sing "*Aeterne Rex altissime*" to celebrate Mankind's entry into the castle (l. 1705a). Generally, noise is the purview of the men. Backbiter *buccinabit cornu*, will blow a horn, to summon Covetousness, and the latter answers, appropriately enough, "why blowe ye so lowde?" (ll. 1852-54). When Flesh wishes to summon his lieutenants, he *clamabit*, will cry aloud, and Lechery's answer is the same: "Why criest thou so schille?" (ll. 1811-13). World bids his trumpets "Howtith hye," proclaim loudly, in summons of the Deadly Sins, and Flesh confirms that he hears a "hidowse whwtinge on hyt" or hideous shouting on high (ll. 1897, 1938). The symbolic irony of these sound effects lies not only in the paradox that the mighty shall be put down from their seats, but in the biblical association of trumpet calls with the "dredful domysday" (l. 3545) when, as God says, "Mihel his horn blowith at my dred dom" (l. 3617). The final trumpet call is thus invoked by the scene at the play's end, with the Father seated in his throne and the singing of the *Te Deum laudamus*.

Gestures provide a similar theatrical contrast of good and evil, and prepare the audience for the benignly ironic reversal in the play's final scene of just judgment. The Deadly Sins are "boistows" or fierce in their gestures, as Belial says of himself: "I champe [gnash my teeth] and I chafe, I chocke on [thrust out] my chinne" (ll. 198-99). A recurrent stage business among the Deadly Sins is their beating of one another for failure in tempting Mankind. "*Tunc verberabit eos in plateam*," reads the stage direction, as Flesh flogs his lieutenants in the platea for letting Man escape (l. 1822). Belial similarly beats his subordinates "*super terram*," on the ground, and World thrashes Covetousness (ll. 1777, 1863). Backbiter's chief function is to turn the Sins against one another in envious detraction. The beatings are slapstick comedy here, as when the Sins are pommeled by the Virtues, but the serious self-destructiveness of wicked behavior is brought home to the audience when Mankind's soul is whipped ignominiously to hell by the Bad Angel (ll. 3114-20). Sin provides its own just punishment, in the form of symbolic stage violence.

The virtuous characters, throughout much of the play, are characterized by sighs, groans, and tears. "I sye sore, and grisly grone," laments the Good Angel, "For his [Mankind's] folye schal make him spilt!" (ll. 449-50). When Mankind betakes him to the company of the Deadly Sins, Confession finds the Good Angel so distraught that he asks him, "Why syest thou and sobbist sore? . . . Why makist thou grochinge under gore?" (ll. 1299-1305). Mercy says she would "wringyn min[e] honde" if God should set aside mercy in his judgment (l. 3449). These trials of the virtuous are in imitation of Christ, "betyn blo and blak/ For trespas that nevere did he" (ll. 2175-76). Mankind himself must "syhe sore" as he dies brokenhearted and pleading for God's mercy (l. 3005). Yet the roles of grieving and of vaunting are reversed in the play's *peripeteia*: at last it is the Sins and the Bad Angel who "sobbe" and "sye sore" at their defeat and are beaten down to hell while the virtuous rejoice (ll. 1866, 3593).

Stage furniture is especially important in juxtaposing images of worldly vice and divine virtue, whereby the paradoxical triumph of seemingly weak innocence over powerful evil gives structural centrality to the final judgment scene. One such piece of furniture, which occupies a dominant visual position in the play as it does in Corpus Christi drama and will later do in many Renaissance plays, is the throne. The biblical text *Deposuit potentes de sede* (l. 2094a) functions, like so many other texts in this play, as a verbal expression of an idea that takes the gestural form of stage action. We see Belial "sitte" enthroned on his scaffold (l. 196). Flesh informs us that Gluttony "sittith semly here by my side" (l. 249). World declares, "Now I sitte in my semly sale [hall];/ I trotte and tremle in my trew trone" (ll. 456-57). Covetousness invites Mankind to ascend his scaffold and "Sit up ryth here in this se" or seat (l. 834). Covetousness' scheme to "set Mankind on a stomlinge stol" (l. 1039) is thus visual as well as metaphorical. Almost 350 lines (ll. 892-1238) are devoted to an elaborate sequence in which the Deadly Sins are summoned to Covetousness' scaffold and are invited up by Mankind to "dwelle by thy side," "With Mankinde to sittyn on lofte" (ll. 1085, 1145).

This tableau of worldly insolence, displaying Mankind in estate surrounded by his new friends, is an apt token of empire that must fail. In its place, the final scene offers us *Pater sedens in trono* and *Pater sedens in juditio* (ll. 3560a, 3597a), while the four daughters ascend *ad tronum* bringing Mankind to "sit" at God's "ryth honde" (l. 3599). God has put down the mighty from their seats, even as he himself assumes the throne of justice. The triumphal figure we see here enthroned is like that of the Ghent Altarpiece by Hubert and Jan van Eyck (1432), where Christ sits in majesty in the upper central panel, splendidly adorned in the scarlet robe and papal tiara of the High Priest, rays of light emanating from his crowned head, the scepter in his left hand while with his right he makes a gesture of benediction.[42] *Les Très Riches Heures of Jean, Duke of Berry* similarly shows God enthroned with orb and crown in its depiction of the Fall of the Rebel Angels.[43]

Stage structures provide the larger context of a *theatrum mundi* in which these divine paradoxes are fulfilled. The castle at the center and its surrounding platea are Mankind's domain, at the focal point of the universe; here is acted out the struggle for salvation of which he is at once the chief object and the most puny of participants.[44] *The Castle of Perseverance* is a play in which the protagonist is central and yet colorless, almost a dramatic device rather than a character, somewhat like Henry VI in Shakespeare's plays about England's great political soul-struggle of the fifteenth century. *The Castle of Perseverance*'s stage reflects the ambivalent centrality and nonentity of its protagonist. Stage structures on the periphery often dominate the action, for it is here that the Deadly Sins muster their forces against Mankind or join him on the scaffold of Covetousness. The play concludes not in the Castle of Perseverance, despite the play's title, but in the East, in heaven, at the throne of God. Meantime the Bad Angel has been thrust down into hell, and all traces of activity have disappeared at the erstwhile bustling thrones of World, Flesh, and Covetousness. Throughout, God's throne in the East is seen to be opposite to World's scaffold in the West, just as the church's altar is in the East and its door, through which the world enters, is in the West.[45] The final tableau of separating the saved from the damned, so familiar in visual representations of judgment, is reinforced by the Boethian staging design of *The Castle of Perseverance*, for hell is in the North, on the left hand of heaven from the audience's point of view as it faces that scaffold.

The castle in the center appears to be of "ston," with mighty "castel walle" (ll. 2042, 2566); it is "strenger thanne any in Fraunce" (l. 1553), and is surrounded by a ditch or moat in which flows the "watyr of grace" (l. 2329). A castle very much like this appears in medieval illustrations of the Castle of Love, as we have seen for instance in the margins of Gothic manuscripts catalogued by Lilian M. C. Randall or in the Peterborough Psalter (fig. 20), where we see women on the battlements of a fortress casting flowers upon the attacking knights below.[46] Katzenellenbogen offers illustrations from about 1175 of five Virtues in a tower.[47]

In *The Castle of Perseverance*, Man's bed is under the castle, further identifying that structure with his spiritual destiny, "and ther schal the sowle lye under the bed tyl he schal ryse and pleye" (stage diagram). The virtuous "holdith him inne" the castle, the bad "wold bringe him owte" (l. 78). The scaffolds of the Sins are imposing and high, as befits their haughty occupants; World is asked to "loke owt" of his scaffold at Mankind below him (l. 575), and the assembling of mighty hosts on these structures, or the sending of ambassadors back and forth between them, provides much of the stage movement in this play. What emerges overall is a theater representative of the divine universe, with little Man at its center and with vast contending forces facing their opposite numbers on every side. The audience is everywhere at once and thus omniscient in its point of view. Divine wisdom too is omniscient; nothing that Man does escapes notice, his smallest acts are cosmically significant. The audience, sharing the perception that Man's trust in worldly prosperity is illusory, is prepared to concur in the justice of the final judgment scene, and to apply the lesson to its own need to think on the "endinge day" (l. 407).

In such a cosmic arena, stage movement cannot fail to suggest a sense of direction or its opposite, wandering, in man's spiritual pilgrimage through life. Action thus literalizes in the theater the journey of meditation described above in Chapter II. "Whom to folwe, wetyn I ne may!" Mankind exclaims (l. 375), as he ponders the conflicting advice of Good and Bad Angels. The question of whom to follow, which way to turn, becomes a matter of blocking for the actor. "Torne not ageyn to thy folye," Confession urges Mankind, but turn he does (l. 1436). "Woldist drawe now to holinesse?" asks the Bad Angel, as Mankind literally takes the step of entering the Castle of Perseverance to "dwelle" there (ll. 1547-73). Yet the Good Angel must later conclude, in tears, that Mankind will "drawe ageyn to dedly sinne" (l. 2547). To "enter" into grace is a metaphor literalized not only when Mankind enters the Castle of Perseverance but finally when he goes to "yone hey place," the throne of God (l. 3217). The grouping of characters yields tableaux of Man's vacillating journey as he alternately joins the Deadly Sins on the scaffold of Covetousness or the sister Virtues in the castle. Such metaphorical and theatrical phrases as "by thy side" (l. 1085), "To the Werld us must gon" (l. 435), "he hath forsakyn us" (l. 2587), "folwyd thine Aungyl that is so Badde" (l. 1525), and "Fro fowle filthe now I fle" (l. 1565) indicate movement from one group to another as Mankind shifts his allegiances. Kneeling alternatively betokens worldly adulation and humble submission to grace (ll. 590, 1493). To "serve" can mean to obey the world's imprisoning counsel or to find true freedom in the service of God.

Perhaps the most telling stage movement is that in the vertical dimension, for it can so effectively suggest spiritual fall and rise. The vertical contrast between scaffold and platea continually lends itself to such movement, and provides once again both a worldly and spiritual meaning: Mankind can mount to the scaffolds of World and Covetousness, where he is crowned with empty glory, or he can aspire to the Castle of Perseverance and to the throne of God. Conversely, he can fall into sin, or humble himself before grace. When Mankind descends together with Folly in the platea ("*Tunc descendit in plateam pariter*"), the audience is invited to identify itself with this fall: "Whoso wil be riche and in gret aray,/ Toward the Werld he schal drawe" (ll. 490-94). Mankind ascends to the World ("*Tunc ascendet Humanum Genus ad Mundum*") to illustrate that Folly can lift up fools: "And I, Folye,/ Schal hyen him hye" (ll. 614, 639-40). When the Deadly Sins join Mankind on Covetousness' scaffold, the vertical emphasis bespeaks haughty aspiration: "I climbe fro this crofte [i.e., the platea]/ With Mankinde to sittyn on lofte," says Envy (ll. 1144-45). Later, when Covetousness tempts Mankind away from the castle, Mankind *"descendit ad Avaritiam"* (l. 2556) to demonstrate how Man "wil to foly falle" (l. 2572).

Yet rising and falling also express the protagonist's uncertain journey toward grace. Confession bids Mankind "cum doun," that is, humble himself, "and speke with Schrifte" (l. 1343). Paradoxically, Mankind sees that confession will "lache me up to livys levene," that is, raise me up to the light of eternal life (l. 1471). He is indeed held from falling while he is able to dwell in the Castle of Perseverance: "whosoevere holde him therinne,/ He schal nevere fallyn in dedly sinne" (ll. 1703-04). This saving paradox of rising and falling visualizes homiletic biblical texts, like so much action in this play: He has put down the mighty from their seats, Whoever exalts himself will be abased (ll. 2094a, 2107a).

The dominant image of fall at the play's end is into death and hell. As a key text informs us, *"Non descendet cum illo gloria eius"* (Psalm 48.18 [49.17]), his glory or wealth will not descend with him into the grave (l. 2625a). Death can "down-bringe to nowth" all humanity, and dwells in a "dale" or "careful cave" (ll. 2793, 2824, 3049), while the damned soul "fallist in fendys folde" or "develys delle," "pitte," or "helle-lake" (ll. 3054, 3125, 3198, 3639). Conversely, the journey to heaven is to "yone hey place" (l. 3217). With the four daughters of God, Mankind ascends to the throne of the Father (l. 3593) where he is "heynyd" or exalted in bounty and bliss (l. 3638), while the Bad Angel is thrust down into hell "In bras and brimston to welle" (l. 3593).

These spatial metaphors of salvation and damnation, familiar in much homiletic commentary, in the visual arts, and in Corpus Christi plays about Last Judgment and Antichrist (see the previous two chapters, above), are theatrically alive in *The Castle of Perseverance*. By giving such metaphors a visual objectivity and narrative excitement in the theater, this play finds in the multilevel nature of allegory its mainspring of convincing dramaturgy, for every action, every character, every structure or stage property is at once symbolic and theatrically "literal" or necessary to the plot. Most of all, the theatrical objectivity of metaphor lends potency to the image of just judgment and its relevance to the audience, for it is the consideration of what will happen to man at "his laste ende" that gives perspective to the cosmic struggle of good and evil dramatized in this play.

NOTES

1. Citations are from David Bevington, ed., *Medieval Drama* (Boston: Houghton Mifflin, 1975), pp. 796-902.

2. W. Roy MacKenzie, *The English Moralities from the Point of View of Allegory* (Boston: Ginn, 1914), and Bernard Spivack, *Shakespeare and the Allegory of Evil* (New York: Columbia Univ. Press, 1958).

3. Richard Kenneth Emmerson, *Antichrist in the Middle Ages* (Seattle: Univ. of Washington Press, 1981), pp. 53, 188-93, and V. A. Kolve, "*Everyman* and the Parable of the Talents," in *Medieval English Drama: Essays Critical and Contextual*, ed. Jerome Taylor and Alan H. Nelson (Chicago: Univ. of Chicago Press, 1972), pp. 316-40.

4. A. Caiger-Smith, *English Medieval Mural Paintings* (Oxford: Clarendon Press, 1963), pp. 45 and 51, pl. XVIII, and E. W. Tristram, *English Wall Painting of the Fourteenth Century* (London: Routledge and Kegan Paul, 1955), pp. 259-60. A similar English allegorical painting of the conditions of the soul of man, seen as part of a larger Last Judgment representation, is to be found on the north wall of Swanbourne Church, Buckinghamshire; see J. Slatter, "Description of the Paintings discovered on the North Wall of Swanbourne Church, Buckinghamshire," *Records of Buckinghamshire*, 3 (1870), 136-40.

5. Craig Harbison, *The Last Judgment in Sixteenth Century Northern Europe* (New York: Garland, 1970), fig. 93; see also ibid., fig. 94. For an example of Death with his dart from the second half of the fifteenth century, see "Le roi mort," Paris, Bibliothèque Nationale, Latin MS. 1160, fol. 151; illustrated in Kathleen Cohen, *Metamorphosis of a Death Symbol: The Transi Tomb in the Late Middle Ages and the Renaissance* (Berkeley and Los Angeles: Univ. of California Press, 1973), fig. 35.

6. Edgar Schell, *Strangers and Pilgrims: From "The Castle of Perseverance" to "King Lear"* (Chicago: Univ. of Chicago Press, 1983), pp. 28f, similarly argues that morality plays such as *The Castle of Perseverance* use a vocabulary of signs, much as do sermons, "to explicate and make persuasive a wide range of moral propositions," translating homiletics into the rhetoric of the theater. David Leigh, "The Doomsday Mystery Play: An Eschatological Morality," in *Medieval English Drama*, ed. Tay-

lor and Nelson, pp. 260-78, usefully shows how the Doomsday play in the cycles, with its unhistorical setting and characters, gives dramatic form to apocalyptic allegory in a way that morality dramatists may well have found useful. On a more incidental literalizing of biblical metaphors (e.g., the cup of sorrow mentioned during the Agony in the Garden) in other pageants of the Corpus Christi cycles, see Clifford Davidson, *From Creation to Doom: The York Cycle of Mystery Plays* (New York: AMS Press, 1984), pp. 5-6.

7. Ernest T. DeWald, *The Stuttgart Psalter* (Princeton, 1930), fol. 6^v and p. 11, fol. 9^v and pp. 13-14; and DeWald, *The Illustrations of the Utrecht Psalter* (Princeton, 1932), sig. F3^v. Art historians do not agree as to whether the illustrations of the Utrecht Psalter are original Carolingian inventions or copies of a lost Early Christian examplar. See Meyer Schapiro, *Words and Pictures: On the Literal and the Symbolic in the Illustration of a Text* (The Hague and Paris: Mouton, 1973), p. 14.

8. Margaret Rickert, *Painting in Britain: The Middle Ages*, Pelican History of Art, 5 (Baltimore: Penguin, 1954), pp. 6-7, 45-46, and Index entry under "Utrecht Psalter."

9. F. P. Pickering, *Literature and Art in the Middle Ages* (Coral Gables: Univ. of Miami Press, 1970), pp. 230-34, and James Marrow, *Passion Iconography in Northern European Art of the Late Middle Ages and Early Renaissance* (Kortrijk, Belgium: Van Ghemmert, 1979), Introduction, p. 5.

10. See Merle Fifield, "The Arena Theatres in Vienna Codices 2535 and 2536," *Comparative Drama*, 2 (1968-69), 259-82.

11. See, for example, "*Deposuit potentes de sede*" ("He hath put down the mighty from their seat," Luke 1.52), and "*Qui se exaltat, humiliabitur*" ("every one that exalteth himself shall be humbled," Luke 14.11 and 18.14), cited at ll. 2094a and 2107a.

12. For similar instances of textual citations relating to the characterization of particular Virtues and Vices in the play, see "*Cum jejunasset quadraginta diebus*" ("when he had fasted forty days," Matthew 4.2), cited at l. 2276a in relation to Abstinence's confounding Gluttony and wanton diet with the bread of the Sacrament, and "*Nunc lege, nunc ora, nunc disce, nunque labora*" ("Read now, pray now, learn now, and work now"), cited at l. 2364a to support the manner in which Busyness or Industriousness confutes Sloth with images of "honeste occupacioun."

13. Other textual citations bearing upon the desertion of Mankind in his covetous old age include "*Et sic relinquent alienis divitias suas*" ("And they [the foolish] shall leave their riches to strangers," Psalm 48.11 [49.10]), "*Non descendet cum illo gloria eius*" ("nor shall his glory descend with him," Psalm 48.18 [49.17]), "*Avarus nunquam replebitur pecunia*" ("He who loves money will never be satiated with money," based on Ecclesiastes 5.9-10), and others. See ll. 2599a-2638a, 2985a.

14. Other such homiletic citations reflecting on the correctness of

God's judgment include *"Non omne qui dicit 'Domine, Domine' intrabit regnum caelorum"* ("Not every one that saith to me, Lord, Lord, shall enter into the kingdom of heaven," Matthew 7.21), *"O Pater misericordiarum et Deus totius consolationis"* ("the Father of mercies and the God of all comfort," 2 Corinthians 1.3-4), and *"Quoniam veritatem dilexisti"* ("For . . . thou hast loved truth," see Psalm 50.8 [51.6]). See ll. 3167a, 3313a, and 3252a.

15. Jacob Bennett, "The 'Castle of Perseverance': Redactions, Place, and Date," *Mediaeval Studies*, 24 (1962), 141-52; but cf. Mark Eccles, ed., *The Macro Plays*, EETS, 262 (London, 1969), pp. xvii-xviii, who concludes that, apart from the banns, one author could have written the rest of the play. The substitution of the four daughters of God for the Virgin Mary in the scene of judgment might be facilitated by the iconographic tradition in which the kissing of Righteousness and Peace was based upon familiar representation of the Visitation of the Virgin by Elizabeth; see DeWald, *The Stuttgart Psalter*, fol. 100^v and commentary. On the literary tradition of the four daughters, see Rosamond Tuve, *Allegorical Imagery: Some Mediaeval Books and their Posterity* (Princeton: Princeton Univ. Press, 1966), p. 67n., and Samuel C. Chew, *The Virtues Reconciled: An Iconographical Study* (Toronto: Univ. of Toronto Press, 1947), esp. chap. II.

16. Moshé Lazar, ed., *Le Jugement Dernier (Lo Jutgamen General): Drame Provençal du XVe siècle* (Paris: Editions Klincksieck, 1971), and DeWald, *The Stuttgart Psalter*, fol. 100^v and commentary.

17. Gordon Kipling, a chapter of a manuscript in preparation for publication on "The Medieval Civic Triumph," Chapter IV, "Third Advent." See also Thomas P. Campbell, "Eschatology and the Nativity in English Mystery Plays," *American Benedictine Review*, 27 (1976), 297-320, and Patrick Cowley, *Advent: Its Liturgical Significance* (London: Faith Press, 1960).

18. DeWald, *The Stuttgart Psalter*, fol. 100^v and commentary.

19. See Bevington, ed., *Medieval Drama*, p. 258.

20. *The Les Très Riches Heures of Jean, Duke of Berry*, Musée Condé, Chantilly, introd. Jean Longnon and Raymond Cazelles (New York: Braziller, 1969), fol. 25^v.

21. Caiger-Smith, *English Medieval Mural Paintings*, pp. 45-49 and pl. XVII, showing a mural of the Three Living and Three Dead Kings from Longthorpe Tower, Northants., c. 1330.

22. For the Bosch, see Walter Gibson, *Hieronymus Bosch* (New York and Washington: Praeger, 1973), pp. 42-47, figs. 31-32. Gibson suggests that Bosch may have been illustrating a proposition in this painting, as exemplified in the passage from Matthew 6.21, "For where your treasure is, there will your heart be also," and in the legend commonly cited in medieval sermons about the miser whose heart is found buried in his strongbox after his unregenerate death. The depiction of "The Deathbed

of Richard Whittington" is from the Mercers' Company, London, MS. "Ordinances of Whittington's Hospital"; see F. R. H. Du Boulay, *An Age of Ambition: English Society in the Late Middle Ages* (New York: Viking, 1970), p. 150.

23. T. W. Craik, *The Tudor Interlude: Stage, Costume, and Acting* (Leicester: Leicester Univ. Press, 1958), chaps. III and IV, and David Bevington, *From "Mankind" to Marlowe* (Cambridge: Harvard Univ. Press, 1962), pp. 48-85.

24. The Bosch *Tabletop* is reproduced in Gibson, *Bosch*, pp. 32-34, fig. 22. For Trotton, see Tristram, *English Wall Painting of the Fourteenth Century*, p. 259, and Caiger-Smith, *English Medieval Mural Paintings*, pl. XVIII. The Deadly Sins are partly defaced.

25. Natalie Crohn Schmitt, "Was There a Medieval Theatre in the Round?" *Theatre Notebook*, 23 (1968-69), 130-42, argues that the color symbolism may owe something to *Le Chasteau d'Amour*, in which the castle of the Virgin itself is painted in white, green, blue, and red, signifying respectively the pure heart of Our Lady, her truth, her hope, and her love, though it must be observed that black is hardly a substitute for blue. Cf. Chew, *The Virtues Reconciled*, pp. 44-49. On color symbolism in the early drama, see Craik, *The Tudor Interlude*, chaps. III and IV, and M. Channing Linthicum, *Costume in the Drama of Shakespeare and His Contemporaries* (1936; rpt. New York: Russell and Russell, 1963), chap. II.

26. Millard Meiss, *French Painting in the Time of Jean de Berry: The Limbourgs and Their Contemporaries* (New York: Braziller, 1974), Text Volume, p. 84, and Illustrations Volume, fig. 304, lower right. The illustration in question is derived from a *Bible Moralisée*, Paris, Bibliothèque Nationale MS. fr. 166, painted by Paul and Jean de Limbourg. Their model was MS. fr. 167, an earlier *Bible Moralisée*, but in the case of this specific image, as Meiss observes, they depart entirely from their model.

27. *Encyclopedia of World Art* (New York: McGraw-Hill, 1967), XIII, 812-15; see also E. H. Gombrich, *Symbolic Images* (London and New York: Phaidon, 1972), fig. 141, showing symmetrically balanced trees of Virtues and Vices.

28. *Encyclopedia of World Art*, XIII, pl. 345; see also Gombrich, *Symbolic Images*, fig. 146, showing the armed conflict of Pudicitia and Libido.

29. Tuve, *Allegorical Imagery*, figs. 14-17, pp. 71-76.

30. Adolf Katzenellenbogen, *Allegories of the Virtues and Vices in Mediaeval Art*, trans. Alan J. P. Crick (1939; rpt. New York: Norton, 1964), p. 55.

31. Morton W. Bloomfield, *The Seven Deadly Sins* (1952; rpt. East Lansing: Michigan State Univ. Press, 1967), pp. 61-66.

32. Katzenellenbogen, *Allegories of the Virtues and Vices, passim*.

33. See, for example, Gertrud Schiller, *Iconography of Christian Art*,

trans. Janet Seligman (Greenwich, Conn.: New York Graphic Society, 1971-72), II, 139, and fig. 452, showing an illustration (c. 1271) of Misericordia and two other Virtues hammering the nails in the Crucifixion.

34. *De vita contemplativa*, III, 19 (Migne, *PL*, LIX, 502), quoted in Katzenellenbogen, *Allegories of the Virtues and Vices*, p. 55.

35. Valenciennes Passion, Paris, Bibliothèque Nationale, MS. Fr. 12536.

36. See illustration by Geoffroy Dumoustier, *The Last Judgment with the Seven Works of Mercy and Lazarus and the Rich Man*, c. 1530-40, frontispiece to the *Cartulaire de l'Hospice Général de Rouen dit Cartulaire de Saint Maclou* (Rouen), illustrated in Harbison, *The Last Judgment*, fig. 53.

37. Tuve, *Allegorical Imagery*, fig. 20, pp. 100-01.

38. Bloomfield, *The Seven Deadly Sins*, p. 104.

39. Gibson, *Bosch*, p. 34, fig. 24.

40. This is the diptych of the Last Judgment in the Metropolitan Museum of Art in New York; see previous chapter.

41. See for example the various illustrations under "Tod" in *Lexikon der Christlichen Ikonographie*, ed. Engelbert Kirschbaum (Rome: Herder, 1968-76), IV, 327-32. See also Merle Fifield, "The Assault on the *Castle of Perseverance*—The Tradition and the Figure," *Ball State University Forum*, 16, no. 4 (1975), 16-26.

42. Elisabeth Dhanens, *Van Eyck: The Ghent Altarpiece* (London: Penguin, 1973), pp. 75-80.

43. *Les Très Riches Heures of Jean, Duke of Berry*, fol. 64ᵛ.

44. On the controversy as to the physical layout of the theater, whether it was entirely in the "round," whether the ditch mentioned in the staging diagram was around the entire playing area or simply around the castle (as seems more likely), see Richard Southern, *The Medieval Theatre in the Round* (London: Faber and Faber, 1957); Merle Fifield, "The Arena Theatres in Vienna Codices 2535 and 2536," pp. 259-82; Schmitt, "Was There a Medieval Theatre in the Round?" *passim*; and Eccles, ed., *The Macro Plays*, pp. xxi-xxiv.

45. Barbara H. Jaye, "Arena Staging and the Boethian Universe," paper presented at the Seventeenth International Congress on Medieval Studies, Western Michigan University, Kalamazoo, May 1982. See Chapter I above for a discussion of the connection between world and judgment in the visual arts.

46. Lilian M. C. Randall, *Images in the Margins of Gothic Manuscripts* (Berkeley and Los Angeles: Univ. of California Press, 1966), p. 75, fig. 96; *The Peterborough Psalter*, ed. Lucy Freeman Sandler (London: Harvey Miller, 1974), p. 31.

47. Katzenellenbogen, *Allegories of the Virtues and Vices*, figs. 46-47. The illustrations are from Hildegard of Bingen's *Liber Scivias* (c. 1175).

VI

"TO PUT US IN REMEMBRANCE": THE PROTESTANT TRANSFORMATION OF IMAGES OF JUDGMENT

Huston Diehl

The history of iconoclasm in Northern Europe in the early Protestant period is complex, and not all Protestants indeed recommended the physical destruction of all the sacred images inherited from the Roman Catholic Church. In England, to be sure, iconoclasm was more severe than in certain continental regions (e.g., Scandinavia) that had adopted the "new religion"; everywhere Protestants were agreed upon the question of veneration to images, which they decried as thoroughly idolatrous. Yet traditional icons of judgment do not disappear in the New Protestant art even in England in spite of polemics against religious images, ordinances which prohibit image worship, and violent outbursts of iconoclasm. These images are not repressed by the Reformers; instead, they are transformed and reinterpreted according to the tenets of the new Protestant faith. The images persist, in other words, but their function changes. They cannot be read in the same way as the images of judgment in medieval art.[1]

Conventional images of Last Judgment, like other sacred images in Protestant art, increasingly occur in emblematic or allegorical pictures of the sixteenth century. Craig Harbison documents this phenomenon in his comprehensive study of Last Judgment iconography in sixteenth-century northern Europe. He shows how many sixteenth-century pictures from Protestant countries combine images of Last Judgment with personifications of such ideas as fortune, death, and justice and with such emblematic motifs as the wheel of life, the wheel of fortune, the four ages of man, the king's scepter and the peasant's spade, and a putto blowing bubbles.[2] This combination of icons of judgment with icons of fortune, earthly existence, and *vanitas* expresses the Christian belief that the transient and unstable human world will come to an end on Judgment Day and reinforces the connection between how man lives his life in this world and the judgment he receives at doomsday.

Pictures such as these that feature allegorical images of *vanitas* or fortune alongside divine images of Christ sitting in judgment or souls rising from their graves at Judgment Day call attention to their man-made nature and thus prevent the viewer from believing them to be efficacious or to have a mystical function. They therefore apparently did not elicit the opposition of those Protestant theologians who forbade images that they believed would inspire idolatry. These pictures function instead as "obvious fictions"; they render sacred events in a self-consciously artificial way and thus satisfy Protestant concerns that the visual image not be confused with the divine thing it signifies. In these allegorical depictions of Last Judgment, sign and thing remain clearly separate. This tendency to transform sacred images of the Middle Ages into allegorical images—images that are obvious fictions and therefore cannot be construed as efficacious or idolatrous—is explicitly sanctioned by Protestant writers in the seventeenth century. Sir Thomas Browne, for example, attacks many Catholic and medieval sacred images because they deceive people, leading the ignorant and superstitious to mistake the sign for the thing, but he approves of allegorical images because they "pretend no corporeal representations; nor could the people misconceive the same unto real correspondencies. So though the Cherub carried some apprehension of Divinity, yet was it not conceived to be the shape thereof."[3]

Many depictions of the Last Judgment in sixteenth- and seventeenth-century Protestant art occur in secondary, or inset, scenes that are part of larger representational scenes of contemporary life. These inset scenes frequently take the form of a framed picture decorating a wall or an engraved picture illustrating a book. By so circumscribing sacred images, the artists distance their viewers from the scene, call attention to the fact that the scene is a man-made representation of a sacred event, and prevent the viewer from believing the image efficacious. Furthermore, because these judgment scenes are juxtaposed to scenes that mirror the real world of the audience, they encourage the viewer to connect the way men live on this earth with divine judgment, the here with the hereafter. These inset scenes thus function as signs that remind the viewer of the Christian belief in a final divine judgment. The aesthetic experience which these pictures create, then, is in line with reformed theology, for the Protestant theologians approve of sacred images that serve only as "memorials unto men, and a remembrance of the testament wherewith God is served in the Spirit," "as laymen's books to remind us of heavenly things," and "to put us in remembrance that there is a Father in heaven," even while the theologians condemn images that inspire worship, idolatry, or superstition. According to the Reformers, images may, quite appropriately, serve as "commemorative aids."[4]

St. Jerome in his Study, a painting attributed to Jan Massys and dated 1535, illustrates this use of the inset scene of Last Judgment (fig. 23). In it Jerome sits at his desk, points to a death's head, and meditates on an illustration of the Last Judgment in his Bible. He is a model of the Christian man, "thinking on his end." The illustration of the Last Judgment and the skull, itself a traditional icon of death that recurs in pictures of Last Judgment, functions as "a remembrance" for both Jerome and the audience. The images call to mind the prophecy of doomsday and encourage the viewer to meditate on death. Because this picture focuses on an individualized human figure, alone with the Scripture, who interprets visible images as signs of death and judgment, it teaches the viewer how to see the image of the Last Judgment in Protestant terms. As a visible sign of a spiritual truth that cannot be seen, the Last Judgment illustration reminds the individual viewer of God's Word without any pretense of embodying the divine spirit. This picture suggests that the fact of the Last Judgment must be accepted on faith, its significance internalized.

Sometimes these Last Judgment inset scenes occur in pictures that seem wholly secular. The central focus of the *Meeting of the Regensburg Town Council* (c.1535) is a secular hall with the councilmen of Regensburg in session (fig. 24). The artist of this engraving seems primarily interested in recording the proceedings of this municipal body. On the wall in the upper right hand corner, however, hangs a framed picture of the Last Judgment. The presence of this small picture calls to mind—for the men in the room and the viewer alike—the Christian prophecy of a final, divine law, and it thus associates the councilmen and the secular law with the divine judge and the sacred law of Christian doctrine. As a small framed picture in a realistic setting, this inset scene does not inspire worship or superstitious belief. Rather, the scene introduces the idea of divine justice into the world of human law. Harbison documents the presence of Last Judgment pictures in many other secular buildings in sixteenth-century Northern Europe, including Town hall chapels, council chambers, the head of stairs leading to the judgment chamber, and murals above the judge's seat in courtrooms.[5] The presence of Last Judgment pictures in secular courts is especially interesting, for it would alter the way the viewer sees the human magistrates in the secular courtroom: these figures become, for the viewer, imperfect images of the divine judge, and the Last Judgment scene would remind the observer that their authority derives from God.

Inset scenes of the Last Judgment in Protestant art may

also reflect ironically on the foreground scene of contemporary life. In an engraving by Jan Sadeler (after Dirck Barendz), titled *Mankind before the Last Judgment* (c.1581), the presence of a background scene of Last Judgment qualifies the foreground scene which depicts men and women at a banquet table, engaged in eating, drinking, and sexual flirtation (fig. 25). The apparent pleasures of the banquet are undercut by the background scene of judgment, suggesting that how men lead their lives in this world has a direct relationship to how men are judged in the next world. Like medieval depictions of Last Judgment that recapitulate all of human history, these pictures emphasize the relation between human history and divine judgment. At the same time, they invert the emphasis of the earlier renderings of Doomsday, focusing on human acts in this world instead of the final divine judgment of those acts and only alluding to, or anticipating, the Last Judgment.

Because the inset scene calls to mind the final reckoning, it influences the way the viewer sees the human activity in the foreground. Juxtaposed to a portrayal of final damnation and salvation, the banqueters seem indulgent, narcissistic, foolish, and unaware. Unlike St. Jerome, they do not see the scene of judgment and, forgetful of the divine, they do not consider their end. This artist thus uses an image of judgment for ethical purposes. The engraving assumes that when the viewer sees the Last Judgment scene, he will realize, and seek to amend, his own sinfulness, but when he forgets—as the banqueters do—he is doomed.

In all three of these examples, the presence of a Last Judgment inset scene alters the way a viewer sees the representational world of the picture, and, by extension, his own world. The pictures encourage man to find in the visible world remembrances of the divine. In *A Lady Weighing Pearls* (c. 1660), Jan Vermeer uses a Last Judgment scene to show how even the ordinary objects of everyday existence may serve to remind man of the spiritual world (fig. 26). In this Dutch genre painting, a woman in contemporary dress weighs pearls on a kitchen balance in a quiet, domestic setting. Behind her, on the wall, hangs a framed picture of the Last

Judgment. When the viewer discovers the framed picture and remembers the prophecy of judgment, he sees that the ordinary objects of this domestic scene are also signs which call to mind the final reckoning. The Last Judgment picture alters the way the viewer sees the literal images of this representational scene, shocking him into the realization that everything in the visible world is potentially a sign of the spiritual, a remembrance of God's higher order. As signs, clearly distinct from the spiritual truths they signify, the visual images of Vermeer's painting satisfy the Protestant criteria for "unabused" or acceptable images. Unlike the "abused" images which the Reformers forbid because they "become ends in themselves," inspire worship, or externalize religion "to please man,"[6] the balance, pearls, and the framed picture in this painting represent heavenly things "under the figure of earthly things, that is to say, under signs familiarly known unto us." Vermeer's techniques thus reflect the Protestant belief that the visible world consists of shadows and signs that man must recognize and interpret. "Our bountiful and gracious Lord," the Protestant theologian Henry Bullinger writes, "did covertly and darkly, nay rather, evidently and notably, set before us to view the kingdom of God in parables or dark speeches; even so by signs it pleased him to lay before our eyes, after a sort, the very same thing, and to point out the same unto us, as it were painted in a table, to renew it afresh, and by lively representation to maintain the remembrance of the same among us."[7] When they reject the Catholic belief in the efficacious image and transubstantiation, Protestants such as Bullinger thus imagine a visible world, filled with signs that are created by God to lead men to spiritual truths. In this Protestant conception of the world, the divine is not present in images but rather is figured forth by images.

Since images may be signs—visible reminders of what is never visible and can, according to Protestant belief, never be adequately expressed—traditional icons of Last Judgment may serve as signs of divine judgment even when they are isolated from scenes of doomsday and are, like the balance and pearls in Vermeer's painting, depicted as part of the representational world. Protestant emblem books frequently present traditional images of Last Judgment like the balance, the judge, and the court of law as isolated images of the human world, then interpret them as signs that call to mind God's judgment. In George's Wither's *Emblemes*, for example, a picture of a balance represents "doome-eternal," according to the accompanying verse (fig. 27). Wither clearly views this visual image as a sign that calls to mind the Last Judgment through analogy, and only imperfectly. He writes of this image, "I, by the *Figure* of this even-scale/ May *partly* show" that God judges the souls of men (italics mine). In his emblem book Francis Quarles similarly uses secular judges and a court of law to represent the idea of divine judgment. In one emblem a personified figure of Justice stands in a court of law with a human figure; in the accompanying epigram, Quarles uses the secular images of the human courtroom to examine questions of divine law and judgment.[8] The viewer of these emblems is asked to look at representational images from his world like the balance or the court of law and to interpret them as signs of God's promised judgment. As in the Vermeer painting, these images function then as remembrances. They call to mind divine truths even as they prevent the viewer from confusing the image with the thing of which it is a sign. Based as they are on analogy rather than identity, these images thus satisfy Protestant criteria for "unabused" images: they reveal resemblances between the familiar human and invisible spiritual worlds but they do not tempt the viewer to believe that the image embodies—or mystically "is"—the divine.

When, in Reformation England, the Protestants began to attack the medieval cycle drama with its culminating play of Last Judgment, their arguments were similar to the arguments they used against the "abused" images of medieval art. Records of the Diocesan Court of High Commission of 1576, for instance, forbid the playing of "God the Father, God the Sonne, or God the Holie Ghoste or the administration of . . . the Sacramentes . . . or anythinge plaied which tende to the maintenaunce of superstition and idolatrie. . . ."[9]

Although government opposition to the Corpus Christi and Whitsun cycles in England eventually ended the annual performances of the plays in the latter part of the sixteenth century, dramatic use of the iconography of judgment did not disappear altogether from the stage. As in the visual arts images of Last Judgment continue to occur in the secular drama of the English Renaissance, but their nature and function change. No longer used to portray the actual judgment day, these images function in Renaissance drama as signs that remind the audience of divine justice, final judgment, and the connection between life in this world and judgment in the next.

A detailed description by an Englishman named R. Willis of a lost morality play written around 1570 reveals that images of Last Judgment appear on the early Protestant stage, as in sixteenth-century Protestant art, in an allegorical context. Willis gives a detailed account of this play, called *The Cradle of Security*, which he had seen in his youth. Focusing on a king who is rocked to sleep in a cradle by three ladies (Pride, Covetousness, and Luxury) only to awaken to discover a "swine's snout upon his face," this play ends with the entrance of "two old men," one in blue with a mace, the other in red with a "drawn sword." The old man with a mace strikes "a fearful blow upon the cradle" where the king lies, whereupon the latter is then "carried away by wicked spirits." In his discussion Willis gives an explicit, straightforward interpretation of this ending: "the Prince," he writes, "did personate in the morall, the wicked of the world . . . the two old men, the end of the world, and the last judgment."[10] The divine events of the end of the world and the Last Judgment thus become personified in this morality play as old men carrying a mace and a sword. Other traditional medieval images of Doomsday—e.g., the sword of justice conventionally carried by Michael, the awakening of the dead, and the demons who carry the wicked down to hell—function here as part of the allegorical narrative alongside such allegorical motifs as the cradle of false worldly security, the sleep of the slothful, and the bestiality of the sinner. Like the allegorical depictions of Last Judgment in sixteenth-century Protestant art, this play connects the way men live in this world with the judgment they receive in the next and presents the dramatic enactment of judgment as an obvious fiction, not to be confused with the actual event. The two old men function as signs that remind the audience of the promised judgment without pretending to present literally that judgment.

A number of existing mid-sixteenth-century morality plays similarly transform medieval images of Last Judgment into allegorical images that act as signs, reminding the audience of doomsday. In a group of plays known as the homiletic tragedies,[11] allegorical figures with names such as "God's Judgment," "God's Pleasure," "God's Visitation," "Justice," "Severity," and "Authority" come on stage, like the two old men in *The Cradle of Security*, and judge the behavior of the characters, often in a final scene of trial. Although these figures act as judges, bestowing rewards and punishments and delivering sentences of eternal salvation and damnation, they clearly do not impersonate Christ the Judge, but rather function as signs reminding the audience of the divine acts of judgment. Because they are so clearly signs, they apparently do not risk Protestant condemnation. These judges divide the virtuous from the erring, praise and reward the good for their devout lives, and condemn and punish the wicked for their sinful lives. In the sentences they pronounce and the judgments they render, these figures refer to doomsday and eternal life, promising "eternal fire," "shame and confusion," "sorrow and care forever" for the wicked (*The Longer Thou Livest*, ll. 1849, 1807, 1822), while offering the virtuous "a greater crown" (*Like Will to Like*, p. 341).

Even though these acts of judgment are presented in an allegorical manner, they occur in scenes that resemble, in design and visual detail, the Last Judgment plays of the great civic cycles (see Chapter IV, above). As in the earlier cycle plays, balance and symmetry predominate in these allegorical scenes of judgment. For each character who has sinned, disobeyed, and misbehaved, a second opposing character of virtue usually exists to offset and balance the wicked. The punishment of Worldly Man in *Enough is as Good as a Feast*, for example, is balanced by the reward of Heavenly Man; the fate of Lust in *The Trial of Treasure* by that of Just; the evil acts of Nicholas Newfangle in *Like Will to Like* by the pious actions of Virtuous Living; the presence of Greediness in *The Tide Tarrieth No Man* by that of Faithful Few. Similarly, the central judging figure associated with heaven is usually balanced by an antagonist of lesser power, associated with hell. While God's Pleasure in *Like Will to Like* pronounces sentences on the human figures, a devil appears to claim Nicholas Newfangle; likewise, God's Judgment in *The Longer Thou Livest* is opposed by Confusion, Justice in *Appius and Virginia* by the vice Haphazard, and Godly Admonition in *All For Money* by Satan. In contrast to the medieval Catholic depictions of Last Judgment, however, these judges are not balanced between intercessors like Mary and John the Baptist. Instead, these plays reflect the new Protestant faith which rejected the idea of intermediaries between man and his God. If the judging figure is accompanied by secondary figures of good, they are personifications of such internal qualities as "Conscience," "Honour," "Humilitie," and "Charitie" rather than Christian saints or other medieval intercessors.

Like the Doomsday plays in the medieval cycles, these final scenes of trial and judgment also employ vertical movement to differentiate the good and the bad. While the virtuous characters remain standing and frequently embrace the judging figure, the wicked characters often fall down and sometimes are even carried down to a symbolic hell on the backs of demons. In *The Longer Thou Livest*, the erring Moros awakes to discover "I cannot stand on my feet for quaking" and falls down; he then gets up only to face God's Judgment, who in a dramatic confrontation strikes him "with this sword of vengeance," causing him to fall down again (ll. 1791-1826). Similarly, in *Like Will to Like* Nicholas Newfangle falls down when he is beaten by "the judge" Severity, then rides off to hell on the devil's back (l. 350), and in *Enough is as Good as a Feast*, Worldly Man "*Fall[s] down*" and Satan arrives to claim him ("O, O, O, O, all is mine, all is mine"), bearing *"him out upon his back"* (ll. 1403, 1428, 1471). In all these scenes, physical falls on stage visually indicate the final, spiritual damnation of the wicked.

Visual images that traditionally appear in medieval depictions of Last Judgment also appear in these moralities' final judgment scenes. There are crowns for the saved, ropes and halters for the damned, a throne of victory, a hell mouth, and tormenting demons. On the other hand, the Protestant faith has caused some subtle changes in these symbolic depictions of Last Judgment. It is interesting to note, for instance, that the sword carried by the archangel Michael in medieval Last Judgment pictures is used in these morality plays not as an attribute of Michael, but as an attribute of a more general personified figure of justice. God's Judgment strikes Moros with a sword (*The Longer Thou Livest*, l. 1791), and Honour gives Virtuous Living a Sword "as a token of victory" (*Like Will to Like*, p. 342). Similarly, there is no direct presentation of the parable of the wise and foolish virgins, but the burning lamps of the wise virgins appear, transformed into an allegorical attribute of Conscience (*Appius and Virginia*, pp. 20-21).

The theme of watchfulness at the heart of this parable also finds symbolic expression in *The Longer Thou Livest* when the sinful Moros wakes from sleep to confront his judge. In an explicit allusion to the scriptural warning in Mark 13.35, "Watch therefore, for ye know not when the master of the house will come . . . if he come suddenly, he should find you sleeping,"[12] Moros wonders aloud when God's Judgment arrives and condemns him, "Am I asleep, in a dream, or in a trance? Ever methinks that I should be waking" (ll. 1823-24). Later, when God's Judgment orders his splendid worldly clothes removed and replaces them with a fool's habit, Moros again connects his past life of sin with sleep, recognizing that he has, in a sense, been asleep: "where is my goodly gear?/ I see well that I was asleep indeed" (ll. 1839-40). The state of sinfulness is here likened to sleep, the sinner's past to a vague and troubled dream, and the moment of judgment to a sudden wakening. The scriptural metaphor of sleeping and waking, literalized here on stage, appeals to Protestant writers in part because it emphasizes the faithful person's need for constant vigilance in a dangerous world racked by human folly and evil. The Christian belief that the second coming of Christ will occur suddenly, without warning, and in an "evil time" (Ecclesiastes 9.12; see also Matthew 24.36-42) thus focuses attention on the way a person lives in this world and on the general unworthiness of mankind, both important Protestant concerns. The motif of sleeping and waking, itself a biblical metaphor for a spiritual condition, thus serves to remind the audience of an event in sacred history without pretending to enact that event.

Since the actual figure of Christ is, of course, forbidden on the Protestant stage, there is in these plays no direct portrayal of Christ's wounds and blood. Nevertheless, in one play, *The Longer Thou Livest*, a cup of wine clearly functions as a sign of the Eucharist and thus reminds the audience of Christ's sacrifice. In that play the wicked Moros, facing death and afraid, asks for a cup of wine: "It was but a qualm came over my heart;/ I lack nothing but a cup of good wine." God's Judgment refuses this unrepentant man wine, however, explicitly connecting the wine with the blood of Christ: "Indurate wretches can not convert," he admonishes, "But die in their filthiness like swine" (ll. 1803-06). Without violating Protestant prohibitions against impersonating Christ, this play thus retains the Last Judgment image of Christ's sacrificial blood by transforming it into a glass of wine that functions as a sign of the Eucharist. It is perhaps significant that the substitution of a glass of wine for the blood of Christ may further reflect a Protestant reinterpretation of the Eucharistic wine. Whereas Catholic theologians teach that the wine is mystically transformed into the blood of Christ— transubstantiated—some Protestant theologians argued instead that the wine is a sign of Christ's sacrifice, a remembrance of the blood that Christ shed, though the Church of England eventually arrived at a compromise position in the Thirty-Nine Articles.[13]

By allegorizing images of judgment, these moralities avoid any charge of idolatry or superstition. Christ is not included in the *dramatis personae*, and no re-enactment of the actual day of judgment takes place. Nevertheless, these plays remind the audience, through traditional icons of judgment, of the Christian belief in a Judgment day and its ethical implications. Swords and crowns and the action of falling down function as visible signs that "put us in remembrance" of what we cannot see.

It is thus not hard to demonstrate how the mid-sixteenth-century moralities adapt and allegorize images of judgment from medieval art and drama. But what about the mature plays of the Renaissance public stage? Do any of these plays retain and use images of the Last Judgment? Twentieth-century readers of Renaissance drama will perhaps be more reluctant to accept the presence of Last Judgment icons in the secular plays of the public theater. Indeed, these plays differ in both method and effect from the morality plays that preceded them, and we would not expect to find in them either the cycle plays' direct presentation of sacred images or the morality plays' allegorical images of judgment. Nonetheless, we can consider the possibility that Last Judgment images survive in the representational and secular drama of the Renaissance public theater, and that a further transformation of this rich iconographic tradition occurred around 1600.

The remaining part of this chapter will draw upon four Jacobean plays—Marston's *The Malcontent* (1603), Shakespeare's *Measure for Measure* (1604), Tourneur's *The Atheist's Tragedy* (1608), and Webster's *The Devil's Law-Case* (1619)—to examine the premise that such a transformation occurred and to explore the nature of such a change, both in the different methods of presentation used by the dramatist and the different methods of interpretation required by the viewer.

Although these four plays are not usually considered together, they do share some important characteristics. Written early in the seventeenth century, all four plays mix tragic and comic elements in ways that do not conform to traditional rules for tragedy, comedy, or Italian tragicomedy. Because their unconventional forms defy usual definitions and generic expectations, many scholars refer to these plays as

191

"problem" plays. Harriet Hawkins, for example, argues that "the first half of *Measure for Measure* . . . is exclusively tragic, while the second half is a network of comic intrigues. And these two dramatic modes of presentation admit no more reconciliation than the original conflict." R. W. Ingram, for another, insists that "*The Malcontent* is as much a problem play as Shakespeare's *Measure for Measure*" because it "plunders all the popular genres of the day." Likewise, Robert Ornstein argues that the tragic pattern of *The Atheist's Tragedy* is undercut by Tourneur's moral intention, while R. J. Kaufmann contends that that play's moral statement is undercut by the playwright's "covert sympathy" for the villain. And Lee Bliss says of the *Devil's Law-Case*: "Comic types and comic expectations repeatedly qualify our sympathetic involvement and deflect us from serious ethical concerns."[14]

In addition all four plays present a dark and confusing world in which disguises, illusions, and deceptions predominate; all explore questions of law, revenge, justice, and judgment; and all reflect a Protestant world view, with a profound sense of man's fundamental unworthiness. These similarities may not be coincidental, for all four plays use traditional images of Last Judgment in their examination of human law, and those familiar images, like judgment icons in Protestant art, function as signs in a representational world, reminding the audience of doomsday. The appearance of conventional images of judgment in Jacobean plays that feature individualized human characters and a world that resembles the audience's own alters the way the viewer sees and interprets that world, encouraging him to interpret physical things as potential signs, remembrances of the divine. Elements of dramatic and artistic renderings of the Last Judgment—in particular, symmetry, recapitulation, and images with culturally-determined meaning—likewise suggest that the mythic pattern of final divine judgment informs all four of these Jacobean plays.

Each of these plays ends in a climactic scene of judgment and revelation in which characters thought to be dead return alive, and each presents in the final scene a cluster of visual images traditionally associated with the Last Judgment. In *The Malcontent*[15] this final scene takes the form of an allegorical masque presented to the members of the court. At the sound of cornets the victims of the usurper Mendoza, all believed to be dead or exiled, enter as ghosts of dukes, led by the classical god Mercury:

> *Mercury.* Cyllenian Mercury, the god of ghosts,
> From gloomy shades that spread the lower coasts,
> Calls four high-faméd Genoan Dukes to come,
> And make this presence their Elysium.
>
> (V.vi.56-59)

The divine messenger of classical mythology, and therefore an intercessor between man and gods, the figure of Mercury sometimes represents, or serves as an analogy to, Christ in Renaissance allegories and emblem books.[16] In this masque, he is called upon to be the erring Aurelia's "advocate" and "lawyer," and thus serves in another capacity that is analogous to Christ, who, according to Calvin, "must appear in court on our behalf, and stand surety for us in judgment."[17]

The villain Mendoza falls "prostrate" at the feet of his victims who tell him he cannot expect "grace" because his condition is one of "gracelessness" (V.vi.126, 127). The dukes "unmask," revealing their identities to the surprised courtiers who had thought them dead, and whom they address as long-estranged "spirits": "You o'er-joyed spirits, wipe your long-wet eyes" (V.vi.159). And Mendoza, realizing that his evil deeds have been exposed, wonders, like Moros in *The Longer Thou Livest*, whether he has just awakened from a long sleep: "What strange delusions mock/ Our senses? Do I dream? or have I dreamt/ This two days' space? Where am I?" (V.vi.117-19).

In this final scene, then, apparently dead men are, through the symbolic action of a masque, "resurrected"; they are led to "Elysium" by a figure of intercession who is called upon to act as a legal representation for a repentant sinner; an evil man falls down, is denied grace, and realizes that his life resembles sleep; and disguised characters reveal their true identities, greeting as spirits loved ones from whom they had been separated by apparent death. Through these motifs of resurrection, revelation, punishment, and reward, the restoration of human justice at the conclusion of this play calls to mind the Christian belief in a final divine judgment. Since these motifs occur in an allegorical masque, they function not as a literal depiction of the Last Judgment, but as obvious fictions, reminding the audience of doomsday without enacting the actual sacred event. They thus enable Marston to explore themes of sacred justice, divine revelation, and human redemption without violating Protestant sanctions against representing God on the stage.

In the other three plays, the final scene also uses familiar images of Last Judgment, but in each case these images occur during a formal trial in a human court of law. Being part of the representational world, they function, like the balance and pearls of the Vermeer painting, as signs that require interpretation. Neither sacred nor allegorical images, they nevertheless remind the audience—that is, they *put it in remembrance of*—the Christian Last Judgment and thus affect the way it understands and evaluates the human world represented on the stage. The conclusion of *Measure for Measure*[18] begins at the city gates with two blasts of the trumpet announcing the "Happy return" (V.i.3) of the absent ruler, Vincentio. A court of justice convenes, officials "sit" in judgment, and Vincentio acts as both judge and lawyer, telling Isabella he is "attorneyed at your service" (V.i.385) even as he orders her to prison. Lies, misunderstandings, indirection, and confusion characterize this trial, and nothing is what it seems. Since the audience knows that Vincentio has in fact been present all along, disguised as a friar, enjoying a position of omniscience, and exercising extraordinary powers, it sees the ensuing misunderstandings ironically. Vincentio forces the characters to confront the problematic and illusory nature of their world and the inadequacy of their own ways of interpreting the world, whereupon he reveals the truth in a series of startling unveilings.

Just as the characters begin to feel hopelessly entangled in a web of lies, deceptions, and false appearances and the audience begins to wonder whether the confusion will ever end, Vincentio masterfully shows how a single truth exists beneath the multiple illusions. He reveals that the veiled woman whom Claudio denies knowing is in fact Mariana, the woman Claudio had betrothed and unwittingly bedded; that he himself is the hooded friar who has seen and heard the secrets of the people in Vienna; that Claudio, the man believed to be executed, in fact lives. Through these revelations, erring characters acknowledge their own failings and prepare for their deserved punishments. Although the Duke condemns their flaws and pronounces the dreadful sentences of the law, however, he allows acts of mercy to supersede the law. Through these actions Vincentio—though he is clearly an imperfect man, a flawed ruler of the human world of Vienna—resembles or calls to mind Christ as judge. He is an absent ruler who in fact is present, an all-seeing though unseen figure of power, a father confessor, a ruler who returns to judge his people, an attorney representing an accused, a revealer of the truth, and a figure of justice and mercy. Though they are not divine acts, Vincentio's revelations serve to remind the audience of the promised revelation of truth at Doomsday. "Therefore judge nothing before the time, until the Lord come," writes Paul, "who will lighten things that are hid in darkness, and make the counsels of the hearts manifest: and then shall every man have praise of God" (1 Corinthians 4.5).

Shakespeare uses the traditional images of Last Judgment in this final trial scene to develop the analogy between the human judge Vincentio and the divine Judge. By doing so, he encourages his audience to consider the human law and justice of Vienna—with all its flaws and imperfections—in the context of the divine law and ultimate sacred justice of Christianity. Shakespeare is not interested in depicting the sacred event of Doomsday on the stage, nor is he writing an allegory in which Vincentio symbolizes Christ. Instead, he uses images of Last Judgment in *Measure for Measure* to inform the human acts of this world, putting the audience "in remembrance" of a spiritual realm that the inhabitants of Vienna cannot see and too easily forget.

In the trial scene at the end of *The Atheist's Tragedy*,[19] icons of Last Judgment also function to remind the audience of a spiritual realm that in this play the atheist D'Amville has explicitly denied. When D'Amville arrives at the trial *"with the hearses of his two sons borne after him"* (V.ii.67sd), his despair at the deaths of his sons is heightened because he believes only in the physical. When he cries in anger for "Judgment, judgment" (V.ii.68), he can imagine only secular law. This scene is ironic, however, for what D'Amville cannot see in his world—visible signs of the divine—are everywhere, reminding the audience of an anticipated final judgment, one that D'Amville, in his concern for worldly things, has denied. At the beginning of this trial, judges sit "above" in a "superior court" known as the "Star Chamber" (V.i.118, 120), and in their elevated position on stage, a position linked through language to the heavenly, they may create for the audience a picture reminiscent of the judging Christ seated on a rainbow in the heavenly court, much as sixteenth-century Protestant pictures of secular judgment mirror pictures of Christ the judge.

The action of rising and falling that commonly occurs in traditional portrayals of Last Judgment also occurs in this trial scene. During the trial characters repeatedly ascend and descend. When D'Amville arrives, he joins the judges "above," but when the defendants Charlemont and Castabella enter, he descends in order to question them. The falsely accused defendants accept impending death, triumphantly assert their ultimate victory in God's eyes, and leap up to the scaffold to await their execution. The troubled D'Amville follows them up, but accidentally strikes himself with the axe he intends for Charlemont and "staggers off the scaffold" (V.ii). The audience thus sees the villainous D'Amville, in a trial presided over by judges who sit above the human drama, twice attempting to ascend but ultimately falling to his death as he foolishly tries to play the judge and executioner of a virtuous man. It also watches the faithful Charlemont (who had earlier been proclaimed dead but is now returned to the living) and the virtuous Castabella ascend to the scaffold where, prepared to die, they find themselves miraculously saved. As in depictions of the Last Judgment, then, falling is here connected with death, rising with salvation. Vertical movement seems to function as a sign, suggesting a final, divine judgment that the flawed human trial only shadows.

Other details in this trial scene resemble traditional icons of judgment. The axe which D'Amville uses to kill himself, for example, connects the human trial with divine justice. Like the sword of Michael, the axe is a conventional image of divine judgment and retribution in sixteenth- and seventeenth-century iconology.[20] Although the unintentional, self-inflicted axe blow to the head seems ludicrous as a literal plot device, it contributes to the symbolic scheme of the trial. Inasmuch as the trial shadows an anticipated Last Judgment, D'Amville's literal act of suicide serves as a sign, reminding the audience that atheism, according to Christian belief, is self-destructive and irrational, that the atheist is ultimately damned.

Like the axe, the cup of wine that D'Amville requests serves as a sign of judgment. Before he kills himself, D'Amville admits he is afraid and asks for a cup of wine to calm his nerves. When the cup of wine is brought on stage, however, it terrifies D'Amville who sees blood, not wine, in the cup:

> Why, thou uncharitable knave,
> Dost bring me blood to drink? The very glass
> Looks pale and trembles at it.
> (V.ii.203-05)

Like Moros in the earlier morality play, *The Longer Thou Livest*, D'Amville calls for literal wine, hoping the physical attributes of alcohol will give him courage, but the cup of wine reminds him of blood instead. To audiences familiar with depictions of Last Judgment that feature blood flowing from Christ's wounds into a cup, this wine which D'Amville mistakes for blood would surely serve as a sign of the Eucharist, a reminder of the sacrificial blood of Christ. It thus closely resembles the cup of wine that is denied Moros in the morality play. For evil characters like D'Amville and

Moros, the wine terrifies rather than comforts: having denied Christ, they face judgment without hope of mercy. The cup of wine, in conjunction with other icons of judgment in this trial scene, thus encourages the audience to find in the visible world before it remembrances of the divine. Although the trial is a secular one, presided over by human judges and subject to all the imperfections of human law, it reminds the audience of the divine justice, the divine judge, and the divine law promised at the Last Judgment. Thus reminded of Last Judgment, the audience sees more fully the inadequacies of the human world. D'Amville's worldly desires—ambition, lust, greed, and the ruthless drive for power—are placed in a larger, spiritual context that qualifies and undercuts them.

In *The Devil's Law-Case*[21] two scenes, the first a trial, the second a trial by combat, likewise use images of divine judgment that qualify the acts and motives of the Machiavellian Romelio and his scheming mother Leonora. Although shrewd, ruthless, and calculating, these two characters fail ultimately to satisfy their desires. The play prepares the audience for this failure. While Romelio and Leonora can imagine only the material world and its physical pleasures, the audience is reminded, through visual and verbal allusions to the Last Judgment, of a spiritual realm that counters their values and undermines their apparent dominance and aggressive energy. During the trials, for example, judges enter a "high Court of Honor" (V.vi.28) and "sit" in judgment (IV.ii, V.vi); a "summons" (V.vi.1) is given and "*two tuckets by several trumpets*" are sounded (V.vi.3*sd*); three men believed to be dead appear alive; hidden truths are revealed; and judgments are pronounced. Though the play enacts a secular trial in a human courtroom, these images of judgment, taken together, serve as visible signs, calling up the promise of divine justice. Through these signs, the play examines human acts of evil and repentance, charity, and forgiveness and encourages the audience to think on its end. Perhaps the dominant theme in this play, in fact, is the importance of acting in the world with the knowledge of a final reckoning. The Capuchin repeatedly urges erring characters to remember their end.

As in *Measure for Measure*, confusion characterizes these two court scenes. Three people who are thought to be dead appear at the trial in disguise. Ercole, believed to be dead at the hand of Contarino, observes the courtroom from a closet, "muffled" (IV.ii.*sd*). Contarino, himself believed to be dead at the hand of Ercole, watches the proceedings disguised as a Dane. Neither knows the other lives, and each suffers guilt and remorse for the "death" he thinks he has caused. A third man, Crispiano, who has created a rumor of his own death in order to spy on his wayward son, enters the courtroom disguised as a judge and presides at the hearing. In all three cases the audience knows who these men really are while the other characters, for the most part, are in the dark. Two surgeons who have witnessed Romelio's attempted murder of Contarino and have pretended to go into exile are also present in disguise.

In addition to these false appearances, false accusations and false evidence abound at this trial. Leonora falsely claims her son Romelio is a bastard in order to disinherit him, and Contilupa confirms her claim by falsely asserting that Crispiano, not Leonora's husband, seduced Leonora and fathered Romelio. Once these multiple illusions and deceptions are established, a sense of utter confusion prevails. In the end, however, the truth is discovered through a series of dramatic revelations: the supposed dead men return to the living, the disguised unmask, the liars, confronted with evidence that exposes their falsehoods, admit their lies. A single truth emerges.

When the "dead" men reveal that they live, their life is seen as a divine miracle, their return to the living as a metaphoric resurrection. "Mercy upon me!" exclaims the still-disguised Contarino when Ercole steps forward, "O, that thou art living/ Is mercy indeed!" (IV.ii.563-64). Adds Romelio, "O, sir, you are happily restored to life" (IV.ii.569). Earlier, the survival of Ercole and Contarino was also viewed by the few who witnessed it as a kind of resurrection. "You are preserved beyond natural reason," the Capuchin tells

Ercole, "you were brought dead out o' th' field, the surgeons ready to have embalmed you. . . . You are divinely informed, sir" (II.iv.1-6). Likewise, the surgeon who observes Contarino's revival regards it as a miracle: "The hand of heaven is in't" (III.ii.164).

While neither man actually died, their apparent death and sudden, unexpected return to life remind the characters of a divine miracle, a resurrection, and thus contribute to the audience's sense that the death and rebirth motif developed in the trial scenes functions as a sign. It is surely not coincidental that the Machiavellian Romelio, when he realizes that his villainy has been discovered, responds like Moros at the end of *The Longer thou Livest* and Mendoza at the end of *The Malcontent*, wondering aloud "If I do not dream" (V.vi.27). For Romelio, as for Mendoza and Moros, this final scene of judgment seems like a dream because he has in a metaphoric sense been caught sleeping.

As in depictions of Last Judgment in medieval art and drama, all four of these plays use symmetry, in particular antithetical balance that juxtaposes good and evil characters. In *The Malcontent* the rightful duke Altofronto is balanced at first by the usurping duke Pietro and later by the second usurper Mendoza; the loyal adviser Celso by the amoral, hypocritical sycophant Bilioso; the faithful wife Maria by the adulterous woman Aurelio; and so forth. Likewise, *Measure for Measure* balances an overgenerous but good ruler and a strict but hypocritical ruler (Vincentio and Angelo), honest and corrupt judges (Escalus and Angelo), a nun and a bawd (Isabella and Mistress Overdone), a woman who is married in every respect except the law and a woman who is legally betrothed but unmarried in every other respect (Juliet and Mariana). Even the title of Tourneur's play—*The Atheist's Tragedy; or, the Honest Man's Revenge*—emphasizes the central juxtaposition of the atheist and the Christian man in that play. And in *The Devil's Law-Case* Webster seems especially intent on setting up antitheses. In that play there are good and bad judges, good and bad advisers, good and bad disguises; there are characters motivated by charity opposing characters motivated by malice; there is a chaste maid who seems to be pregnant and a fallen nun who really is pregnant.

Unlike their medieval predecessors, however, these plays do not use such symmetry to express the division of souls into the damned and the saved. Instead, after setting up such oppositions, all of these plays except *The Atheist's Tragedy* break down the distinctions between good and bad. This breakdown of such elaborately constructed symmetry is disorienting; while the audience has learned to distinguish honest from deceitful, loyal from betraying, and chaste from lustful, in the end virtuous and erring alike are grouped together. A series of miraculous conversions unites everyone in *The Malcontent* except Mendoza. Laws that condemn violators to death are not enforced in *Measure for Measure*; instead, erring characters are brought back into the society and are united with the more virtuous who, surprisingly, see themselves as erring, too. All of the villains in *The Devil's Law-Case* are likewise exposed but are not treated with the harshness their acts seem to warrant.

These tragicomic resolutions, allowing as they do for the union of good and bad, have disturbed many modern readers, who argue that the endings of these plays are flawed and dissatisfying, that they violate the integrity of the dramatic action. Poetic justice does not appear to be realized. Although these endings, in their eradication of a carefully built symmetry, violate the audience's expectations, they reflect, in significant ways, Protestant attitudes toward divine judgment, and they thus complete these plays' allusions to the Christian Last Judgment. When it rejected the belief that a person could contribute to his salvation through good deeds, Protestantism emphasized the fundamental unworthiness of all humans. Tainted by original sin, every person was considered by nature sinful, fallen, undeserving, and therefore, under the law, condemned. Protestant thinkers insisted therefore that only God, through his grace and because of his infinite mercy, can intervene and save man. Salvation can result only from divine, not human, action. "For since no perfection can come to us so long as we are clothed in this flesh," writes Calvin, "and the law moreover announces death and judgment to all who do not achieve perfect righteousness in works, it will always have grounds for accusing and condemning us unless, on the contrary, the Lord's mercy counters it, and by continual forgiveness of sins repeatedly acquits us."[22] Protestant Last Judgment art manifests this Reformed theology by dropping altogether the image of psychostasis or the weighing of souls.[23]

It is this relation between fallen man and a God of mercy that these Renaissance playwrights seem interested in exploring. Pietro, Ferenze, and Aurelio err, yet through no act or intention of their own they are, in the end, redeemed, and Marston's play celebrates that redemption. Angelo, who uses the law to condemn another man for the very act he himself also has committed, deserves death according to the law, yet he is forgiven through an act of mercy. And Romelio and Leonora outdo each other in maliciousness and viciousness, yet they too are allowed to live. When the Capuchin tries to prevent them from succeeding in their villainy, he is struck by the impotency of his own action, asserts that human will is corrupt by nature, and calls on heaven:

> O, look upwards rather:
> Their deliverance must come thence. To see how
> heaven
> Can avert man's firmest purpose!
>
> (V.v.14-16)

Webster's play repeatedly shows how "presumptuous and hidden sins" (V.v.21) may pervert man's good intentions, yet it nevertheless concludes with a happy ending that seems to be heavenly ordained. "If I do not dream," says the villain Romelio after he is inexplicably moved to free the Capuchin, "I am happy too" (V.vi.27). The violation of the symmetry these plays establish is thus not a flaw in dramatic plotting, but rather part of the overall design, reinforcing the presence of the judgment images and exploring Protestant ideas of human error and divine mercy.

As in earlier plays that depict the Last Judgment, these Renaissance plays also examine the relation of divine judgment to human history, but they invert the emphasis by focusing on particular individuals and their behavior in this world while alluding, through visual and verbal references, to an anticipated judgment. In their discussion of "recapitulation," David Bevington and Pamela Sheingorn have shown how "events in human history are seen in relation to the final day of reckoning" in medieval cycle drama (Chapter IV, above). In these four Renaissance plays, on the other hand, the foreground action presents human acts in time while allusions to Doomsday and images from the representational world remind the audience of an expected divine judgment at the end of time. In *The Malcontent*, for example, Malevole reminds Mendoza that "I once shall rise . . . at the resurrection" (I.v.15f), and the word "fall" is repeatedly used for ironic effect in scenes with a prostitute. *Measure for Measure* is filled with similar allusions to final judgment, including references to "the tooth of time," "the razure of oblivion," and "the end of reckoning" (V.i.5-46) as well as a richly developed pattern of legal images. Similar language also alerts the audience to the expectation of a final judgment in *The Atheist's Tragedy*; in one scene, for instance, characters speak of calling men "to account," "pay[ing] dearly for 't," "reckoning," and dreading bills "that we are not able to discharge" (IV.v.45-50). Likewise, in *The Devil's Law-Case* characters refer to "a strict account" (I.ii.63-65), a "hereafter" and "after-reckonings" (IV.ii.553-54), "the last day" (II.iii.138), rising to "judgment" (IV.i.115), and "the day of judgment" (IV.i.117). Such imagery reminds the audience of doomsday, encouraging it to see the human behavior enacted on the stage in relation to a final divine judgment.

In contrast to the medieval cycle plays with their depiction of all who have lived throughout human history, these plays focus on only a few highly particularized characters. Under the influence of Protestantism, these Renaissance plays personalize human history, heightening the audience's identification with the individual and his anticipated judgment. The audience of these plays is thus encouraged to see the individual and his personal history in the context of divine history, in conformance with Protestant belief. "The general and particular judgment, calamities, and punishments," insists the Protestant writer Thomas Draxe in *An Alarum to the Last Judgment* in the early seventeenth century, "both in the old and the new Testament, and in all succeeding ages, are Types, Similitudes, and Foresignifications" of the Last Judgment.[24]

All of these plays thus employ traditional icons of judgment, but they adapt these images to a Protestant vision of the world. Judgment images that appear on the Renaissance commercial stage do not serve as a straightforward enactment of a future Doomsday, as in the cycle plays, nor do they present an allegorical depiction of divine judgment, as in the morality plays. Instead, they occur as natural phenomena in a representational world. That world, in accordance with Protestant belief, is a dark and illusory one where images may not signify and humans must of necessity interpret what they see, even though they are fallen creatures and prone to error. Visible images in these stage worlds—and in the actual world which such fictional worlds represent—are thus potential signs that may reveal the divine order of things. As external, physical objects, however, they are also unreliable and potentially dangerous.

Protestant theologians repeatedly urge men and women to interpret "the book of nature," to find in the visible world God-made signs of a higher, spiritual realm, even as they insist on the fallibility of all human interpretation. Error defines the human condition for the Protestant believer; nevertheless, God communicates to fallen man through signs, and man must therefore constantly engage in acts of interpretation. Thus, while Calvin warns that physical things may delude, dazzle, and blind, he also writes that "since we are creatures who always creep on the ground, cleave to the flesh, and do not think about or even conceive of anything spiritual . . . [God] leads us to himself even by these earthly elements, and in flesh itself causes us to contemplate the things that are of the spirit."[25]

Calvin sharply distinguishes between the flesh and the spirit, but he nevertheless bases his covenant theology on the belief that God uses physical things as signs to lead man to him. "The term 'sacrament'," he writes, "embraces generally all those signs which God has ever signalled to men to render them more certain and confident of the truth of his promises." For Calvin, then, visible images like the rainbow are sacraments, serving, in his words, as "a reminder" of God's promises.[26]

The worlds of the four plays examined in this chapter reflect the paradoxical Protestant belief that the physical world is at once illusory and potentially significant. In all four plays characters and audience alike experience the problematics of sight. Disguises, false appearances, and deceptions emphasize the untrustworthy nature of the visible world. Characters misinterpret and misunderstand what they see, and at times utter confusion threatens to prevent the characters from ever discovering the truth behind the multiple illusions. In the final act of *Measure for Measure*, for example, Shakespeare creates a situation in which nothing is as it appears to be: Angelo, Isabella, the Duke, and Lucio all lie; Angelo seems to be the honorable magistrate, Isabella to be mad, Mariana to be lying, the Duke to be ignorant, the friar to be a trouble maker. In this scene dramatic irony enables the audience to see the discrepancies between appearances and truth and to realize the illusory nature of the physical world. Dramatic irony works in a similar way in the other plays as well, especially when the audience knows the true identities of disguised figures. At other times, however, the audience knows no more than the characters themselves. In *The Malcontent*, for instance, the audience believes that Ferenze and later Malevole die when they fall to the ground and are pronounced dead. It is therefore surprised and startled to realize these characters are alive when they suddenly stand up and speak. In scenes such as these the audience is led to believe in an appearance, then forced to confront the false nature of that appearance. These plays thus make the audience aware of the human condition, of seeing through a glass darkly, and at times they create that very condition when the audience experiences directly the uncertainty of knowledge.

Unlike the medieval plays of judgment, then, the plays of the commercial Renaissance stage use images of Last

205

Judgment as signs within fictional worlds that represent the fallen world as the Protestants conceived it. Although such plays depict the sensuous universe as confusing and illusory, they encourage their audiences to recognize and interpret visible things as signs of the divine. Courtrooms, judges, physical falls, cups of wine, and veils exist as literal things in the fallen world of man, but they also serve as remembrances, signs of a promised day of judgment.

Significantly, it is the experience of seeing through a glass darkly that Christian doctrine promises will be eradicated at Doomsday. "For now we see through a glass, darkly," writes Paul, "but then shall we see face to face: now I know in part; but then shall I know even as I am known" (1 Corinthians 13.12). All four plays discussed here anticipate this moment. After presenting a world of illusions and deceptive appearances, they dramatize—in physical time and space— a moment of revelation when disguises are stripped away, lies are exposed, and the truth is made manifest. This moment, characterized in each play by a series of sudden and surprising unmaskings and unveilings, serves as the culmination of the recurring icons of judgment, for it reminds the audience of the promised revelation that will end the need for signs and the danger of misinterpreting what one sees. The audience, however, can experience that revelation only indirectly, through an imaginative act, for it cannot transcend the dark and uncertain phenomenological world. Protestant drama does not attempt to enact the final day of judgment, but rather to remind the audience of that anticipated day through visible signs from the natural world.

NOTES

1. See especially John Phillips, *The Reformation of Images: Destruction of Art in England, 1535-1660* (Berkeley and Los Angeles: Univ. of California Press, 1973), *passim*.

2. Craig Harbison, *The Last Judgment in Sixteenth-Century Northern Europe* (New York: Garland, 1976), pp. 17, 184-86.

3. *Pseudodoxia Epidemica*, in *The Works of Sir Thomas Browne*, ed. Geoffrey Keynes (Chicago: Univ. of Chicago Press, 1964), II, 389.

4. William Tyndale, *An Answer to Sir Thomas More's Dialogue*, ed. Henry Walter (1850); *Ten Articles* (1536); Thomas Cranmer *et al.*, *Bishop's Book*; as cited in Phillips, *Reformation of Images*, pp. 45, 54, 56-57.

5. Harbison, *Last Judgment*, pp. 52-61.

6. Phillips, *Reformation of Images*, p. 46, paraphrasing William Tyndale, *An Answer to Sir Thomas More's Dialogue*.

7. Quoted by Andrew D. Weiner, *Sir Philip Sidney and the Poetics of Protestantism: A Study of Contexts* (Minneapolis: Univ. of Minnesota Press, 1978), pp. 42-43.

8. Francis Quarles, *Emblemes* (London, 1635), p. 160.

9. *Court Book 1575-1580*, fol. 19, as quoted in Harold C. Gardiner, *Mysteries' End: An Investigation of the Last Days of the Medieval Religious Stage* (New Haven: Yale Univ. Press, 1946), p. 78.

10. *Mount Tabor, or Private Exercises of a Penitent Sinner* (London, 1639), pp. 111-13.

11. David Bevington uses the term "homiletic tragedy" to describe a group of popular mid-sixteenth-century moralities that end in the defeat of a central protagonist; see *From "Mankind" to Marlowe* (Cambridge: Harvard Univ. Press, 1962), p. 161. These plays include: R. B., *Appius and Virginia*, in *Early English Dramatists*, ed. John S. Farmer (London: Early English Drama Society, 1908); Ulpian Fulwell, *Like Will to Like*, in *Old English Plays*, ed. W. Carew Hazlitt (London: Reeves and Turner, 1874), III; *The Trial of Treasure*, *Old English Plays*, III; W. Wager, *"The Longer Thou Livest" and "Enough is as Good as a Feast,"* ed. R. Mark Benbow (Lincoln: Univ. of Nebraska Press, 1967); George Wapull, *The Tide Tarrieth No Man* (London, 1576).

12. All citations to the Bible in this chapter refer to the Geneva Bible (Geneva, 1560).

13. See *Articles of Religion*, XXVIII, for the assertion that, while transubstantiation is not involved in the Eucharist, neither is the Eucharist merely a sign. The idea that the Eucharist is a sign only was held by the followers of Zwingli. For a useful review of Eucharistic controversies, see F. L. Cross, ed., *The Oxford Dictionary of the Christian Church*, 2nd ed. (Oxford: Oxford Univ. Press, 1974), pp. 475-77.

14. Harriet Hawkins, *Likenesses of Truth in Elizabethan and Restoration Drama* (Oxford: Clarendon Press, 1972), p. 76; R. W. Ingram, *John Marston* (Boston: Twayne, 1978), p. 99; Robert W. Ornstein, *The Moral Vision of Jacobean Tragedy* (Madison: Univ. of Wisconsin Press, 1960), p. 121; Lee Bliss, *The World's Perspective* (New Brunswick: Rutgers Univ. Press, 1983), p. 175.

15. All citations of this play are to John Marston, *The Malcontent*, ed. George K. Hunter (London: Methuen, 1975).

16. See, for example, Geoffrey Whitney, *A Choice of Emblemes* (Leyden, 1586), p. 2.

17. John Calvin, *Institution of the Christian Religion*, trans. Ford Lewis Battles (Atlanta: John Knox Press, 1975), p. 47.

18. All citations of this play are to *The Riverside Shakespeare*, ed. G. Blakemore Evans *et al.* (Boston: Houghton Mifflin, 1974).

19. All citations of this play are to Cyril Tourneur, *The Atheist's Tragedy*, ed. Irving Ribner (Cambridge: Harvard Univ. Press, 1964). For an extensive analysis of this play, see my article, " 'Reduce Thy Understanding to Thine Eye': Seeing and Interpreting in *The Atheist's Tragedy*," *Studies in Philology*, 78 (1981), 47-60.

20. See, for example, Cesare Ripa, *Iconologia* (Rome, 1603).

21. All citations of this play are to John Webster, *The Devil's Law-Case*, ed. Frances A. Shirley (Lincoln: Univ. of Nebraska Press, 1972).

22. Calvin, *Institution*, p. 45.

23. Harbison, *Last Judgment*, pp. 131-35.

24. Thomas Draxe, *An Alarum to the Last Judgment* (London, 1615), p. 4.

25. Calvin, *Institution*, p. 118.

26. Ibid., p. 125.

L'ENVOI

David Bevington

> Christianity was born apocalyptic and has remained so, not in the sense that apocalyptic hopes exhaust the meaning of Christian belief, but because they have never been absent from it.
> —Bernard McGinn, *Visions of the End*, p. 11

Without attempting to summarize the various arguments this book has advanced about iconography of Judgment and how it developed during the Middle Ages and Renaissance, we might conclude with a glance at the very process of change in visual language. Do we observe alterations during our period in the conception of visual language and the way in which it signifies? Scholars have recently presented evidence for a transformation in verbal language during the Middle Ages and the Renaissance. Joseph Porter and R. Macdonald, for example, see in Shakespeare's verbal language a reflection of changing ideas about kingship and social order.

The shift in Shakespeare's great historical plays about Richard II, Henry IV, and Henry V is from the medieval and ceremonial language of Richard to the Renaissance and practical language of the Henrys, from the linguistic absolutism of a king who believes in the magical validity of names to a world of proliferating tongues and vulgar dialects, of incessant coining of names, of wordplay and artful public utterance. Hotspur, like Richard II, ties his ear to his own tongue and its world of figures; Falstaff claims that honor is a word and that words are lacking in universal essence. Hence the linguistic playfulness, the punning, the holiday irresponsibility in speech acts. Prince Hal learns from Falstaff to be aware of a variety and versatility of tongues, but he also learns to speak seriously in the language of promising, of giving his word in order to keep it.[1]

As Hal senses, those who do not grow in language are destined to be defeated by history. Aware that his father has destroyed the privileged sanctity of a king's name by stealing the crown, Hal must forge a language for a new world of usurpation. He must exploit all the pragmatic resources of irony, understatement, wary hyperbole, and deft paronomasia, foregoing the simple grandiloquence of his grandfather John of Gaunt and the absolute distinction of "No" or "Aye" for a more realistic language of "either/or."[2] The tragic death of a sacramental view of nature and its kindred poetic sensibility gives way, as Eric La Guardia observes, to a new order of detachment and political expediency; an overly reliant faith in symbol and the magical oneness of the symbolic with the objective must yield to a new symbolic order of monarchy created by Prince Hal out of the malleable and subjective materials of persuasive speech.[3]

Can a similar shift be perceived in the visual language studied in this book? Much evidence seems indeed to confirm such a process.[4] Linguistic absolutism is essential to the idea of the visual attribute in medieval iconography. The implements of the Passion prominently featured both in drama and in pictorial renditions of the Last Judgment in Gothic art are invariable and unambiguous signs identifying Christ as King in judgment amidst the visual tokens of his suffering for mankind. The extensive similarities between drama and other visual arts derive from a fixed language of religious iconography, and communicate with audience or viewer by means of unquestioned sacred truths. Meaning is enriched by multiple correspondences between sacred art and the entirety of sacred history, especially those events such as the Fall of Man and the Flood that typologically anticipate the final Judgment. Certitude grows out of a sense of fixed place and occasion rooted in Scripture and liturgy. God's sacred word in Scripture provides fixity of meaning upon which interpretation of visual signs can confidently rest. The principles of design with which this book has been concerned—symmetry, hieratic ordering, a portraiture that is at once personalized and generic, recapitulation—derive their strength in drama and other visual arts alike from understood ideas of one-to-one correspondence and an unchanging opposition between truth and falsehood.

When, on the other hand, in Renaissance drama and art the images of the Judgment are denied their essential validity as sacred icons, they become instead the visual means to put us in remembrance of the Judgment. They become tokens of apocalypse commenting upon the mutable world now at the center of the play or work of art. Detachment and irony figure importantly in the visual language of juxtaposition thus created, and the mutability of human affairs vastly increases the potential range of paronomasia and theatrical illusion. Increased use of vernacular language in Renaissance drama is accompanied by a new flexibility in the kinds of images now permitted on stage or in the graphic and plastic arts.

Nevertheless, too simplified a view of this change can obscure continuity and complexity in the design. We need go no further than the Antichrist to realize the extent to which late medieval art is beset by problems of ambiguity in visual signs. Truth may be whole and indivisible, but Antichrist is fearfully adept at counterfeiting truth. Because his life is a parody of Christ's, he can entrap the unwary into misreading the potentially deceptive language of outward signs. In the theater, where illusion is paramount, visual imitation and deception are an essential part of the actors' vocabulary, and hence lend themselves to a testing of those very certitudes by which medieval art makes visual communication possible. Even though St. Augustine and other Church Fathers provide a theological perspective with which to confront evil masquerading as truth, and even though the visual language of medieval art generally survives the test of illusion by reestablishing its scriptural authority, the problem of certitude does become the very stuff of dramatic conflict.

Conversely, Renaissance art does not embrace a new visual language of proliferating and desanctified images without many a backward glance. The remembrance of fixed and eternal meaning gives perspective on the mutabilities of history, even if the artist's center of focus is now the brazen world of contingent event and temporality. Without a due appreciation of continuity in pictorialism, without an awareness of a medieval heritage through which spiritual truths are imaged forth in the material language of this world, we are apt to insist too much on the secularism of Renaissance art. Nowhere are the continuity and the change more clearly seen than in stage images of the drama as it moves from the eternal ceremoniousness of divine order to the existential flow of human event.

NOTES

1. Joseph Porter, *The Drama of Speech Acts: Shakespeare's Lancastrian Tetralogy* (Berkeley: Univ. of California Press, 1979).

2. Ronald R. Macdonald, "Uneasy Lies: Language and History in Shakespeare's Lancastrian Tetralogy," *Shakespeare Quarterly*, 35 (1984), 22-39.

3. Eric La Guardia, "Ceremony and History: The Problem of Symbol from *Richard II* to *Henry V*," *Pacific Coast Studies in Shakespeare*, ed. Waldo F. McNeir and Thelma N. Greenfield (Eugene: Univ. of Oregon Press, 1966).

4. Clifford Davidson, "Gesture in Medieval Drama with Special Reference to the Doomsday Plays in the Middle English Cycles," *EDAM Newsletter*, 6, No. 1 (Fall 1983), 8-17, and Julian Plante, "More on Gesture," *EDAM Newsletter*, 7, No. 1 (Fall 1984), 1-2.

ILLUSTRATIONS

1. Separation of the Sheep and the Goats. Early Christian sarcophagus lid. 4th century. The Metropolitan Museum of Art, Rogers Fund, 1924.

2. The Last Judgment. Romanesque tympanum, Church of St. Faith, Conques.   12th century.

3. The Last Judgment. Anglo-Saxon Ivory. Late 8th or early 9th century.
Victoria and Albert Museum.

4. St. Foy asks God's forgiveness. Detail from tympanum, Church of St. Faith, Conques.

5. Poacher receives his reward. Detail from tympanum, Church of St. Faith, Conques.

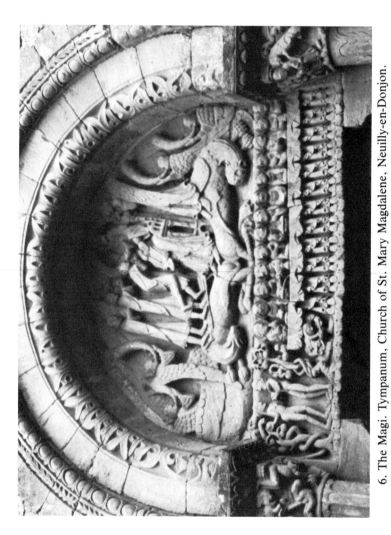

6. The Magi. Tympanum, Church of St. Mary Magdalene, Neuilly-en-Donjon.

7. Resurrection of the Witnesses. Cloisters Apocalypse, fol. 18ᵛ. The Metropolitan Museum of Art, Cloisters Collection, 1968.

8. Ascension (center panel), Biblia Pauperum. Library of Congress.

9. Pentecost (center panel), Biblia Pauperum. Library of Congress.

10. Life of Elias. Oxford, Bodleian Library MS. 270b, fol. 168.

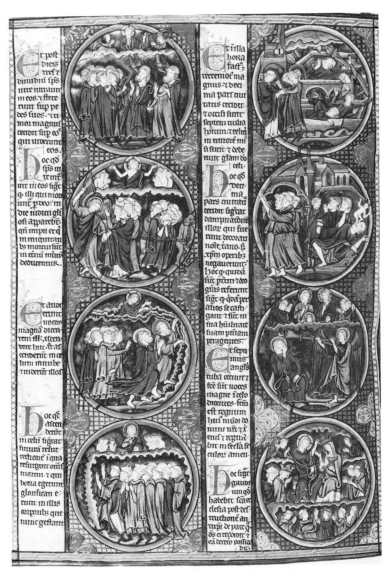

11. Two Witnesses. British Library, Harley MS. 1527, fol. 132ᵛ.

Dar nach ſo füren die tüfel den Enntokriſt in die hell· Wann ſyn
erſtez anfang iſt von des tüfelſʒ rod vnd vnploſung·

12. Destruction of Antichrist. Woodcut. *Vita Antichristi.*

Last Judgmᵗ aᵗ domeſtdai

13. The Last Judgment. Bolton Hours. York Minster Library MS.
   Add. 2, fol. 208. c. 1420.

14. The Last Judgment. Wall painting (restored), St. Thomas of Canterbury
Church, Salisbury. c. 1500. Photograph courtesy of National
Monuments Record.

15. Rogier van der Weyden, *Last Judgment Altarpiece*. Beaune, Hôtel-Dieu. 1443-52. Photograph courtesy of Bildarchiv Foto Marburg.

16. Hubert and/or Jan van Eyck, *The Last Judgment*. Panel painting.
c. 1420-25. Metropolitan Museum of Art, Fletcher Fund, 1933.

17. The Last Judgment. Church of St. Peter, Wenhaston. Formerly in chancel arch. c. 1500. Photograph courtesy of National Monuments Record.

Irma Beate Birgitte: De Syon. ☨ ..

18. The Last Judgment. Devotional woodcut, from Brigittine convent at Syon, founded by Henry V. Bodleian Library MS. Rawl. D. 402.

19. The coming together of Peace and Righteousness. Illustration of Psalm 84.11 (85.10). Stuttgart Psalter, detail of fol. 100^v. Photograph courtesy of Bildarchiv Foto Marburg.

20. The Castle of Love. Peterborough Psalter, detail of fol. 91^v. Bibliothèque Royale, Brussels.

21. Hieronymus Bosch, *Death of the Miser*. Panel painting. National Gallery of Art, Washington, D.C., Samuel H. Kress Collection, 1952.

22. Staging Design for the Valenciennes Passion. Paris, Bibliothèque Nationale, MS. Fr. 12536, fols. 239ᵛ-240ʳ.

23. Attributed to Jan Massys, *St. Jerome in His Study*. Panel painting. c. 1535. Prado, Madrid.

24. Hans Mielich, *Meeting of the Regensburg Town Council*. Engraving.
c. 1535.

25. Jan Sadeler (after Dirck Barendsz), *Mankind before the Last Judgment*. Engraving. c. 1581.

26. Jan Vermeer, *A Lady Weighing Pearls*. Painting. c. 1660. National Gallery of Art, Washington, D.C., Widener Collection.

What ever God *did* fore-decree,
Shall, without faile, fulfilled be.

27. Emblem from George Wither, *A Collection of Emblemes* (London, 1635), Book II, No. 33.

INDEX

213